Great Western
Branch Line Termini

GREAT WESTERN BRANCH LINE TERMINI

Volume One

by Paul Karau

Oxford Publishing Co.

Copyright © 1977 Oxford Publishing Co. and Paul Karau
Reprinted 1985
All rights reserved

ISBN 0-86093-369-5

2-6-2T No. 4502 at Tetbury.   *W.A. Camwell*

Printed in Great Britain by
Netherwood Dalton & Co. Ltd., Huddersfield, Yorks.

Published by
Oxford Publishing Co.
Link House
West Street
POOLE, Dorset

Contents

Additional structure drawings (originally reproduced on fold-out sheets) pertaining to these stations appear in the supplementary section at the rear of this combined volume.

Introduction

Over the years the histories of many of our branch lines have appeared in various books and magazines often accompanied by a few general illustrations, but to date, very little has been published to record the physical appearance of these lines, many of which have now disappeared.

In compiling this book I have attempted to present a portrait of just five Great Western branch line termini which no longer exist.

Each station is presented using a sequence of notes and photographs which is intended to give the reader some idea of how it once appeared. My own drawings of the track plans and buildings have also been included and these are based mainly on personal surveys and official plans.

I sincerely hope that this book may help to enlighten those who have never had the opportunity of visiting these stations and perhaps restore a few memories to those who once knew them.

Paul Karau   1977

DEDICATION

To all those whose kindness has made this book possible.

Fairford station,
17 June 1961.
D. Thompson

Acknowledgements

I cannot claim any credit for the majority of photographic material included within this volume, indeed I am indebted to the many photographers with whom all credit must remain. I should like to express my deepest thanks to Tony Smith, not only for the many outings we have shared exploring these stations, but for his constant help and encouragement; also to Keith Steele for his help in the early stages of compiling this volume.

I should also like to thank the following:— Mrs. J.H. Ahern, Dr. Ian C. Allen, P. Bartlett, I.D. Beale, A.E. Bennett, F. Bolton, L. Bolton, K. Bowler, F.M. Butterfield, W.A. Camwell, R. Carpenter, H.C. Casserley, R.M. Casserley, R. Chown, J. Church, Mrs. Clarke, M.S. Cross, J.E. Cussen, J.J. Davis, B.L. Davis, M.J. Deane, N. de Courtais, R. England, M.J. Esau, D. Esau, Mr. Farmiloe, C. Fuller, E. Glidden, V. Harris, J. Holden, C. Hopkins, H. Humphries, D. Hyde, D.K. Johnson, P. Kelley, C.P. Legg, F. Lindstrom, R. Luckett, P. Maunder, G.E. Membury, J.H. Meredith, K. Montague, J.H. Moss, Miss J. Munday, G. Nicholson, L. Nicolson, R.T. Parham, Hon. J. Parker, M.J. Parsons, J. Penfold, M. Robinson, R.G. Rose, J.H. Russell, P.G. Rymer, T.B. Sands, T. O'Shay, R.H.G. Simpson, A. Smith, C. Strevens, Messrs. F. Tappin & Sons, D. Thompson, T. Tunnycliffe, C. Turner, B. Wall, M.B. Warburton, Mrs. Watts, C.F.D. Whetmath, I.M. Wilson, Bristol Museum, British Railways, Locomotive & General Railway Photographs, Lens of Sutton, Photomatic, Public Record Office.

Finally I should like to thank my wife for her tolerance and all the help she has given me in compiling this book.

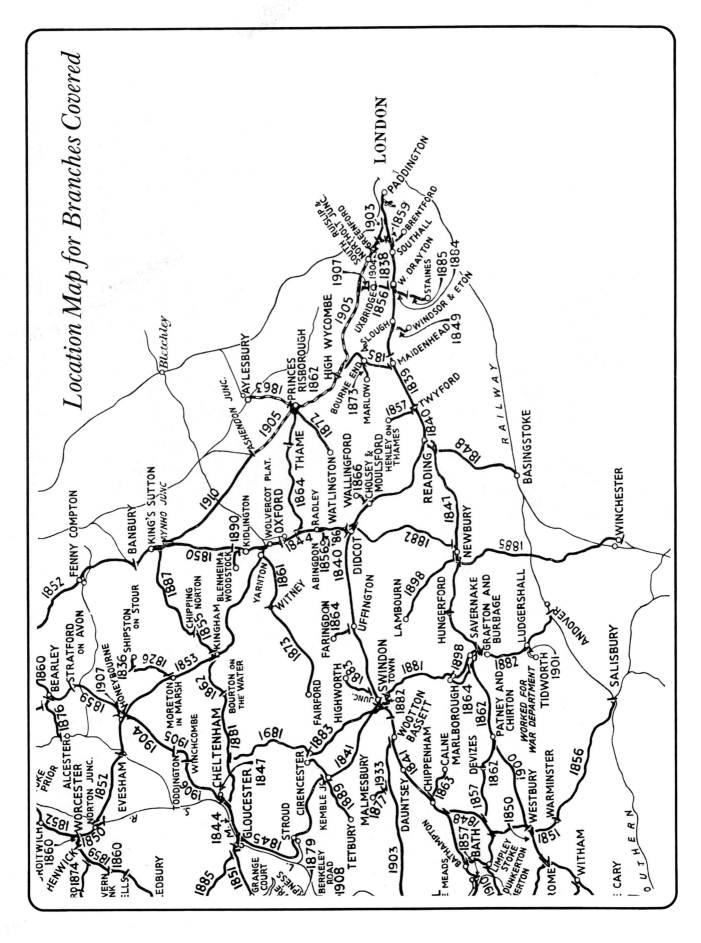

Location Map for Branches Covered

7

Fig. F1 0-6-0 Pannier tank No. 7411 at Fairford 13th September, 1958. *A.E. Bennett*

FAIRFORD

KEY FACTS

Companies of Origin	Witney Railway Co. East Gloucestershire Railway Co.	Length of Branch	21 Miles 57 Chains
Date of Opening	Witney Railway 14th November, 1861 East Gloucestershire Railway 15th January, 1873	Ruling Gradient	1 in 100
		Route Colour	Yellow
Purchased by GWR	1st July, 1890	Overall Speed Restriction	50 mph
Date of Closure	18th June, 1962 Yarnton to Witney remaining open for goods traffic until 2nd November,1970	Single Line Worked by	Yarnton to Brize Norton-Electric Tablet. Brize Norton to Fairford- Electric Train Staff

ORIGIN

Despite bitter opposition from the Great Western Railway, the Witney Railway Act received Royal Assent on 1st August, 1859 and authorised the construction of a line from Yarnton, on the Oxford Worcester and Wolverhampton Railway, a distance of 8 miles 13 chains to Witney, a busy town on the edge of the Cotswolds renowned for its blanket industry.

The GWR opposed the scheme, fearing the possibility of a future extension to Cheltenham, which could have provided a competitive through route from London to Cheltenham via the London and North Western Railway to Yarnton.

Construction began on 5th May, 1860 and the OWWR, which was to have worked and maintained the line, was absorbed by the West Midland Railway during the same year, the WMR taking over the agreement. (The West Midland Railway was itself absorbed by the GWR in 1863.) The Witney Railway was first opened to passenger and coal traffic on 14th November, 1861 but it was not until 1st March, 1862 that the completion of facilities allowed the line to be opened to other goods traffic. Intermediate stations were provided at Cassington, Eynsham and South Leigh.

The proposed East Gloucestershire Railway was an ambitious scheme to construct a line from Cheltenham to Faringdon, with a branch to Witney, thus creating the competitive route from London to Cheltenham via the LNWR as previously feared by the GWR. The Great Western Railway offered to guarantee capital for the EGR in return for the abandonment of the branch to Witney, in favour of one to Bourton-on-the-Water. Terms were agreed, and the East Gloucestershire Railway received Royal Assent on 7th August, 1862, however the GWR later withdrew from

the scheme, believing it to be an unnecessary financial risk, leaving the East Gloucestershire Railway Co. quite powerless.

An attempt to revive the EGR in its original form was made in 1863, with financial support from the Midland Railway. This attempt was authorised by an act of Parliament on 29th July, 1864, but as a result of objections raised by the GWR to the Midland Railway's involvement in the East Gloucestershire Railway, Parliament refused to allow the Midland Railway to subscribe to the scheme and again the EGR was left in abeyance.

An Act of Parliament on 15th July, 1867 granted the EGR an extension of time to complete the works, but taking stock of its financial position the company resolved to temporarily abandon the Cheltenham to Faringdon section and to concentrate on the completion of the section from Witney to Fairford.

The East Gloucestershire Railway was finally opened on 15th January, 1873, the line extending from a new station at Witney, with intermediate stations at Brize Norton & Bampton, Alvescot and Lechlade. A new station was opened at Kelmscott & Langford in 1907 and in 1944, during the 2nd World War, a station was provided at Carterton to serve the nearby aerodrome at Brize Norton. The line was worked by the GWR until 1st July, 1890 when this company absorbed both the Witney and East Gloucestershire Railway Companies. Hopes for any extension of the line to Cheltenham gradually faded and the total result of the ambitious proposals of the EGR, was a 21 mile branch line, which ran through sparsely populated countryside and terminated in a meadow a mile or so from the little town of Fairford.

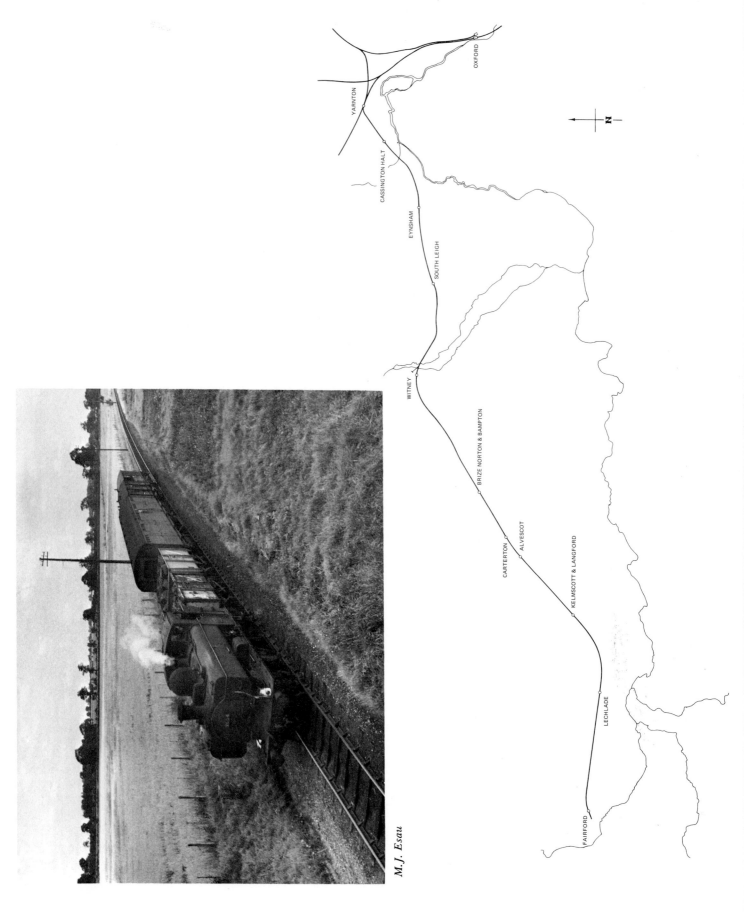

M.J. Esau

10

A peaceful study at Fairford station in 1955.
M.J. Deane

OPERATION

The Fairford branch was single track throughout and operated using an electric tablet system between Yarnton and Brize Norton and electric train staff between Brize Norton and Fairford. Two locomotives were provided from Oxford and sub-shedded at Fairford for branch duties. Boiler washouts and maintenance were carried out as necessary at Oxford, but the locomotives were generally returned to service the same day. With turntables at both Oxford and Fairford even tank locomotives were turned to face the direction of travel at each end of the 25 mile journey and coal was taken at Oxford, as certainly since the mid-1920's, there was no coal stored at Fairford.

Because of the numerous staff changes the operation of the branch timetable is not easy to explain, but it is hoped that the following notes which apply to the 1937 timetable may be of some guidance:

There were four drivers and four firemen based at Fairford to cover the daily shifts and two cleaners in overnight attendance.

A typical weekday began with one of the cleaners leaving the shed, just before 4.30 am, to call the early turn driver for duty. The first crew booked on at 5.30 am and pumped water to fill the supply tank, after which they collected the first set of coaches from the run round loop in the yard and departed with the 7.10 am to Oxford.

The second crew booked on at 8.0 am and again pumped water before collecting their coaches from the siding alongside the shed. Following the arrival at 9.00 am of the 5.50 am goods from Oxford, the second crew departed with the 9.18 am which conveyed the local milk in a vehicle at the rear of the train.

The 5.50 am goods was sorted until the return of the first crew with the 9.22 am from Oxford, which arrived at 10.27 am. The crews changed over and the Fairford men worked straight out again with the goods, leaving the Oxford men to turn and water the branch loco and work back to Oxford with the 11.00 am passenger (which overtook the goods at Lechlade).

The first Fairford crew remained with the Oxford bound goods as far as Bampton, where they changed over with the second Fairford crew returning from Oxford with the 12.00

mid-day. This change enabled the first crew to return to Fairford and book off duty. The second crew then continued with the up goods to Witney where they changed over with an Oxford crew on the 12.35 pm down goods (this was the second branch goods train) and worked this train back to Fairford to complete their duty.

The third Fairford crew had booked on at 1.20 pm and departed with the 2.12 pm passenger and the fourth crew who booked on at 4.05 pm took over the sorting of the 12.35 pm goods, which had arrived at 3.50 pm.

The 4.22 pm from Oxford, which was manned by the third Fairford crew as far as Witney, arrived at Fairford in the charge of an Oxford crew at 5.24 pm. The Oxford men worked straight out again with the 5.30 pm goods, and left the fourth Fairford crew to turn and water the branch loco and work the 6.32 pm to Oxford and back.

The third crew, which were last mentioned at Witney worked back to Oxford with the 4.38 pm from Bampton and finally returned to Fairford with the 6.15 pm, which arrived at 7.25 pm. After their arrival, they shunted the coaches into the siding alongside the loco shed and turned the loco in readiness for the morning. The fire was thrown out as there was no one in attendance at this time and the third crew booked off, leaving the loco inside at the rear of the shed.

The fourth crew arrived at 10.40 pm with the last train from Oxford. The coaches from this train were left in the run round loop, the loco was turned and left inside the shed with a low fire, as by this time the cleaners had arrived and the fourth crew booked off.

An interesting feature of operation at Fairford during the 1920's was the steel towing cable used when running round excursion trains which were too long for the run round loop (excursion trains were run to Fairford carnival each year). The locomotive would draw its train into the yard as usual, then run onto the track alongside and use the 30 - 40 yd long cable to pull the train further down the yard, towards the buffer stops, in order to clear the loop entry points. It is not clear how long this practice continued for.

Fig. F2 0-6-0PT No. 4676 on arrival at Fairford station.

J.H. Moss

Fig F3 0-6-0PT No. 7411 and 2-6-2T No. 4513 at the entrance to the loco shed at Fairford.

Real Photographs

SECTION.		Number of Wagons exclusive of Brake Van.												
		2-8-0			2-6-2 T			2-6-0			Ordinary Engines.				
											Tender.			Tank.
From	To	Coal.	Goods.	Empties.	Coal.	Goods.	Empties.	Coal.	Goods.	Empties.	Coal.	Goods.	Empties.	Coal.	Goods.	Empties.
Fairford Branch.																
Oxford	Fairford	...	...	...	...	...	...	...	...	...	24	36	48	26	39	50
Fairford	Oxford	...	...	...	...	...	...	...	...	...	24	36	48	26	39	50

Extract from GWR "Maximum Loads" 1908

MOTIVE POWER

During the early years of the line the following classes were officially listed for use on the branch:—

Metro class 2-4-0T, 1076 class 0-6-0PT (Buffalo), 2721 class 0-6-0PT and 645 class 0-6-0PT.

As seen in *Fig. F5*, at least one 517 class 0-4-0T was used on the branch, although the Metro class 2-4-0T's came to be used almost exclusively, certainly from the early years of this century until the 1940's.

Fairford's allocation for 1920/21 is listed here as an example.

1450	Metro class 2-4-0T	Jan - Dec
1491	" " "	Jan - March
1498	" " "	April
1491	" " "	May
1498	" " "	June
1491	" " "	July - Aug
1498	" " "	Sept
1491	" " "	Oct - Jan 1921

Other Metro class 2-4-0T's employed on the branch included:— Nos. 626, 654, 926, 3508, 3564, 3565, 3568, 3588, 3589, 3592.

The ex MSWJ Rly. 2-4-0's Nos. 1334, 1335 and 1336 were apparently employed for a short time on the line around 1926.

74XX class 0-6-0PT's Nos. 7404, 7408, 7411, 7412 succeeded the Metros on branch services and remained in regular use until the final years, although Nos. 9653 and 9654 0-6-0PT's of the 57XX class were actually employed at the time of closure.

No. 5754 saw occasional service on the branch and Diesel Railcars had worked through to Fairford, but were generally only used between Oxford and Witney. Goods services were usually worked by Dean Goods class 0-6-0's No. 2579 in particular, but these were later succeeded by the Collett 2251's.

'Dukedogs' and Collett 0-4-2T's Nos. 1420, 1435, 1432 and 1450 also saw occasional service on the branch, after nationalisation.

Figs. F4 & F5 Two views of Fairford Station on the opening day of the East Gloucestershire Railway, 15th January, 1873. Subsequent views in this chapter make an interesting comparison, but notice (upper view) the slotted post signals with the lever frame on the platform and (lower view) the original cattle dock just visible beyond the goods shed.

The horse drawn coach, just visible in the station forecourt, was owned by the Bull Hotel in Fairford and used to carry passengers into the town.

During the winter months in the early years of the line, hot stones, heated in a fire devil by the station porter are said to have been wrapped up and placed in the carriages to warm the passengers' feet.   *Courtesy R. Luckett*

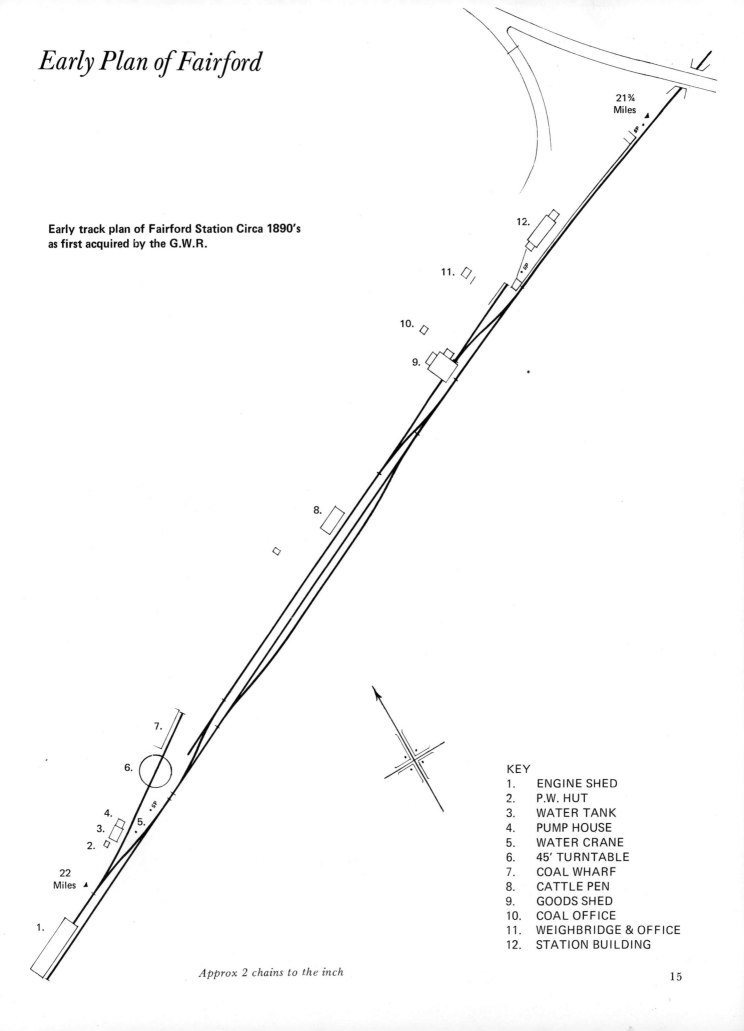

Early Plan of Fairford

**Early track plan of Fairford Station Circa 1890's
as first acquired by the G.W.R.**

21¾
Miles

12.

11.

10.

9.

8.

7.

6.

4.

3.

5.

2.

22
Miles

1.

KEY
1.   ENGINE SHED
2.   P.W. HUT
3.   WATER TANK
4.   PUMP HOUSE
5.   WATER CRANE
6.   45' TURNTABLE
7.   COAL WHARF
8.   CATTLE PEN
9.   GOODS SHED
10. COAL OFFICE
11. WEIGHBRIDGE & OFFICE
12. STATION BUILDING

Approx 2 chains to the inch

15

Fig. F6 Looking west from the road bridge at some time between 1930 and 1935 with a Metro class 2-4-0T (possibly No. 982) awaiting departure at the head of a three coach train of clerestory stock. An 0-6-0 Pannier tank can just be seen in the yard beyond.

L. & G.R.P.

WITNEY & EAST GLOUCESTERSHIRE BRANCH.

Single Line between Yarnton Junction and Fairford worked by the Electric Staff and Electric Tablet.

STAFF SECTIONS.

Yarnton and Eynsham / Eynsham and Witney Station / Witney Station and Bampton } Electric Tablet.

Bampton and Lechlade / Lechlade and Fairford } Electric Train Staff.

The Crossing Stations are :—Yarnton, Witney, Bampton and Fairford. Goods Trains to carry one Head Light in centre of buffer plank.

‡ Streamlined Car must stop dead at Yarnton Junction Signal Box to receive or hand over the Tablet.

Distance from Oxford M	C	Mile Post Mileage M	C	DOWN TRAINS. STATIONS.	Ruling Gradient. 1 in	Time allowances for Ordinary Freight Trains—see page 262. Point to point times.	Allow for stop.	Allow for start.	WEEK DAYS. K Goods. arr.	dep.	B Passenger. arr.	dep.	B Passenger. arr.	dep.	B 9.30 a.m. P. Risboro. Diesel R. Car arr.	dep.	B Passenger. arr.	dep.	B Diesel Rail Car. SO arr.	dep.	K Goods SX arr.	dep.	K Goods. SO arr.	dep.
M	C	M	C			Mins.	Mins.	Mins.	A.M.	A.M.	A.M.	A.M.	A.M.	A.M.	A.M.	A.M.	P.M.	NOON	P.M.	P.M.	P.M.	P.M.	P.M.	P.M.
..		63	40	**Oxford**	—	—	—	1	—	5 50	—	**7 57**	—	**9 22**	**10 22**	**10 25**	—	**12 0**	—	*12 20*	—	12 35	—	*12 45*
3	65	67	25	Yarnton	240R	10	1	1	6 1	**Y**6 6	8 4	X8 5	9 29	9 30	10 31‡	10 31½	12 7	12X 8	*12 26‡*	*12 26½*	12 44		*12 57*	X *1 24*
4	79	68	39	Cassington Halt	—	—	—	—	—	—	8 8	8 9½	9 33	9 34½	10 34	10 34½	12 11	12 12½	*12 29*	*12 29½*	—	—	—	—
7	12	70	52	Eynsham	100 F	8	1	1	6 16	6 37	8 14½	8 15½	9 39½	9 40½	10 38	10 38½	12 17½	12 18½	*12 33*	*12 33½*	12 55	1 5	*1 35*	**Z***1 43*
9	22	72	62	South Leigh	132R	6	1	1	**C**	**R**	8 20½	8 21	9 45½	9 46	10 42½	10 43	12 23½	12 24	*12 37½*	*12 38*	1 13	1 23	*1 51*	*2 1*
11	75	75	35	Witney	100R	8	1	1	6 55	**R**7X45	8 26	8 29	9 51	X9 54	10 48	—	12 29	12 32	*12 43*	—	1 33	1 54	*2 11*	X *2 43*
15	51	79	11	Bampton	100R	9	1	1	7 55	8 5	8 36	—	10 0	10 1			12 38	12X39			2 5	X 2 55	*2 53*	*3 5*
17	59	81	19	Alvescot	100R	6	1	1	8 12	8 22			10 5	10 7	..	..	12 43	12 44		..	3 3	3 18	*3 13*	*3 28*
19	68	83	28	Kelmscott & Langford P.	100 F	—	—	—	**C**	**R**	....	....	10 11½	10 13	....	....	12 49	12 50	....	..	—	—	*3 34*C	**R***3 44*
22	23	85	63	Lechlade	100R	10	1	1	8 31	• 8 52		..	10 18	10 21	..	..	12 55	12 56	..		3 30	3 42	*3 50*	*4 17*
25	42	89	2	**Fairford**	100R	6	1	—	9 0	X			**10 27**	¶	....	....	**1 2**	—			3 50	—	*4 25*	—

DOWN TRAINS. STATIONS.	WEEK DAYS—cont. B Passenger. arr.	dep.	B Passenger. arr.	dep.	B Passenger. arr.	dep.	B 7.15 p.m. Didcot Diesel Rail Car arr.	dep.	B Passenger. SX arr.	dep.	B Passenger. SO arr.	dep.	B Passenger. SO arr.	dep.			SUNDAYS.		B Passenger. arr.	dep.		
	P.M.	P.M.	P.M.	P.M.	P.M.	P.M.	P.M.	P.M.	P.M.	P.M.	P.M.	P.M.	P.M.	P.M.					P.M.	P.M.		
Oxford	—	**3 25**	—	**4 22**	—	**6 15**	**7 35**	**7 38**	—	**9 35**	—	*9 35*	—	*11 15*	....	....	....	....	—	**5 10**	....	....
Yarnton	3 32	3 33	4 29	X4 30	6 22	6 23	7 44‡	7 44½	9 42	9 43	*9 42*	*9 43*	*11 22*	*11 23*	....	.	..	..	**C**	**S**	..	..
Cassington Halt	3 36	3 37½	4 33	4 34½	6 26	6 27½	7 47	7 47½	9 46	9 47½	*9 46*	*9 47½*	*11 26*	*11 27½*	....	....	....	....	5 19	5 20½	....	....
Eynsham	3 42½	3 43½	4 39½	4 40½	6 32½	6 33½	7 51	7 51½	9 52½	9 53½	*9 52½*	*9 54*	*11 32½*	*11 33½*	..	..	..	..	5 25½	5 26½	..	..
South Leigh	3 48½	3 49	4 45½	4 46	6 38½	6 39	7 55½	7 56	9 58½	9 59	*9 59*	*10 0*	*11 38½*	*11 39*	....	....	....	....	5 31½	5 32	....	....
Witney	3 54	X3 57	4 51	X4 54	6 44	X6 50	8 1	—	10 4	10 7	*10 5*	*10 15*	*11 44*	*11 48*	..	..	..	..	5 37	5 40	..	..
Bampton	4 4	—	5 0	5 1	6 56	X7 0			10 13	10 14	*10 22*	*10 23*	*11 55*	—	....	....	....	....	5 46	5 47	....	....
Alvescot			5 5	5 6	7 4	7 5	..	..	10 18	10 19	*10 28*	*10 29*			..	..	..	..	5 51	5 52½	..	..
Kelmscott & Langford P.	....	....	5 11	5 12	7 10	7 12	....	....	10 24	10 27	*10 34*	*10 37*	....	....	....	....	....	....	5 57	5 58	....	....
Lechlade	..	..	5 17	5 18	7 17	7 19	..	..	10 32	10 34	*10 42*	*10 44*	..	..	..	..	..	..	6 3	6 4	..	..
Fairford	....	....	**5 24**	X —	**7 25**	¶	....	....	**10 40**	—	*10 50*	—	....	....	....	....	....	....	**6 10**	—	....	....

R Train to put off at Witney only and berth Shed Traffic. Not to dress yard. **Y** Pick up Newspapers for Fairford Line.

¶ Fairford arrive 3 mins. later on Saturdays. Extra time allowed for increased load.

WITNEY & EAST GLOUCESTERSHIRE BRANCH.

UP TRAINS. STATIONS.	Ruling Gradient 1 in	Time allowances for Ordinary Freight Trains.—See page 262 Point to point times.	Allow for stop.	Allow for start.	WEEK DAYS. B Passenger. arr.	dep.	B Passenger. arr.	dep.	B Passenger. arr.	dep.	B Diesel Rail Car. arr.	dep.	K Goods arr.	dep.		B Passenger. arr.	dep.	B Diesel Rail Car. SO arr.	dep.
		Mins.	Mins.	Mins.	A.M.	A.M.	A.M.	A.M.	A.M.	A.M.	A.M.	A.M.	A.M.	A.M.		A.M.	A.M.	P.M.	P.M.
Fairford	—	—	—	1	—	**7 10**	.	..	—	X**9 18**		..	—	10 35		—	**11 0**	..	..
Lechlade	100R	6	1	1	7 16	7 17	...	...	9 24	9 26	...	....	**10 43**	**V11 25**		11 6	11 7	....	....
Kelmscott & Langford	117R	—	—	—	7 21	7 22	..	..	9 31	9 33	..	..	-	—		11 11	11 12		.
Alvescot	100R	10	1	1	7 26	7 28	....	..	9 38	9 39	....	....	**11 37**	**11 42**		11 16	11 17	...	...
Bampton (Oxon)	100R	5	1	1	7 32	7 34	..	8 47	9 43	9 44	..	..	**11 59**	X**12 40**		11 21	11 22	..	..
Witney	100R	9	1	1	7 40	7X43	8 54	9 0	9 50	X 9 53	—	11 2	**12 51**	X **3¶55**		11 28	11 32	....	*1 5*
South Leigh	100R	8	1	1	7 48	7 48½	9 5	9 5½	9 58	9 58½	11 7	11 7½	—	—		11 37	11 37½	*1 10*	*1 10½*
Eynsham	132R	6	1	1	7 52½	7 53½	9 9½	9 10½	10 2½	10 3½	11 11½	11 12	**C**	**S**		11 41½	11 42½	*1 14½*	*1 15½*
Cassington Halt	—	—	—	—	7 58½	8 0	9 15½	9 17	10 8½	10 10	11 15½	11 16	—	—		11 47½	11 49	*1 19*	*1 19½*
Yarnton	100R	8	1	—	8 3	X 8 4	9 20	9 21	10 13	10 14	11 18½	‡11 19	4 23	X 4 40		11 X52	11 53	*1 22*	X *1‡23*
Oxford	—	10	1	—	**8 11**	—	**9 28**	—	**10 21**	—	**11 26**	—	4 52	—		**12 0**	—	*1 30*	—

V If Lechlade unable to shunt train to yard, it must follow 11.0 a.m. Passenger from Fairford.

¶ For alternative times from Witney on alternate Thursdays see below.

UP TRAINS. STATIONS.	WEEK DAYS—cont. B Passenger. arr.	dep.	B Passenger. arr.	dep.	K 10.35a.m Goods ex Fairford. arr.	dep.		K Goods. SO arr.	dep.	K Goods. SX arr.	dep.	B Passenger. arr.	dep.	B Diesel Rail Car. arr.	dep.	B Passenger. SO arr.	dep.		SUNDAYS. B Passenger. arr.	dep.		
	P.M.	P.M.	P.M.	P.M.	P.M	P.M.		P.M.	P.M.	P.M.	P.M.	P.M.	P.M.	P.M.	P.M.	night	night		P.M.	P.M.		
Fairford	—	**2 12**	..	..	Alternative		..	—	X *5 30*	—	X 5 30	—	**6 32**	..	..	..	..	..	—	**6 42**		..
Lechlade	2 18	2 19	...	....	times from		....	*5 38*	*5 48*	5 38	5 48	6 38	6 40	....	....	....	...	...	6 48	6 51		....
Kelmscott & Langford	2 23	2 24	..	..	Witney on		..	*5 54*C	R*6 0*	5 54C	R6 0	6 45	6 47		..	..	..	..	6 56	6 58		..
Alvescot	2 28	2 29	....	...	alternate		....	*6 6*	*6 16*	6 6	6 16	6 51	6 53	....	....	....	....	....	7 2	7 3		....
Bampton (Oxon)	2 33	X 2 34	..	4 38	Thursdays.		..	*6 23*	*6 38*	6 23	6 38	6 58	X 7 3	..	..	—	*12 5*	..	7 7	7 8		..
Witney	2 40	X 2 43	4 44	X 5 2	*12 48*	*5 22*	....	*6 47*	X *6 48*	6 47	•8X 35	7 10	7 19	—	8 15	*12 12*	*12 17*	....	7 15	7 17		....
South Leigh	2 48	2 48½	5 7	5 7½	*5 32*	*5 40*	..	**C**	**R**	8 43	8 53	7 24	7 24½	8 20	8 20½	*12 22*	*12 22½*	..	7 22	7 22½		..
Eynsham	2 52½	2 53½	5 12½	5 13½	*5 48*	*5 56*	....	*7 3*	*7 14*	9 1	9 12	7 29½	7 30½	8 24½	8 25	*12 26½*	*12 27½*	....	7 26½	7 27½		....
Cassington Halt	2 58½	3 0	5 18½	5 20	—	—	..	—	—	—	—	7 35½	7 37	8 28½	8 29	*12 32½*	*12 34*	..	7 32½	7 34		..
Yarnton	3 3	3 5	5 23	5 24	**C** 6 5	**S**	....	**C** 7 30	**R**	**C** 9 22	**S**	7 40	7 41	8 31½	‡ 8 32	*12 37*	*12 38*	....	7 37	7§38		....
Oxford	**3 13**	—	**5 32**	—	*6 15*	—	..	*7 45*	—	9 30	—	**7 50**	—	**8 39**	—	*12 45*	—	..	**7 45**	—		..

§ Calls if required to set down.

Later Plan of Fairford

Fairford Station 1950
This plan shows the station in its final form, although
the "basic layout" dates from at least as far back as 1925.
Note: The extra goods siding 'A' was added during the
Second World War and the larger turntable, which was
probably constructed alongside the original, was installed about 1948.

21¾
Miles

16.
15.
14.
13.
12.
17.
11.
10.
9.
8.
7.
6.

A

5.

4.
3.
22
Miles
2.
1.

Approximately 2 chains to 1 inch

R. FRED. COLE
COAL & COKE   MERCHANT
Nº 11   FAIRFORD & LECHLADE

KEY
1. ENGINE SHED
2. LOCO. DEPT. MESS HUT
3. P.W. HUT
4. WATER TANK
5. 55' TURNTABLE
6. CRANE (6 TON)
7. LOADING GAUGE
8. GOODS SHED
9. COAL OFFICE
10. WEIGHBRIDGE & OFFICE
11. SIGNAL BOX
12. STATION BUILDING
13. PARCELS SHED
14. BICYCLE SHED
15. P.W. HUT
16. P.W. HUT
17. OIL HUT

OXFORD, WITNEY and FAIRFORD.

SINGLE LINE between Yarnton Junction and Fairford, worked by the Electric Tablet and Electric Staff.

Staff Sections.

Yarnton and Eynsham Eynsham and Witney Station } Electric Tablet. Witney Station and Brize Norton	Brize Norton and Carterton Carterton and Lechlade } Electric Train Staff. Lechlade and Fairford

The Crossing Stations are :—Yarnton, Eynsham, Witney, Brize Norton, Carterton, Lechlade, and Fairford.

At Lechlade it is only possible to cross one passenger train and one freight train or two freight trains. The Passenger Train must be kept on the running line.

Down Trains.   Week Days.

Distance from Oxford. M. C.	Mile Post Mileage. M. C.	STATIONS.	Ruling Gradient 1 in	Point to point times. Mins	Allow for Stop. Mins.	Allow for Start. Mins.	K Freight. arr. a.m.	dep. a.m.	C Parcels. arr. a.m.	dep. a.m.	B Passenger. arr. a.m.	dep. a.m.	B Passenger. arr. a.m.	dep. a.m.	B Passenger. arr. a.m.	dep. a.m.	K Fairford Freight. arr. a.m.	dep. a.m.	B Passenger. arr. p.m.	dep. p.m.
—	63 40	OXFORD	—	—	—	—	—	5H40	—	6 45	—	8 2	—	—	—	—	‡	9 26	—	12 12
3 65	67 25	Yarnton	240 R	10	1	1	C5	56S	C6	52S	8 9	8 10	—	—	9 33	9 34	C10	34S	12 19	12 20
4 75	68 35	Cassington Halt	—	—	—	—	—	—	—	—	8 13½	8 14	—	—	9 37½	9 38	—	—	12 23½	12 24
7 12	70 52	Eynsham	100 F	8	1	1	C6	4S	7 0	7 10	8 19	8 20	—	—	9 43	9 44	10 44	11 12	12 29	12 30
9 22	72 62	South Leigh	132 R	6	1	1	—	—	7 15	7 20	8 25	8 26	—	—	9 49	9 50	CR	—	12 35	12 36
11 75	75 35	Witney	100 R	8	1	1	6 20	7 5	7 25X	V7 55	8 31	8 35	—	—	9 55X	10 1	11 30	X2 45	12 41	12 46
15 51	79 11	Brize Norton & Bampton	100 R	9	1	1	7 16X	7 37	8 2	8 10	8 42	X8 48	—	—	10 8	10 9			12 53X	12 55
17 3	80 43	Carterton	100 R	—	—	—	CS	—	8 13	—	8 51	—	X9 40	—	10 12	10 13	See below for continuation.		1 5	1 6
17 59	81 19	Alvescot	100 R	6	1	1	7 45	8 0	—	—	—	—	9 43	9 44	10 16	10 17			1 11	1 11
19 68	83 28	Kelmscott & Langford	100 F	—	—	—	8 7C	R8 15	—	—	—	—	9 49	9 50	10 22	10 23			1 17	1 18
22 23	85 63	Lechlade	100 R	10	1	1	8 22	8 45	—	—	—	—	9 56	9 57	10 29	10 30				
25 42	89 2	FAIRFORD	100 R	6	1	1	8 55	—	—	—	—	—	10 5	—	10 37	—			1 25	—

H—Hinksey Yard.   V—Engine to take water on arrival.   Train to be shunted to Up Platform for unloading after departure of 7.0 a.m. Fairford.   ‡—Oxford Station 10.21 **CG** 10.23 a.m.

Down Trains.   Week Days—continued   Sundays.

STATIONS.	K 10.15 a.m. Hinksey Freight. (continued). arr. p.m.	dep. p.m.	B Passenger. arr. p.m.	dep. p.m.	B Passenger. arr. p.m.	dep. p.m.	B Passenger. arr. p.m.	dep. p.m.	B Passenger. arr. p.m.	dep. p.m.	B Passenger. arr. p.m.	dep. a.m.	B Passenger. arr. p.m.	dep. p.m.
OXFORD	—	·♦··	—	3 35	—	4 16	—	6 18	—	10 10	—	11 50	C10	10 35
Yarnton			3 42	3 43	4 23	4 24	6 25	6 26	10 17	10 19	CS		42S	
Cassington Halt			3 46½	3 47	4 27½	4 28	6 29½	6 30	10 22½	10 24	12 0	12 1	10 45	10 47
Eynsham			3 52	3 53	4 33	4 35	6 35	6 36	10 29	10 31	12 6	12 8	10 52	10 54
South Leigh			3 58	3 59	4 40	4 41	6 41	6 42	10 36	10 38	12 13	12 14	10 59	11 1
Witney	—	2X45	4 4	4 10	4 46X	4 52	6 48X	6 56	10 43	10 49	12 19	12 24	11 5	11 12
Brize Norton and Bampton	2 56	3 15	4 17	4 20	4 59	5 1	7 3	7 5	10 56	10 58	12 31	12 34	11 19	11 22
Carterton	CS	—	4 23	—	5 4	5 6	7 8X	7 10	11 1	11 4	12 37	12 40	11 25	11 28
Alvescot	B23	3 47			5 9	5 10	7 13	7 14	11 7	11 9	12 43	12 44	11 31	11 33
Kelmscott & Langford	3 54C	R4 0			5 16	5 17	7 20	7 21	11 14	11 15	12 49	12 50	11 38	11 40
Lechlade	4 7	4 17			5 22	5 24	7 26	7 28	11 20	11 23	12 57	12 59	11 46	11 48
FAIRFORD	4X25	—			5 31	—	7 35	—	11 30	—	1 6	—	11 55	—

FAIRFORD, WITNEY and OXFORD.

Up Trains.   Week Days.

STATIONS.	Ruling Gradient 1 in	Point to point times. Mins.	Allow for Stop. Mins.	Allow for Start. Mins.	B Passenger. arr. a.m.	dep. a.m.	B Passenger. arr. a.m.	dep. a.m.	B Passenger. arr. a.m.	dep. a.m.	B Passenger. arr. a.m.	dep. a.m.	K Hinksey Freight. arr. a.m.	dep. a.m.	B Passenger. arr. p.m.	dep. p.m.
FAIRFORD	—	Mins.	Mins.	Mins.	—	7 0	—	—	—	9 15	—	11 7	—	11 15	—	12 35
Lechlade	100 R	6	1	1	7 7	7 8	—	—	9 22	9 23	11 7	11 8	11 23	11 52	12 42	12 43
Kelmscott & Langford	117 R	—	1	1	7 12	7 13	—	—	9 27	9 28	11 12	11 13			12 47	12 48
Alvescot	100 R	10	1	1	7 18	7 19	—	—	9 33	9 35	11 18	11 19	12 13	12 20	12 53	12 54
Carterton	100 R	—	1	1	7 22	7 23	—	8 40	9 38X	9 40	11 22	11 23	CS	—	12 57	X1¶4
Brize Norton & Bampton	100 R	5	1	1	7 26	X7 27	8 43X	8 47	9 43	9 45	11 26	11 27	12 27X	1 30	1 7	1 9
Witney	100 R	9	1	1	7 34X	7 40	8 54	9 0	9 52X	9 58	11 34X	11 40	See below for continuation.		1 16	1 22
South Leigh	100 R	8	1	1	7 44	7 45	9 4	9 5	10 3	10 4	11 44	11 45			1 26	1 27
Eynsham	132 R	6	1	1	7 49	7 51	9 9	9 10	10 8	10 9	11 49	11 50			1 31	1 32
Cassington Halt	—	—	—	—	7 57	7 58	9 16	9 17	10 15	10 16	11 56	11 57			1 38	1 39
Yarnton	100 R	8	1	1	8 1	8 2	9 20	9 22	10 19	10 20	12 0	12 1			1 42	1 43
OXFORD	—	10	1	—	8 10	—	9 30	—	10 28	—	12 8	—			1 50	—

¶—Advertised departure from Carterton 12.59 p.m.

Up Trains—Week Days—continued.   Sundays.

STATIONS.	B Passenger. arr. p.m.	dep. p.m.	K 11.15 a.m. Fairford Freight. (continued). arr. p.m.	dep. p.m.	B Passenger. arr. p.m.	dep. p.m.	B Passenger. arr. p.m.	dep. p.m.	K Freight. arr. p.m.	dep. p.m.	B Passenger. arr. a.m.	dep. a.m.	B Passenger. arr. p.m.	dep. p.m.
FAIRFORD	—	2 2					6 17	6 10	—	6 20	—	9 6	—	6 36
Lechlade	2 9	2 10					6 17	6 18	6 28	6 36	9 9	9 14	6 43	6 44
Kelmscott & Langford	2 14	2 15					6 22	6 23	CR	—	9 19	9 20	6 49	6 50
Alvescot	2 20	2 21					6 28	6 30	6 48	6 58	9 25	9 30	6 55	6 56
Carterton	2 24	2 26		1 30		4 38	6 33	6 34	7 2CX	S7 12	9 30	9 32	6 59	7 1
Brize Norton & Bampton	2 29	2 31	1 41X	2 6	4 41	4 43	6 37X	6 39	7 17	7 24	9 36	9 38	7 4	7 5
Witney	2 38	2 43	2 16C	R2 24	4 50X	5 5	6 46X	6 54	7 34	7 50	9 45	9 50	7 12	7 16
South Leigh	2 47	2 48	2 32C	R2 40	5 9	5 10	6 58	6 59	CR	—	9 55	9 56	7 20	7 21
Eynsham	2 52	2 53	2 50	3 30	5 15	5 16	7 3	7 4	8 6	8 13	10 0	10 1	7 25	7 27
Cassington Halt	2 59	3 0			5 26	5 27	7 10	7 11	—	—	10 7	10 8	7 33	7 34
Yarnton	3 3	3 5	2 50	3 30	5 26	5 27	7 14	7 15	C8	22S	CS	—	7 37¶	7 38
OXFORD	3 13	—	3H45	—	5 35	—	7 22	—	8H37	‡—	10 20	—	7 45	—

H—Hinksey Yard.   ¶—Stop not advertised.   ‡—**CR** at Oxford South Yard.

Taken from Original Timetables

Fig. F7 Fairford Station entrance,
2nd February, 1957.

R.M. Casserley

Fig. F8 The station building was similar in design to those at Lechlade, Alvescot and Witney and was constructed using the local Cotswold stone with a tiled roof. The slate roof on the gentlemen's convenience was a later addition by the GWR.

British Railways

Fig. F9 Another official view of the station forecourt taken on the same dismal day in January, 1932. The signal box, which had been a later addition by the GWR was constructed of blue brick with a slate roof. Part of the rear wall of this building was angled to give access to the end loading bank which of course resulted in the unusual roof.

Notice the posts for the Tilley Lamps which were installed about 1930; lamp oil was locked in the corrugated iron shed which is just visible on the extreme right of *Fig. F6*.   *British Rail*

Fig. F10 A closer view of the station building in 1947 after the installation of gas lighting. The conspicuously new corrugated asbestos shed just beyond the main building was installed for use as a parcels office, and erected on the site of the loading bank referred to in *Fig. F13*. The extension to the foreground of this picture had until this time served as the parcels office, next was the porters' room, followed by the station master-cum-ticket office, general waiting room, ladies' and gentlemen's lavatories.

J.H. Russell

Fig. F11 An overall view of Fairford Station during the 1930's. The recently constructed platelayers shed, at the foot of the platform, replaces the smaller one illustrated in *Fig. F6*. This shed was subsequently enlarged with a new and higher roof as seen in *Fig. F12*, no doubt to accommodate the larger Wickham Trolley. The shunt arm on the starter signal was added around 1930 to facilitate shunting movements in and out of the yard.

Lens of Sutton

Fig. F12 An interesting comparison view to *Fig. F11*, taken in 1958. Note the GWR pattern milepost which only replaced the original EGR example after nationalisation.

M.J. Esau

Fig. F13 The station buildings and platform, January 1932. The ramp beside the corrugated iron pagoda shed was used by local farmers for unloading milk churns onto the platform. Apparently the taller 17 gallon churns slid well down the ramp (lubricated with milk!), but the later 10 gallon churns had a tendency to topple over and by 1930 the milk was unloaded beside the signal box.

British Railways

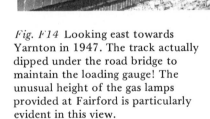

Fig. F14 Looking east towards Yarnton in 1947. The track actually dipped under the road bridge to maintain the loading gauge! The unusual height of the gas lamps provided at Fairford is particularly evident in this view.

J.H. Russell

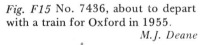

Fig. F15 No. 7436, about to depart with a train for Oxford in 1955.

M.J. Deane

Fig. F16 Signalman/Porter Bert Hawtin inside the signal box at Fairford in 1926.

Courtesy of G.E. Membury

Fig. F17 0-6-0PT No. 7412 in the station platform at Fairford 17th June, 1961. The wet tank sides and footplate are evidence of well filled tanks in readiness for the journey to Oxford.

D. Thompson

Fig. F18 The corrugated iron pagoda shed, so favoured by the GWR, was installed at the station for use as a bicycle shed.

R. Chown

Fig. F19 An example of each of three common styles of GWR platform trolleys makes an interesting if not unusual display together on the platform. Every available wall space on the platform frontage of the main station building was clad with advertisement hoardings, even the signal box did not escape this fate.

British Railways

Fig. F20 The signalman's view of the yard with No. 7436 about to draw its train into the platform. Only the first crossover at the foot of the platform and the protecting catchpoint, were controlled from the signal box, all other turnouts being operated by 'yard levers' similar to the example in the foreground of *Fig. F21*.

M.J. Deane

Fig. F22 The opposite end of the goods shed in later years.

Photoscript — Deddington

Fig. F21 Local stone was again employed in the construction of the Goods Shed which was one of the original buildings of the EGR. The roof was corrugated iron (although it is said to have originally been tiled) but the doors shown here, in 1947, were later damaged in a shunting accident and subsequently replaced with those illustrated in *Fig. F20*.

The 1 ton 10 cwt crane housed in the building was the only crane at the site until the Second World War alterations.

The old coach body just visible on the extreme right of this view was used for the storage of wheat and flour.

J.H. Russell

Fig. F23 The weighing machine and weigh-house.
R. Chown

Fig. F24 A further view of the goods shed on 18th July, 1959 with the sliding doors to the loading bay just visible beneath the canopy.

Station coal was kept in the enclosure just in front of the lorry.
J.J. Davis

Fig. F25 0-6-0PT No. 9653 at the head of a train in the yard.

D. Esau

Fig. F26 An official view taken on 16th November, 1944 before the installation of the yard crane and showing the new siding which was added to cope with the increased volume of wartime traffic for the nearby aerodrome.

There were two coal merchants at Fairford, namely James Marriott and Bernard T. Frost, both of whom had offices in the yard. Marriott's office was the nearer to the station building and is just visible behind the signal box in *Fig. F19*.

British Railways

Fig. F27 The 6 ton yard crane was only installed subsequent to the yard alterations (probably 1945).

R. Chown

Fig. F28 A 2251 class engine runs past its train. Note the restriction board beside the buffer stop. The siding in the foreground originally served a cattle dock which disappeared in later years, possibly at the time of the wartime alterations to the yard.

R.H.G. Simpson

Fig. F29 0-6-0PT No. 4676 being turned in readiness for the return journey to Oxford.

The iron water tank was installed by the GWR soon after the turn of the century and was fed from a well situated on the opposite side of the turntable siding. A pump inside the well was used to fill the tank and was powered by steam from the branch locos. At one time locos allocated to the branch are said to have been fitted with an additional steam pipe for this purpose (which projected through a hole in the fireman's side of the cab) to which the flexible pipe from the pump was connected.

Early plans show the original water tank as being rectangular in plan with a pump house alongside.

J.H. Moss

Fig. F30 An ex Great Western 12 ton ventilated van which was stabled at the end of the main goods siding at one time during the 1950's and inscribed 'For use at FAIRFORD only'.

This vehicle is said to have been in use as a fertilizer store.

Photoscript – Deddington

Fig. F31 No. 7411 alongside the water tank in 1947. The 45′ turntable illustrated here could only just accommodate a Dean Goods and was replaced shortly after this date with the larger 55′ version shown in *Fig. F29*. The main goods siding was shortened and the new turntable was installed a little further east, towards the station.

J.H. Russell

Fig. F32 No. 2236 pumping water beside the well.
It was at this point that the fires were dropped from the branch locos before going on shed.
Branch locos were coaled at Oxford as, certainly from the 1920's onwards, loco coal was not stored at Fairford.
M.J. Deane

Fig. F33 A view of the rear of the platelayers hut, which was situated alongside the turntable siding.
R. Chown

Fig. F34 The end of the line, looking towards Cheltenham, the unattainable goal of the East Gloucestershire Railway. The loco shed was constructed of timber with very low foundation walls of red brick. There was no interior lighting in the building, for even when a gas supply was laid to the station, the loco dept. was left to manage with two Tilley lamps.

Occasionally a larger loco of the Dean Goods class or a small Prairie tank would be sent from Oxford in place of one of the regular branch locos, but this was most unpopular with the overnight cleaners, especially during the winter months, because the extra length of the intruder prevented the shed doors from being closed.

C.F.D. Whetmath

Fig. F35 The horsebox body illustrated here served as a replacement engineman's cabin. Previously a mess hut had been situated inside the rear of the loco shed but this disappeared one morning when one of the crews experienced difficulty in raising steam in a loco and in desperation used part of the dividing wall for firewood!

Photoscript – Deddington

Fig. F36 A detail view of the south wall of the loco shed.
Author

Fig. F37   M.S. Cross

The Fairford branch was closed on 18th June, 1962
but the line between Yarnton and Witney remained
open for goods traffic until 2nd November, 1970.

Fairford Station itself has now completely disappeared
with the exception of the main station building, which
remains in use as the office of a frozen foods company who
now occupy the site.

Further sources of reference:
Railway Magazine Vol. 68 *P191 1931*
Railway Magazine Vol. 106 *P677 1960*
Railway World Vol. 23 *P337 1962*

SCALE DRAWINGS OF BUILDINGS AT FAIRFORD

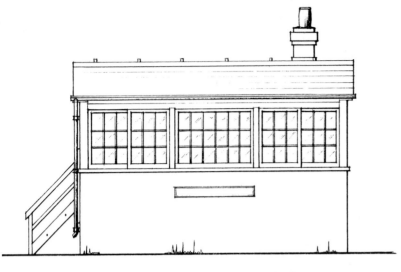

ELEVATION TO PLATFORM

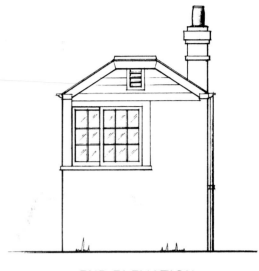

END ELEVATION
FACING EAST

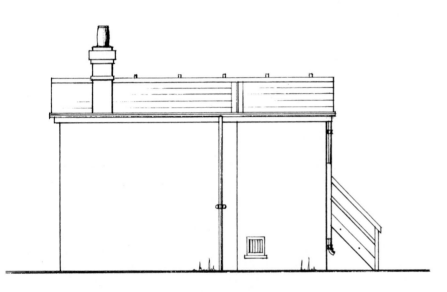

ELEVATION TO FORECOURT

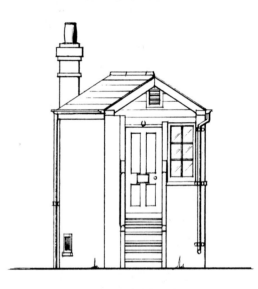

END ELEVATION
FACING WEST

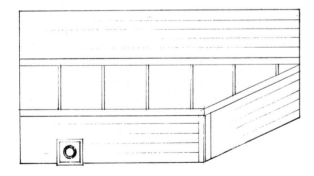

PLAN VIEW OF ROOF

Fairford Signal Box

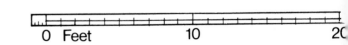

0   Feet   10   20

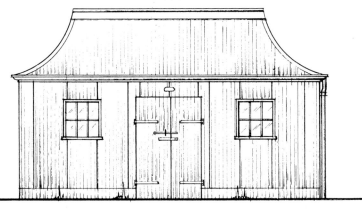
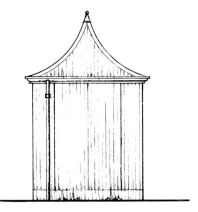

Fairford Cycle Shed

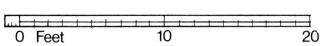

0 Feet   10   20

Fairford station, January 1932.   *British Railways*

Fig. L1 Railcar No. 19 leaves Lambourn on 15th October, 1949 with brake third No. 5494 in tow.

J.H. Meredith

LAMBOURN

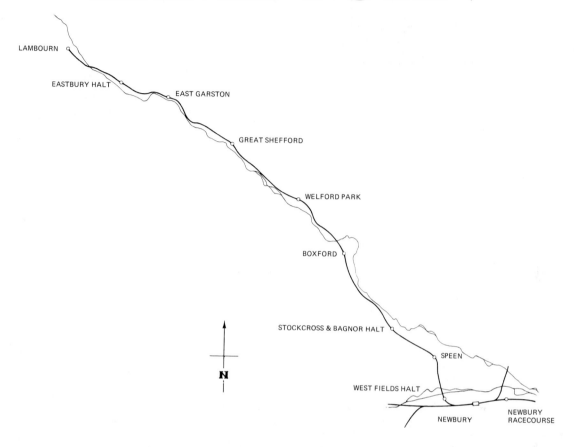

KEY FACTS

Company of Origin	Lambourn Valley Railway Co.
Date of Opening	2nd April, 1898
Purchased by GWR	1st July, 1905
Date of Closure	4th January, 1960 Newbury to Welford Park remained open for freight to US Airforce Base until 3rd November, 1973
Length of Branch	12 Miles 32 Chains
Ruling Gradient	1 in 60
Route Colour	Uncoloured (Yellow Engines permitted subject to strict observance of speed limit)
Overall Speed Restriction	30 mph (15 mph Goods Trains)
Single Line Worked by	Electric Token System

ORIGIN

The Lambourn Valley Railway was authorised by an Act of Parliament on 2nd August, 1883, but difficulties experienced in raising capital delayed the start of construction until 18th June, 1888. Progress was slow; in 1890 the Lambourn Valley Railway Company took legal action against its contractor who had failed to meet his obligations and the necessary raising of additional capital further delayed proceedings. Construction was recommenced in 1897 and the line was first open to public traffic on 4th April, 1898.

The LVR operated its own services with a few items of rolling stock which had been purchased by the company chairman and a locomotive hired from the GWR. Traffic was healthy from the outset, with racehorse traffic soon becoming an important source of revenue, but the financial burden of over-capitalisation prevented the railway from showing a profit and the undertaking sold out to the GWR on 1st July, 1905.

The line extended from Newbury to Lambourn, a distance of 12 miles 32 chains along the shallow valley of the River Lambourn, with intermediate stations at Speen, Stockcross & Bagnor, Boxford, Welford Park, Great Shefford, East Garston and Eastbury. A new halt was opened at Newbury West Fields by the GWR in 1907.

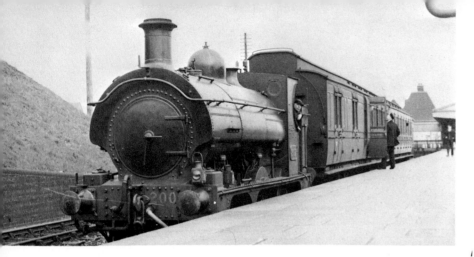

Fig. L2 850 class 0-6-0ST No. 2007 waits at the head of the Lambourn train in the branch bay at Newbury. (The fireman is Bill Bayliss.)

Lens of Sutton

Fig. L3 Lambourn branch staff pose on one of the ex MSWJ Rly. 2-4-0's. The fireman and driver are Charlie Fuller and Mr. Price respectively. The guard in the left hand foreground is Jack Greenaway with Arthur Smith and son Eric at his side.

Courtesy A. Smith

OPERATION

The single line was operated using an electric token system, with a locomotive shedded at Lambourn.

The following notes apply to the operation of the line on a typical weekday of 1933, there were two train crews based at Lambourn at this date and an overnight loco cleaner:

The first train of the day departed from Lambourn at 7.42 am and often conveyed a tail load of one or two horse boxes to Newbury. (Only cattle traffic is mentioned for this train in the working timetable.) The 10.40 am and 12.43 pm return passenger services completed the duty of the early turn crew who were relieved at Lambourn at 3.00 pm.

The 3.12 pm departure returned from Newbury with local school children and the last return passenger train, which departed at 6.00 pm, returned in the charge of a Reading loco and crew, leaving Newbury at 7.20 pm. The Lambourn crew collected the branch goods from Newbury yard and left for Lambourn at 8.15 pm, calling at intermediate stations as required. Following the arrival of the 7.20 pm at Lambourn, the Reading crew shunted the yard and returned to Newbury with the pick-up goods, crossing with the Lambourn bound goods at Welford Park. When the Lambourn crew finally reached the terminus, the wagons were placed and the loco was taken on shed for disposal. On Saturdays, the Lambourn crew worked the 7.20 pm from Newbury themselves together with a late return trip known locally as the 'boozer,' which left Newbury at 10.15 pm, and the Reading men worked the branch goods in each direction. The only Sunday service was a train from Didcot which arrived at Lambourn at 5.39 pm and departed again at 6.55 pm. The ex MSWJ Rly. 2-4-0's were regularly employed on this turn with Didcot crews and were required to pump water to fill the conical tank during their stay.

Lambourn shed was closed in 1936 when passenger services were taken over by Diesel Railcars. Railcar No. 18 was built in 1937 and delivered to the branch for trials, this was the first Railcar to be fitted with buffers and drawgear and was capable of hauling a tail load of 60 tons. (A later batch of Railcars Nos. 19 to 34 were similarly equipped as a result of the trials.) Railcars were based at Reading and with the exception of the newspapers conveyed in the mornings, ran as empty stock to and from Lambourn each day. The 4.35 pm from Newbury, which conveyed local school children, continued as a steam hauled service with the locomotive returning light engine to Newbury, having left the coaches at Lambourn.

Following the closure of Lambourn shed the branch goods was re-scheduled and worked during the early afternoon and locomotives for the branch came to be supplied from Reading.

For many years Auto trailer No. 58 was used for passenger services supplemented by two clerestory coaches. The spare coaches were used to increase the accommodation of the 7.40 am from Lambourn and the 4.35 pm from Newbury. They were also brought into use as required on Thursdays, which was market day, and Saturdays for shoppers.

MOTIVE POWER

The Lambourn Valley Railway Company hired a Locomotive from the GWR for the opening of the line, a 'Sharp Stewart' 2-4-0T No. 1384 (ex Watlington and Princes Risborough Railway).

Within months the Company had purchased two outside cylinder 0-6-0T's from Chapman and Furneaux, *Aelfred* and *Ealhswith*, a third and similar loco *Eadweade* being purchased from the Hunslet Engine Company in 1903. All three locomotives were sold to the Cambrian Railways in 1904, when two steam railmotors, hired from the GWR were substituted as an economy measure. Having sold its own motive power, the LVR found the railmotors had become troublesome, due to the high proportion of chalk present in the water supply, and reverted to hiring locomotives from the GWR.

When the Great Western took over the line in 1905 locomotives from Didcot shed were sub-shedded at Lambourn on a weekly basis. 850 class 0-6-0 Pannier and Saddle tanks were used on the line and Lambourn's allocation during 1920/21 is listed here as an example:

1953	850	class	0-6-0	PT	Jan - April
2002	"	"	"	ST	May
2003	"	"	"	PT	June - Sept
1912	"	"	"	ST	Oct
2003	"	"	"	PT	Jan 1921

The ex MSWJ Rly. 2-4-0's Nos. 1334, 1335 and 1336 were frequently used on the line and sometimes shedded at Lambourn for branch duties.

Lambourn shed was closed in 1936, when Diesel Railcars took over passenger services, and locomotives for the branch were later supplied from Reading shed.

Nos. 2532, 2573 and 2579 were among the 0-6-0 Dean Goods regularly employed on the branch, only being succeeded during the final years by the later Collett 2251's which had not previously been permitted on the line.

Diesel Railcars Nos. 18 and 19 worked passenger services for many years but steam hauled passenger workings were later restored with 57XX class Pannier tanks.

1933 Working Timetable

LAMBOURN VALLEY LINE.

Single Line worked by Electric Tablet System.   Crossing Stations are Newbury, Welford Park and Lambourn.
Worked by Engine and Branch Car (one class only) on weekdays, and by engine and train on Sundays.

Down Trains — Week Days / Sundays

Distance M·C	STATIONS	Ruling gradient one in	Point to Point times (Mins.)	Allow for Stop (Mins.)	Allow for Start (Mins)	B Pass. A.M.	B Pass. A.M.	B Pass. P.M.	B Pass. P.M.	B Pass. P.M.	B Pass. SO P.M.	K Goods SO arr. P.M.	K Goods SO dep. P.M.	K Goods SX arr. P.M.	K Goods SX dep. P.M.	B Pass. dep. P.M.
—	Newbury .... dep.	—	—	—	2	9 25	11 47	2 0	4 35	7 20	10 15		8 15		8 15	4 40
—·57	Newbury W.F. Halt ,,	63 R	—	—	—	9 28	11 50	2 3	4 38	7 23	10 18	¶8 20	OW8 25	¶8 20	OW8 25	4 43
1·53	Speen ,,	75 R	—	—	—	9 33	11 54	2 7	4 42	7 27	10 22	—	—	—	Z	4 49
2·60	Stockcross & Bagnor ,,	84 R	—	—	—	9 36	11 57	2 11	4 46	7 30	10 26	—	—	—	—	4 53
4·56	Boxford ,,	82 R	17	1	1	9 43	12 2	2 17	4 51	7 36	10 31	8 40	8 50	8 50	Q9 0	5 0
6·19	Welford Park ,,	62 R	3	1	1	9 49	12 8	2 23	4 57	7 41	10 37	8 55X	9 15	9 7	X10 10	5 5
8·14	Great Shefford ,,	210 R	5	1	1	9 58	12 15	2 30	5 4	7 47	10 44	9 22	9 35	10 17	10 35	5 15
9·74	East Garston ,,	89 R	5	1	1	10 4	12 20	2 36	5 10	7 52	10 50	9 42	9 50	10 42	10 50	5 23
11·2	Eastbury ,,	60 R	—	—	—	10 8	12 25	2 41	5 15	7 56	10 55	—	—	—	—	5 30
12·33	Lambourn arr.	62 R	13	—	—	10 12	12 30	2 46	5 20	8 3	11 0	10 5	—	11 5	—	5 39

Up Trains — Week Days / Sunday

STATIONS	Ruling gradient one in	Point to Point times (Mins.)	Allow for Stop (Mins.)	Allow for Start (Mins.)	B Mixed A.M.	B Pass. A.M.	B Pass. P.M.	B Pass. P.M.	B Mixed P.M.	B Pass. SO P.M.	K Goods SX arr. P.M.	K Goods SX dep. P.M.	K Goods SO arr. P.M.	K Goods SO dep. P.M.	B Pass. dep. P.M.
Lambourn .. dep.	—	—	—	1	7 42	10 40	12 43	3 12	6 0	8 45		8 45		11 5	6 55
Eastbury ,,	62 R	—	—	—	7 47	10 45	12 47	3 17	6 5	8 50	—	—	—	—	7 2
East Garston ,,	60 F	16	1	1	7 52	10 49	12 51	3 21	6 10	8 54	9 3	9 13	C	R	7 10
Great Shefford ,,	89 F	5	1	1	7 59	10 55	12 56	3 27	6 16	9 0	9 20	9 38	C	R	7 17
Welford Park .. ,,	167 F	5	1	1	8 5	11 1	1 2	3 32	6 21	9 X 7	9 45	X10 0	C	R	7 24
Boxford ,,	62 F	5	1	1	8 10	11 6	1 8	3 37	6 26	9 12	10 7	10 20	—	—	7 30
Stockcross & Bagnor ,,	61 R	—	—	—	8 14	11 12	1 13	3 43	6 32	9 18	—	—	—	—	7 37
Speen ,,	84 F	—	—	—	8 19	11 16	1 18	3 47	6 36	9 23	—	Z	—	—	7 42
Newbury W. F. Halt ,,	76 F	—	—	—	8 22	11 20	1 21	3 50	6 40	9 27	—	—	Gates.		7 47
Newbury arr.	63 F	10	—	2	8 25	11 23	1 24	3 53	6 43	9 30	10 45	—	12 5	—	7 50

Q To shunt out traffic for 8.45 p.m. Lambourn to pick up at one shunt.   Z 5 minutes allowed in running for opening and closing gates at Speen Station.
The 7.42 a.m. and 6.0 p.m. trains ex Lambourn may be run as "Mixed" Trains for the conveyance of Cattle traffic only.   ¶ These times apply to Newbury West Box.

1950 Working Timetable

NEWBURY AND LAMBOURN.

Single Line worked by Electric Token System.   Crossing Stations are Newbury, Welford Park, and Lambourn.
Worked by Diesel Car on week days (except 4.15 p.m. Newbury).
The 8.0 a.m. and 6.5 p.m. trains ex Lambourn may be run as "Mixed" Trains for the conveyance of Cattle traffic only.

ENGINE WORKING.—0-6-0 engines in the 23XX, 24XX and 25XX classes may work in emergency between Newbury and Lambourn subject to the observance of a special overall maximum speed restriction of 25 m.p.h. and of the permanent speed restrictions of 15 m.p.h. when employed for the haulage of goods trains ; also adherence to the 20 m.p.h restriction at either end of the branch in the case of passenger trains and of 15 m p.h. at Welford Park " down line through station loop " (vide page 162).

DOWN TRAINS — WEEK DAYS.

Dist. M·C	STATIONS	Ruling Gradient 1 in	Diesel Car P-to-P Mins.	Steam Loco P-to-P Mins.	Freight P-to-P Mins.	Allow Stop Mins.	Allow Start Mins.	B News & Parcels dep. a.m.	B Pass. dep. a.m.	B Pass. dep. a.m.	K Freight arr. p.m.	K Freight dep. p.m.	B Pass. dep. p.m.	B Pass. dep. p.m.	B Pass. dep. p.m.	B Pass. dep. p.m.	B Pass. SO dep. p.m.
—	NEWBURY .... dep.	—	—	—	—	—	2	6 50	9 25	11 45		12 10	2 0	4 15	5 12	7 25	10 15
—·57	Newbury W. F. H. ,,	63 R.	2	2	—	—	—		9 28	11 43	12‖150	W1220	2 3	4 18	5 15	7 28	
1·53	Speen ,,	75 R.	2½	3	—	—	—		9 31	11 51		Z	2 6	4 21	5 18	7 31	10 21
2·60	St'kcross & B'gnor ,,	84 R.	2½	3	—	—	—	7 0	9 35	11 55		—	2 10	4 25	5 22	7 35	10 25
4·56	Boxford ,,	82 R.	4½	5	17	1	1	CR	9 40	12 0	12 40	12 45	2 15	4 30	5 27	7R40	10 R30
6·19	Welford Park ,,	62 R.	4½	5	3	1	1	7G813	9 46	12 6	12 59	X 1 5	2 21	4 36	5X33	7 46	10 36
8·14	Great Shefford .. ,,	210 R.	4½	5	5	1	1	7 22	9 52	12 12	1 12	1 28	2 27	4 42	5 39	7 52	10 42
9·74	East Garston ,,	89 R.	3	4	5	1	1	—	9 57	12 17	1 35	1 40	2 32	4 47	5 48	7 57	10 47
11·2	Eastbury ,,	60 R.	3	4	—	—	—	10 1	12 21			2 36	4 51	5 48	8 1	10 51
12·33	LAMBOURN arr.	62 R.	3½	4	13	—	—	7 35	10 5	12 25			2X40	4 55	5 52	8 5	10 55

UP TRAINS — WEEK DAYS.

STATIONS	Ruling Gradient 1 in	Diesel Car P-to-P Mins.	Steam Loco P-to-P Mins.	Freight P-to-P Mins.	Allow Stop Mins.	Allow Start Mins.	B Mixed dep. a.m.	B Pass. dep. a.m.	B Pass. dep. p.m.	K Freight arr. p.m.	K Freight dep. p.m.	B Pass. dep. p.m.	G Engine to Reading dep. p.m.	B Mixed dep. p.m.	B Empty Diesel SX dep. p.m.	B Pass. SO dep. p.m.	B Empty Diesel SO dep. p.m.
LAMBOURN .... dep.	—	—	—	—	—	1	8 0	10 40	12 40		X	2 47	3 10	5‖ 8	6 5	8 45	11†10
Eastbury ,,	62 R.	3	4	—	—	—	8 4	10 44	12 44			3 14		6 9	8†15	8 49	
East Garston ,,	60 F.	3	4	16	1	1	8 8	10 48	12 48			3 18		6 13	—	8 53	
Great Shefford ,,	89 F.	4	6	5	1	1	8 15	10 53	12 53	C	R	3 23		6 20	—	8 58	
Welford Park ,,	167 F.	4½	5	5	1	1	8 23	11 0	1X 0	C	R	3 30	5X34	6R33	80832	9 5	1105‖7
Boxford ,,	62 F.	4½	5	5	1	1	8 28	11 5	1 5	C	R	3 35		6R33	—	9R10	
Stockcross & Bagnor ,,	61 R.	2½	3	—	—	—	8 34	11 11	1 11			3 39		6 39	—	9 17	
Speen ,,	84 F.	2½	3	—	—	—	8 38	11 15	1 15	—	Z	3 45		6 43	—	9 20	‡
Newbury W. F. Halt ,,	75 F.	2	3	—	—	—	8 41	11 18	1 18			3 48		6 47	—	9 23	‡
NEWBURY arr.	63 F.	2	2	10	—	2	8 45	11 20	1 20	3 30		3 50	5‖52	6 50	8†50	9 25	11†45

R—Treated as a Halt.   Z—5 minutes allowed in running for opening and closing of gates at Speen Station.
¶—These times apply to Newbury West Box.   ‡—To call at West Fields to open or close Halt.

Taken from original timetable

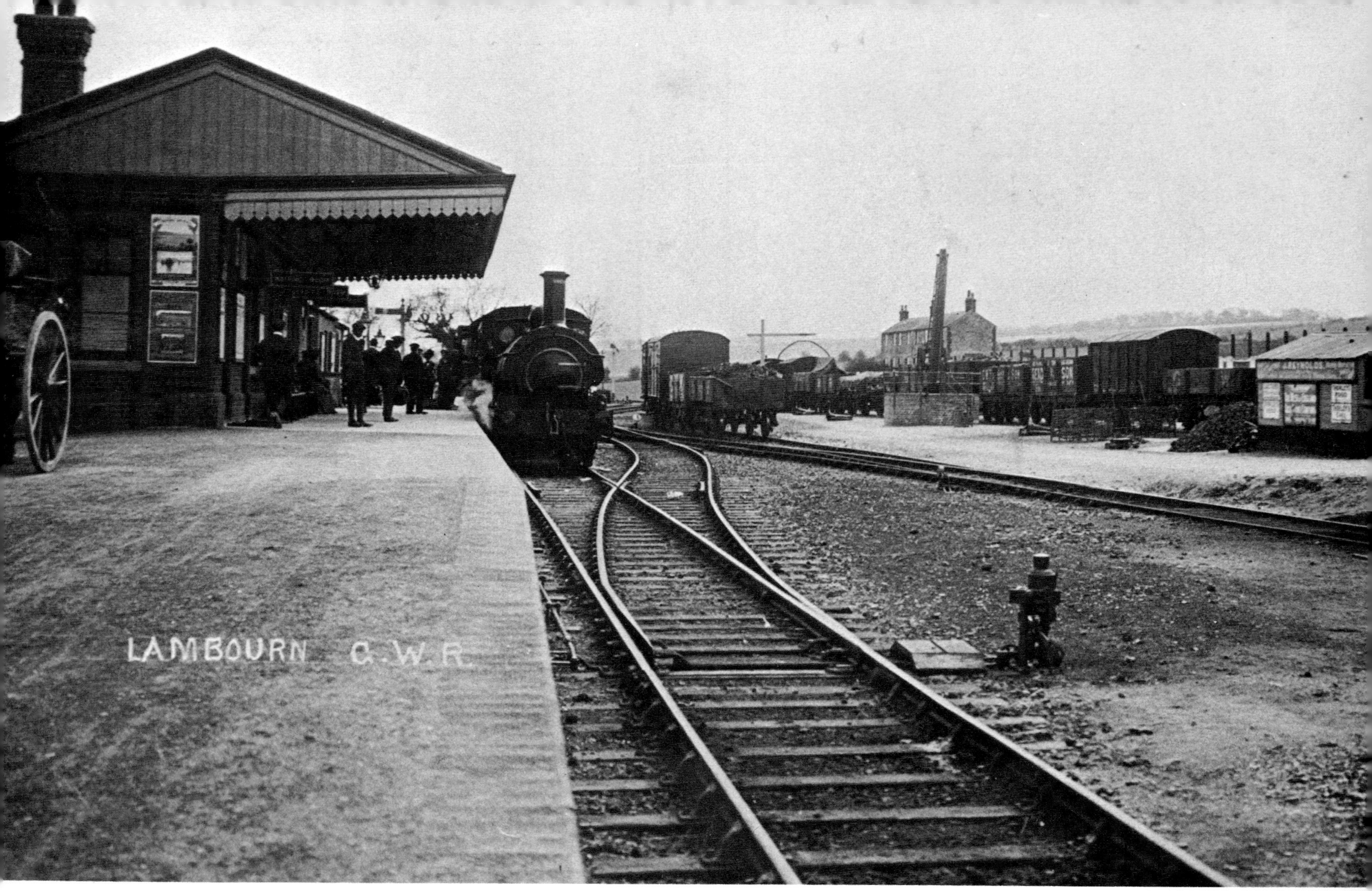

LAMBOURN G.W.R.

Fig. L4 An unidentified 850 class saddle tank shortly after arrival at Lambourn. This photograph, taken sometime between 1910 and 1919, illustrates the early style ground signal, wooden coal merchants office, 5 ton yard crane and the timber built loading gauge, all of which subsequently were replaced.

Early Plan

Early Track Plan Showing Lambourn Station as first constructed by the Lambourn Valley Railway Co.

KEY
1. WEIGHBRIDGE & OFFICE
2. WATER TANK
3. ENGINE SHED
4. GOODS SHED
5. STATION BUILDING
6. COAL OFFICE
7. CATTLE PEN
8. CRANE
9. CARRIAGE SHED

Lambourn Station, subsequent to the improvements carried out by the G.W.R. Circa 1911

Approximately 2 chains to 1 inch

12¼ miles

KEY
1. WEIGHBRIDGE & OFFICE
2. STORES
3. WATER TANK (CONICAL)
4. ENGINE SHED
5. GOODS SHED
6. STATION BUILDING
7. STORE
8. PARCELS
9. COAL OFFICE
10. CRANE (5 TON)
11. CATTLE PEN
12. LAMP HUT
13. COAL
14. P.W. HUT
15. SIGNAL BOX
16. LOADING GAUGE

Later Plan

Fig. L5 Railcar No. 18 at Lambourn.   *M.B. Warburton*

Fig. L6 A 57XX class 0-6-0PT approaches Bockhampton crossing with a goods train for Lambourn in 1956.

L. Nicolson

Fig. L7 The same train passing over the crossing tackles the final gradient of 1 in 63, easing to 1 in 100 before reaching Lambourn Station.

A brick built crossing keeper's hut which stood at the site was manned at short intervals by a junior member of staff dispatched from the station before the arrival of the train.

L. Nicolson

Fig. L8 Lambourn Station on the Public opening day 4th April, 1898.

British Railways

Fig. L9 The original station building and platform. The lightly laid trackwork shown in these early views was constructed of flat bottom rail spiked directly to the sleepers and ballasted over.

British Railways

Fig. L10 No. 1384 shortly after arrival at Lambourn. Note the original timber water tank at the site of the well and the loco coaling stage outside the shed. The coaling stage was later removed and locomotives were coaled straight from the wagon.

British Railways

Fig. L11 The Lambourn Valley Railway's first public train at Lambourn. The four Brown Marshall coaches were purchased by the Company Chairman and the locomotive, No. 1384 (ex Watlington & Princes Risborough Railway) was hired from the GWR. The livery of the coaches is reputed to have been blue with gold lettering.

Courtesy L. Nicolson

Fig. L13 The ground fell away sharply behind the platform and was inlaid with granite blocks for support, whilst the main station building was supported on extensive brick arch foundations. The picture was taken in 1919 and just shows the siding which ran off behind the signal box and the original siting of the starter signal on the platform.

Fig. L14 An official photograph of 1910 showing the GWR replacement station buildings and platform, just after completion. The new platform was actually constructed behind the original, thus increasing the area of trackage. The main building was constructed of red brick with moulded reveals to the windows and doorways and Taylors Patent roofing, constructed of a steel framework clad with traditional matchboarding. The nearer of the two supplementary buildings was used as a store whilst the other served as a parcels office.

British Railways

Fig. L15 Railcar No. 19 on the 3.10 pm to Newbury, 4th October, 1948.

W.A. Camwell

Fig. L16 No. 2007 at Lambourn during winter months with her crew preparing for the draughty bunker-first trip to Newbury.

Photomatic

Fig. L17 Ex MSWJ Rly. No. 1334 on arrival at Lambourn during January 1935. The loco shed in the background was closed in 1936, when diesel railcars were first introduced on the branch. The building was said to have been dismantled for further use and moved to Didcot in 1939. The corrugated iron shed alongside the buffer stop covered a well. Water was raised by a Pulsometer pump, powered by steam from the branch locos, and stored in the conical topped tank, which additionally fed the 'NOT DRINKING WATER' supply to the station. For many years Station Staff collected drinking water from nearby houses (visible behind the crane in *Fig. L4*) as it was not until after the Second World War that a mains water supply was laid to the site and fed both the station and the conical tank.

Dr. Ian C. Allen

Fig. L18 The layout of the site, as seen from the buffer stops after the removal of the loco shed.   *M.J. Deane*

Fig. L19 No. 2579 awaiting departure with a three-coach train to Newbury.

   W.A. Camwell

Fig. L20 The station buildings and goods shed, still bearing GWR colours just prior to their repainting in 1953/54.

The 20 ton weighing machine was installed in 1948, together with a pre-cast concrete office just visible beyond the water tank. This replaced a much outdated cart machine and a small wooden office which had previously stood at the site. The new machine, No. WR8675, was sent to Gloucester Eastgate after closure.

The small corrugated iron office featured in these views was occupied by the local coal merchant, L.J. Bodman & Son.

J.H. Moss

Fig. L21 The original LVR goods shed survived throughout the life of the branch. It was constructed of timber with a corrugated iron roof and sliding doors. The canopy which overhung the track was cut to the shape of the standard load gauge and may have been originally intended for use as such. The access road to the loading bay skirts the foreground of this view.

Photoscript – Deddington

Fig. L22 Lambourn Station yard in 1954 with 0-6-0PT No. 7777 running round its train. The extensive loading bank in the foreground was necessary to contend with the high percentage of racehorse and cattle traffic.

The Pacos (horseboxes) stabled in the yard were a familiar sight at Lambourn, some of the vehicles being allocated to particular trainers whose names appeared on the sides.

The gas lighting in these vehicles was replenished from a Cordon (gas tank wagon) which was usually kept in the yard. Note the vehicle crossing on the siding to the goods shed.

T.B. Sands

Fig. L23 During the reconstruction of Lambourn station, around 1910, the GWR replaced the original 1 ton 10 cwt yard crane with the 5 ton crane illustrated in *Fig. L4.* The yard crane illustrated in these views was an even later replacement that had a lifting capacity of only 3 tons.

Photoscript – Deddington

Fig. L25 The small wooden signal box at Lambourn appears to have been a standard GWR groundframe erected at minimum cost during the reconstruction of the station and installation of signalling around 1910.

Note the signalman's bicycle leaning against the porch.

Courtesy C.P. Legg

Fig. L24 This wooden-posted signal was originally sited on the station platform (as seen in *Figs L4* and *L13*). Following the removal of the siding (around 1936) which ran behind the signal box it was repositioned here, but never fully repainted before its removal some 18 years later! Note the position of the balance weight on the post, this was because in the signal's former position, the normal arrangement could have been a hazard to passengers.

I.D. Beale

Fig. L26 The signalman's view of the station showing the corrugated iron lamp hut which stood at the foot of the platform.

J.H. Moss

Fig. L27 No. 7777, a regular engine on the branch during the 1950's, gently eases towards the platform to collect its train. The tubular steel starting signal installed in 1953/4, replaced that shown in *Fig. L24.*

T.B. Sands

Fig. L28 A further view of the signal box.
It is interesting to note the lofty stove pipe, and the arrangement whereby water from the front guttering is piped to run away at the rear.
M.B. Warburton

Fig. L29 A general view of the yard with a Dean Goods awaiting departure in the loop, just clear of the crossing.

J.H. Moss

Fig. L30 The line approached the station across the downs on a gradient of 1 in 100 which levelled at the throat of the station yard. A platelayer is seen lubricating the pointwork just prior to the arrival of the passenger train which would have enabled the Dean Goods in the previous view to make its departure.

J.H. Moss

S. Fletcher

Lens of Sutton

The Lambourn branch was closed to all traffic on 4th January, 1960, with the exception of goods workings to the U.S. Airforce base and Welford Park, which continued until 3rd November, 1973.

At the time of writing the line to Welford remains derelict and overgrown. Lambourn station itself has completely disappeared and almost ironically become the base of Lambourn Ridgeway Transport Ltd., horse carriers.

Further sources of reference:
Railway Magazine Vol. 11 *P47 1902*
Railway Magazine Vol. 100 *P739 1954*
'The Lambourn Valley Railway',
by *M.R.C. Price, Oakwood Press.*

SCALE DRAWINGS OF BUILDINGS AT LAMBOURN

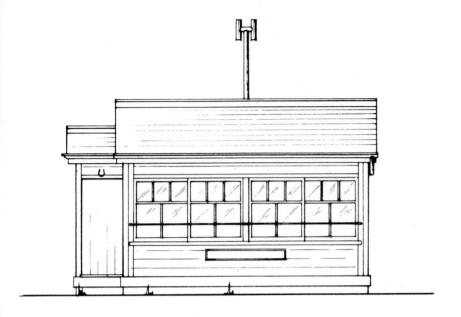

ELEVATION TO SOUTH WEST

END ELEVATION
FACING SOUTH EAST

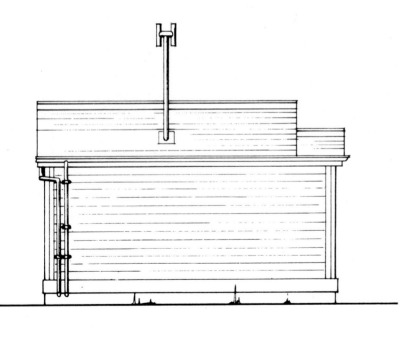

REAR ELEVATION

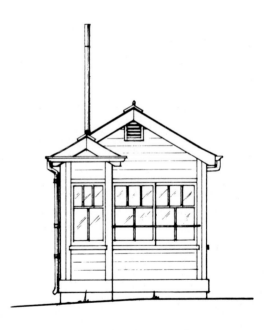

END ELEVATION
FACING NORTH WEST

Lambourn Signal Box

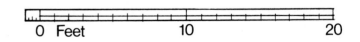

0 Feet   10   20

Lambourn Weighbridge Hut

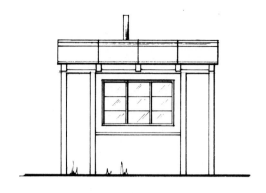

ELEVATION TO SOUTH EAST

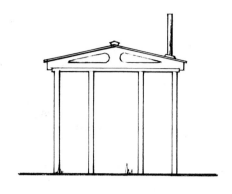

END ELEVATION
FACING NORTH EAST

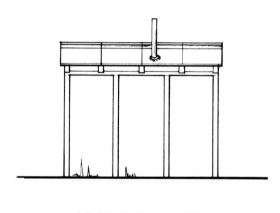

REAR ELEVATION

END ELEVATION
FACING SOUTH WEST

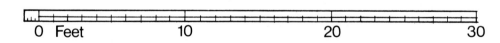

0 Feet   10   20   30

Lambourn Lamp Hut

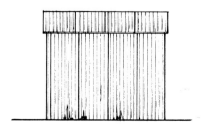

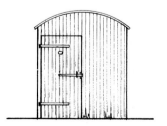

Fig. T1 Collett 0-4-2T No. 5806 at Tetbury in 1948. *M.J. Deane*

TETBURY

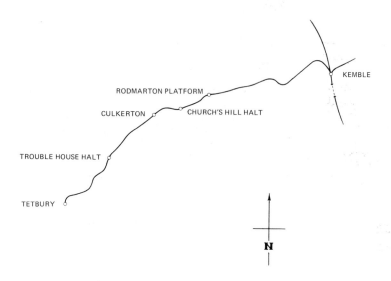

KEY FACTS

Company of Origin	Great Western Railway
Date of Opening	2nd December, 1889
Date of Closure	Closed to Goods — Tetbury to Culkerton 1st July, 1963 Culkerton to Kemble 4th August, 1963 Closed to passengers 4th April, 1964
Length of Branch	7 Miles 19 Chains
Ruling Gradient	1 in 69
Route Colour	Yellow
Overall Speed Restriction	40 mph
Single Line Worked by	Train Staff and One Engine in Steam or two coupled together (the line was originally worked by an electric token system)

ORIGIN

The Tetbury branch was authorised by an Act of Parliament on 7th August, 1884 and unlike the other lines included in this volume was constructed by the Great Western Railway. The line was opened on 2nd December, 1889 and ran from Kemble which was also the junction for the Cirencester branch, a distance of 7 miles 19 chains to Tetbury with one intermediate station at Culkerton.

Additional halts were later opened at various dates — these were namely: Jackaments Halt, Rodmarton Platform, Church's Hill Halt and Trouble House Halt.

Fig. T2 70' trailer No. W47 at Tetbury, 15th July, 1951.

Roye England

OPERATION

The Tetbury branch was operated on the 'One Engine in Steam' principle, using a wooden train staff. Tetbury itself was a sub-shed of Gloucester although locomotives were actually supplied by Swindon shed and branch crews were based at Tetbury.

A typical weekday of 1953:

The early turn fireman booked on at 6.30 am and relieved the overnight shedman. After the arrival of the driver, the loco was oiled up and moved off shed to join the auto trailer in the platform, taking water alongside the shed on the way.

The first train departed at 8.00 am, conveying school children and often returned with a parcels van in tow. The second departure at 9.30 am returned as a mixed train and was often late back to Tetbury after setting down churns of drinking water at Culkerton and shunting the yard there as required. The yard was shunted at Tetbury and the early turn crew were relieved after their return from the 12.10 pm which ran mixed to Kemble, conveying empties. The fresh crew began their duty by further shunting of the yard and if time allowed, pumping water to fill the water tank at the shed. The 3.40 pm worked out as a mixed train and returned with the school children. The 6.5 pm and 7.40 pm return passenger workings completed the day's timetable.

During the later years there was no overnight shedman at Tetbury and locomotives were lit up each morning by the fireman. Problems arose when they overslept and were subsequently late in raising steam; on such occasions the loco was moved off shed, under low pressure using a pinch bar and the first train often departed with just enough steam to hold off the brakes!

Passenger services were usually worked by an Auto Trailer, but push pull working was rare because of the shunting requirements of mixed train operations. A standby coach was kept in the head shunt beyond the platform to strengthen services as required, but special trains for Westonbirt School are said to have comprised of some six or seven coaches and were even double headed.

During shunting operations the Auto Trailer was usually stabled on the running line, beyond the neck of the yard, to act as a stop against which the train was made up. The station was on a falling gradient towards the buffer stops, so when completed trains were too long for the loco to pass on the run round loop, stock was propelled just beyond the neck of the yard and allowed to return to the platform by gravity, running past the locomotive which had hastily retreated into the run round ahead of the moving train.

MOTIVE POWER

0-4-2 tank locomotives of the 517 class were allocated to Tetbury during the early years of the line, the official allocation for 1920/21 being listed here as an example:—

1154	517 class	0-4-2T	Jan - May
529	,,	,, ,,	Jun - Oct
1154	,,	,, ,,	Nov
529	,,	,, ,,	Dec/Jan 1921

Both the 48XX (later renumbered 14XX) and the non auto fitted 58XX classes of the later Collett 0-4-2T's succeeded the 517's and remained in service on the line until closure.

Post War allocations included:—
Nos. 1404, 1433, 5804, 5805, 5806

45XX class 2-6-2T's were occasionally provided when 0-4-2T's were not available.

During the 1950's a number of 0-6-0 pannier tanks of the 57XX, 74XX and 16XX classes saw regular service on the branch and lightweight diesel railbuses worked passenger services from 1959 until closure.

Fig. T3 No. 1436 shortly after arrival at Tetbury with the 10.35 am from Kemble, 4th October, 1948.
W.A. Camwell

1933 Working Timetable

KEMBLE AND TETBURY BRANCH.

Worked by Train Staff, only one Engine in Steam at a time or 2 or more coupled together between Kemble and Tetbury. **Culkerton Station.**—The Sidings at Culkerton are locked by a key fixed in end of the Train Staff.

Distance M.	C.	DOWN TRAINS.		Statn. No.		Mixed T (A.M.)		Mixed (A.M.)		Pass. (P.M.)		K RR Goods (P.M.)		Pass. N (P.M.)		Pass. (P.M.)		Pass. (P.M.)	Pass. (P.M.)		Sundays				Pass. (P.M.)
—	—	Kemble	dep.	2503	..	8 40	..	10 30	..	1 23	..	3 40	..	4 0	..	5 23	..	6 47	8 35	..	..	..	..		8 15
3	3	Rodmarton Platfm ...	,,	2505	...	—	...	10 38	....	1 30	....	R	....	4 7	....	5 30	...	6 54	8 42	....	....	....	....	..	8 22
4	31	Culkerton	arr	....	..	8 49	..	10 43	..	1 33	..	—	..	4 11	..	5 33	..	6 57	8 45	..	..	..	..	...	8 25
			dep	2506	...	8 50	...	10 46	....	1 36	....	4 0	....	4 12	....	5 34	....	6 58	8 46	....	....	...	....	..	8W28
7	19	Tetbury	arr	2507	..	8 56		10 53	..	1 42	..	4 10	..	4 19	..	5 40		7 4	8 52	..		..	..	..	8 34

Distance M.	C.	UP TRAINS.		Pass. (A.M.)		Pass. (A.M.)				Mixed Q (P.M.)		K RR Goods (P.M.)		Mixed N (P.M.)		Mixed (P.M.)		Pass. (P.M.)	Pass. (P.M.)		Sundays				Pass. (P.M.)
—	—	Tetbury	dep	7 52	Culkerton arr. 7.59.	9 15	..	..	....	12 15	..	2 40	..	3 10	..	4 40	..	6 10	7 35	..	..	..	..	....	5 30
2	68	Culkerton	,,	8* 0		9 23	....	....	..	12 24	....	3 0	....	3 19	....	4 53	....	6 18	7 42	....	....	....	....	..	5 40
4	16	Rodmarton Platfm	,,	8 3		9 26	..	..	....	12 30	..	R	..	3 25	..	4 59	..	6 21	7 46	..	..	..	..	....	5 43
6	57	Stop Board.	,,	—		—	....	....	..	—	....	3P13	....	—	....	—	...	—	—	....	....	....	....	..	—
7	19	Kemble	arr.	8 10	*	9 33	..	..	....	12 37	..	3 16	..	3 32	..	5 6	..	6 28	7 52	..	..	..	..	....	5 50

Engines of 2-4-0 T. type may work over this Branch. **N** Runs on Tetbury Monthly Market day, Second Wednesday in month. **Q** To run as a Passenger train on Tetbury Monthly Market day. **R** Will not run on Tetbury Monthly Market days.
Mixed Trains.—When required to stop at Stop Board 5 minutes additional time allowed for running and Stop Board purposes.
T When run as Mixed 14 minutes allowed between Kemble and Culkerton. **W** Guard to close station and extinguish lamps.

Taken from original timetable

1953 Public Timetable

Table 107 KEMBLE and TETBURY—(Third class only)

Miles	Week Days only	am	am	am		pm S	pm	pm	
	105London (Pad.) dep	5 30	7R30	11R5	..	..	2 15	4R55	..
—	**Kemble** .... dep	8 45	10 30	1p18	....	3 22	5 10	6 54	..
3	Rodmarton Platform	8 53	10 40	1 27	..	3 29	5 18	7 1	
4½	Culkerton	8 56	10 48	1 33	....	3 33	5 21	7 5	..
7¼	**Tetbury** .. .. arr	9 5	11 0	1 42	..	3 41	5 29	7 13	..

Miles	Week Days only	am	am	pm	pm S	pm E	pm S	pm	
—	**Tetbury** ... .. dep	7 52	9 30	1215	2 5	3 40	3 48	6 5	..
2¾	Culkerton	7 59	9 38	1223	2 12	3 49	3 55	6 12	....
4½	Rodmarton Platform	8 2	9 41	1228	2 15	3 54	3 58	6 15	..
7¼	**Kemble** .... arr	8 11	9 49	1239	2 24	4 7	4 7	6 24	....
98¼	**105London** (Pad.) arr	10 28	12 25	3R 0	5R35	6R55	6R55	9 20	..

E Except Saturdays. *p* pm. **R** Refreshment Car Train. **S** Saturdays only.

SECTION. From	To	2-8-0 Coal.	2-8-0 Goods.	2-8-0 Empties.	2-6-2 T Coal.	2-6-2 T Goods.	2-6-2 T Empties.	2-6-0 Coal.	2-6-0 Goods.	2-6-0 Empties.	Ordinary Engines Tender. Coal.	Tender. Goods.	Tender. Empties.	Tank. Coal.	Tank. Goods.	Tank. Empties.	
Tetbury Branch.																	
Kemble Junction ...	Tetbury	...	...	...	...	...	...	...	...	...	...	...	...	10	15	25	Passenger tank engine.
Tetbury	Kemble Junction ...	...	...	...	...	...	...	...	...	...	...	...	...				

(Number of Wagons exclusive of Brake Van.)

Extract from GWR "Maximum Loads" 1908

RAILWAY STATION TETBURY

Fig. T4 Tetbury Station at the beginning of the century with, what would appear to be, a 517 class 0-4-2T at the head of a mixed train. This view, taken prior to the platform extension, shows the original station building, the loco shed as first constructed with the water tank in a lower position, the platelayers hut opposite the platform and evidence of the signalling which was later removed.

Courtesy M.J. Deane

Track Plan

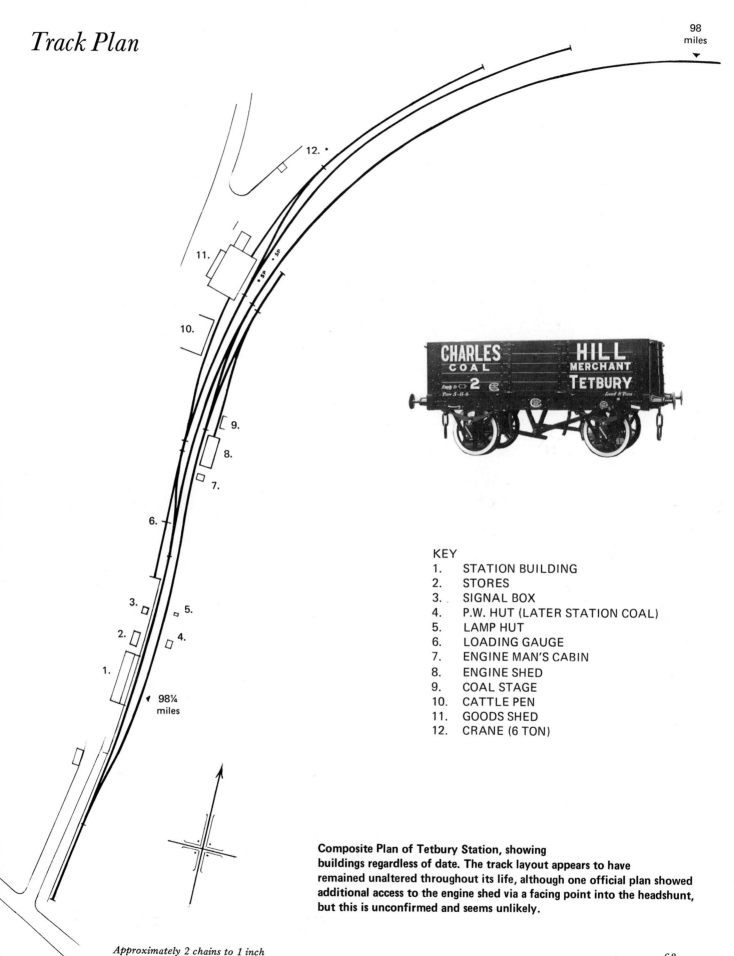

12. •

11.

10.

9.

8.

7.

6. •

3. ◻   5.

2. ◻   4.

1.

◄ 98¼
miles

KEY
1.   STATION BUILDING
2.   STORES
3.   SIGNAL BOX
4.   P.W. HUT (LATER STATION COAL)
5.   LAMP HUT
6.   LOADING GAUGE
7.   ENGINE MAN'S CABIN
8.   ENGINE SHED
9.   COAL STAGE
10. CATTLE PEN
11. GOODS SHED
12. CRANE (6 TON)

**Composite Plan of Tetbury Station, showing
buildings regardless of date. The track layout appears to have
remained unaltered throughout its life, although one official plan showed
additional access to the engine shed via a facing point into the headshunt,
but this is unconfirmed and seems unlikely.**

Approximately 2 chains to 1 inch

Fig. T5 The intending passenger's view of the station as seen from the Malmesbury road.   *A.E. Bennett*

Fig. T6 An undated view of the station, probably taken during the 1930's. A standby coach and horseboxes were generally stabled at this end of the headshunt and severely restricted shunting movements in and out of the yard. The points at this end of the run round were permanently sprung in favour of the loop since the removal of the signalling.

Note: The trees behind the retaining wall (alongside the access road) were later removed.

Lens of Sutton

Fig. T7 The station approach, 3rd September, 1962, after the removal of the station entrance gates (as seen in *Fig. T6*) which were re-sited at the head of the drive. Note railbus at platform.

C. Strevens

Fig. T8 The main station building was constructed around 1915/16 to replace the original wooden building shown in *Fig. T4*. It was constructed of red brick with a tiled roof and many of the doors and windows from the previous building were utilised at the discretion of the contractor. The parcels office doorway which is just visible behind the telephone battery cabinet is said to have been disused for many years.

R.T. Parham

Fig. T9 0-6-0PT No. 7418 shortly after arrival at Tetbury with a mixed train from Kemble, 27th April, 1955.

H.C. Casserley

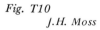

Fig. T10
J.H. Moss

Fig. T11 The rear of the station buildings after closure.

N. de Courtais

Fig. T12 This small brick building served as the station stores-cum-bicycle shed and was erected on the site of a corrugated iron shed which had previously served the same purpose.

R.G. Rose

Fig. T13 The station buildings and platform in 1949. Station coal had previously been stored in a wooden pen, situated opposite the platform, which may have been the remains of the platelayers hut shown in *Fig. T4*. This was replaced by the concrete-block built pen, which is illustrated on the left of this view, shortly after construction. The aperture in the face of the platform is almost certainly evidence of the former signal box.

L. & G.R.P.

Fig. T14 Looking towards Kemble from the station platform.   *M.J. Deane*

Fig. T15 A further view of the station in the mid 1950's.   *M.J. Deane*

Fig. T16   *C. Strevens*

Fig. T17 A closer view of the end loading bank. The corrugated iron lamp hut, which was almost surrounded by bushes, is just visible on the extreme left of the picture.

R.T. Parham

Fig. T18 Tetbury Station was situated on a falling gradient of 1 in 264 towards the buffer stops. Vehicles destined for the end loading bank were often propelled over the yard entry crossover and left to run back onto the buffer stop with the guard applying the brakes alongside.

J.H. Moss

Fig. T19 The water tank mounted on the loco shed was supplied from a well which lay between the enginemen's cabin and the rear of the shed. Water was raised by a small surface steam pump, powered by the branch loco and situated beneath the tank inside the building.

R.T. Parham

Fig. T20 A rural scene at Tetbury in 1955.   *M.J. Deane*

Fig. T21 The loco shed and coal stage, as seen from the goods shed looking towards the station with the cattle dock in the right hand foreground.

J.H. Moss

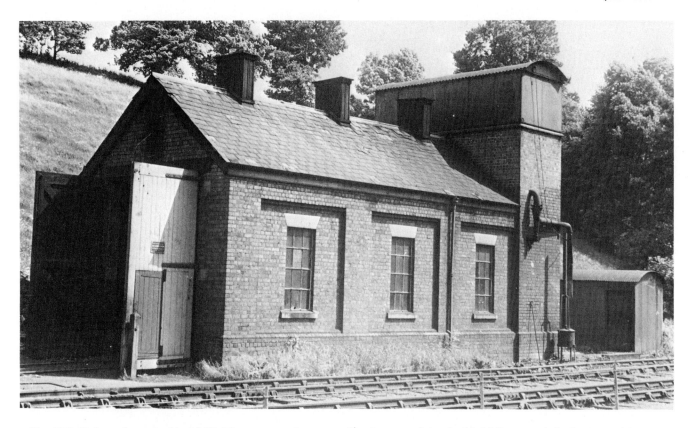

Fig. T22 Tetbury loco shed in 1947. The water tank mounted at the rear of the shed initially occupied a lower position, as mentioned in *Fig. T4*. This building was constructed of blue brick with a slate roof, but the fresh brickwork beneath the tank was a lighter shade of purple-brown.

J.H. Russell

Fig. T23 Tetbury goods shed was an extensive structure by branch line standards. It was constructed of blue brick to the same basic design as those at Maidenhead and Twyford and incorporated a weigh-house and a 30 cwt crane.

Public Record Office

Fig. T24 From the same spot as *Fig. T18*, but looking in the opposite direction, towards Kemble. In common with other stations of this volume, the doors at this end of the goods shed were smashed in a shunting accident of later years. For some months, whilst awaiting repairs, a tarpaulin was religiously hung in the doorway each night.

J.H. Moss

Fig. T25 The six ton yard crane. *R.G. Rose*

Fig T26 A view of the goods yard looking towards the station. The road vehicle crossing place can just be seen at the crossover in the sidings and 'The Dolphins' coal merchants office is situated on the extreme right hand side.

R.T. Parham

Fig. T27 The pointwork at the neck of the run round loop was controlled by a ground frame, housed in the small wooden cabinet on the right of the picture (beside the loco siding) whilst the yard entry crossover in the foreground was controlled by the other ground frame illustrated in *Fig. T14*.   *M.J. Deane*

Fig. T28 A very desolate scene in the goods yard looking towards Kemble just prior to closure.

R.T. Parham

Fig. T29 A 16XX class 0-6-0 pannier tank is seen here leaving Tetbury with the branch train for Kemble in 1955.

M.J. Deane

N. de Courtais

The Tetbury branch was closed to passengers on 4th April, 1964. Part of the yard at Tetbury, including the goods shed, remains in use as a depot for The Dolphins Coal Company, but with this exception, the station has completely disappeared.

Further sources of reference:
    Railway Modeller Vol. 5 *P286 1954*
    Railway World Vol. 16 *P47 1955*
    Model Railway News Vol. 33 *P210 1957*
    Railway World Vol. 19 *P367 1958*
    Railway Magazine Vol. 110 *P742 1964*

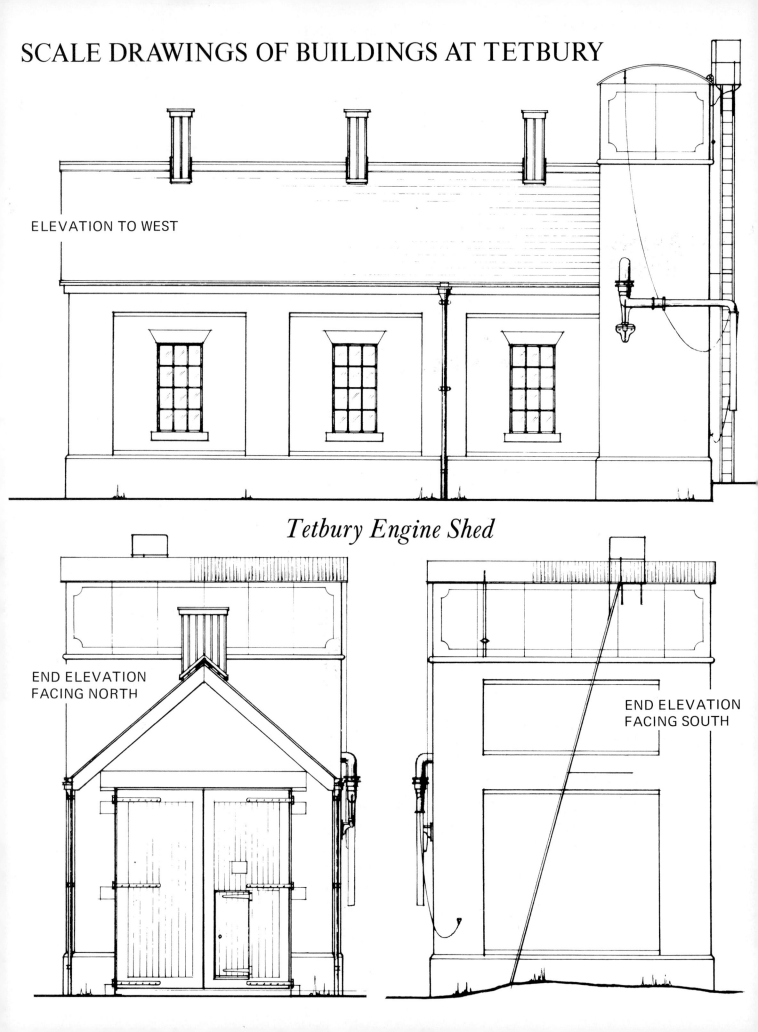

SCALE DRAWINGS OF BUILDINGS AT TETBURY

ELEVATION TO WEST

Tetbury Engine Shed

END ELEVATION
FACING NORTH

END ELEVATION
FACING SOUTH

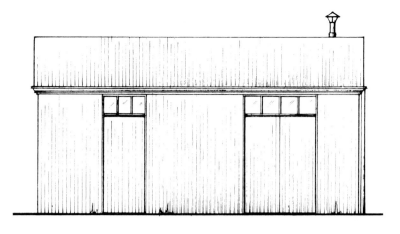

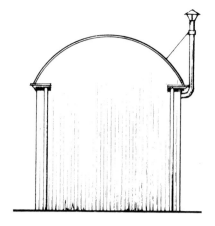

Tetbury Original Lamp Room and Stores (GWR 1888)

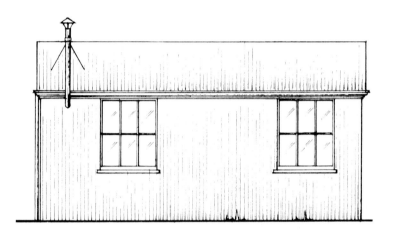

Detail views of the goods shed and yard crane at Tetbury during the final years.

R.T. Parham

Fig. WL1 Collett 0-4-2T No. 4862 stands just outside the loco shed at Wallingford Station on 6th June, 1937.

W.A. Camwell

WALLINGFORD

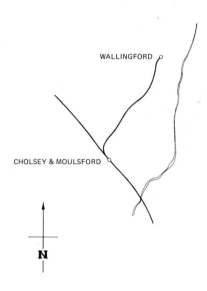

WALLINGFORD

CHOLSEY & MOULSFORD

N

KEY FACTS

Company of Origin	Wallingford & Watlington Railway Co.
Date of Opening	2nd July, 1866
Purchased by GWR	2nd December, 1872
Date of Closure	15th June, 1959 Remaining open for goods traffic until 13th September, 1965
Length of Branch	2 Miles 49 Chains
Ruling Gradient	1 in 202
Route Colour	Uncoloured
Overall Speed Restrictions	30 mph
Single line worked by	Train Staff & One Engine in Steam or two coupled together

ORIGIN

The Wallingford and Watlington Railway Act of July 1864 authorised the construction of a line from the GWR main line near Cholsey, 3 miles 24 chains to Wallingford. The line was to continue to Watlington, a further distance of some six miles and terminate in a field just outside the town, but insufficient financial support prevented the fulfilment of the scheme and in the event, only the Wallingford section was completed.

The line to Wallingford was opened on 2nd July, 1866 and worked by the GWR. The junction with the main line had originally been at Wallingford Road, then renamed Moulsford, but the branch was effectively shortened when this station was replaced with a new one which was constructed in the 1890's some ¾ of a mile to the west and named Cholsey and Moulsford.

The Wallingford and Watlington Railway Company soon found itself in financial difficulties and subsequently sold out to the GWR on 2nd December, 1872.

There were no intermediate stations on the line, gradients were easy and the 2½ miles to Wallingford were without engineering works of any size.

Fig. WL2 No. 1405 pauses at the entrance to the gasworks siding, opposite the station platform.

J.H. Russell

OPERATION

The single line was operated on the One Engine in Steam principle, with a locomotive from Reading shed being sub-shedded at Wallingford each week. There were two drivers and two firemen based at Wallingford together with an overnight cleaner. The Wallingford loco department were proud in their work and apparently locos which came from Reading each Monday, were returned in spotless condition the following week. (Locomotives generally faced up the branch, the trailer being propelled towards Wallingford.)

The following notes apply to the weekday timetable of 1937:

The first train out of Wallingford in the morning was the 7.08 am passenger, which returned as the first of the three mixed trains from Cholsey. The wagons in tow were detached on arrival at Wallingford and left in the yard with little time for sorting. Three return passenger trips then followed before shunting could be resumed. The 10.22 am returned as the second mixed train and the yard was sorted for almost three quarters of an hour. During this time a milk tank wagon was collected from the C.W.S. Creamery's private siding and later taken to Cholsey at the rear of the 11.35 am. The next departure at 12.28 pm returned with an empty milk wagon in tow. A total of no less than 18 return trips were made in all each weekday, with the 4.58 pm and the 7.48 pm departures from Wallingford running as mixed trains. The last departure of the day was at 9.45 pm but this train waited at Cholsey not arriving back at Wallingford until 11.42 pm.

There were no trains on Sundays other than one trip into Cholsey with the milk tank from the Creamery, for the sole purpose of which the Wallingford loco was specially steamed. The intensive weekday service proved most demanding on loco crews, water and coal being taken as and when time permitted, but with the almost continual demand for shunting movements and the auto coach not being permitted into the yard, the auto gear (apparently being considerable trouble to couple) was frequently left disconnected, so that when propelling towards Wallingford the fireman would unofficially drive from the loco and the driver would control the braking from the front of the auto trailer.

80

MOTIVE POWER

Throughout the life of the branch auto fitted four coupled tank locomotives were used almost exclusively and proved most suitable for the mixed traffic workings, 517 class 0-4-2 tank locomotives being employed in the earlier years. Wallingford's official locomotive allocation for 1920/21 being listed here as an example:—

1443	517 class 0-4-2T			Jan - March
1484	,,	,,	,,	April - July
519	,,	,,	,,	Aug - Sept
526	,,	,,	,,	Oct - Jan 1921

The later Collett 0-4-2T's succeeded the 517's and worked the line until the withdrawal of passenger services.

Post War allocations included:—
Nos. 4844, 4847, 4848, 1444 and 1447.

At least one Dean Goods is said to have worked the line and even one of the ex MSWJ 2-4-0's No. 1336. However, such occasions were extremely rare. During the later years of the line locomotives were supplied from Didcot shed and following the closure of Wallingford shed in 1956 Collett 2251's and various 0-6-0 pannier tanks were often to be seen at Wallingford.

517 class 0-4-2T No. 1479 on Wallingford branch duties, at Cholsey in January 1931. *Dr. Ian C. Allen*

Fig. WL3 No. 1442 leaving Cholsey with the 6.10 pm to Wallingford on 29th July, 1955. The auto trailer No. W81W was built in 1912.

P. Kelley

1937 Working Timetable

WALLINGFORD BRANCH. RAIL-AUTO CAR—ONE CLASS ONLY.

No Block Telegraph on this Line. Form of Staff, Square; Colour, Brown.
SINGLE LINE worked by Train Staff, and only one Engine in Steam at a time, or two coupled together.

Distances.	Mile Post Mileage.	STATIONS.	Ruling gradient 1 in	Point to point times. Mins.	Allow for stop. Mins.	Allow for start. Mins.	B Auto. Mixed. A.M.	B Auto. Pass. A.M.	B Auto. Pass. A.M.	B Auto. Pass. A.M.	B Auto. Pass. A.M.	B Auto. Pass. A.M.	B Auto. SO P.M.	B Auto. Pass. P.M.	B Auto. SX P.M.	B Auto. SO P.M.	B Auto. SX P.M.	B Auto. Mixed P.M.	B Auto. Pass. P.M.	B Auto. Pass. P.M.	B Auto. Pass. P.M.	B Auto. Pass. P.M.	B Auto. Pass. P.M.	B Auto. Pass. P.M.	B Auto. Pass. P.M.	B Auto. Pass. P.M.	B Auto. P.M.	SUNDAYS. C Milk E'ties. P.M.	G Eng. P.M.
— 48 37	Ch'ls'y&M.dep	—	—	—	1	7 35	8 16	8 52	9 20	10 45	11 55	12 51	12 56	1 28	2 8	2 29	3 8	4 6	5 40	6 20	6 56	7 29	8 3	8 25	9 16	11¶36	12 V 5	3 ||10
2 52 51 8	Wallingf'rdarr 202F	—	—	—	—	7 42	8 22	8 58	9 26	10 54	12 1	12 57	1 3	1 34	2 14	2 29	3 14	4 12	5 46	6 26	7 2	7 35	8 9	8 31	9 22	11¶42	12 V 12	3 ||16

STATIONS.	Ruling gradient 1 in	Point to point times. Mins.	Allow for stop. Mins.	Allow for start. Mins.	B Auto. Pass. A.M.	B Auto. Pass. A.M.	B Auto. Pass. A.M.	B Auto. Pass. A.M.	B Auto. Pass. A.M.	B Auto. Pass. A.M.	B Auto. Mixed A.M.	B Auto. Pass. P.M.	B Auto. SO P.M.	B Auto. Pass. P.M.	B Auto. Pass. P.M.	B Auto. Pass. P.M.	B Auto. Mixed P.M.	B Auto. Pass. P.M.	B Auto. Pass. P.M.	B Auto. Pass. P.M.	B Auto. Mixed P.M.	B Auto. Pass. P.M.	B Auto. Pass. P.M.	B Auto. P.M.	C Milk. A.M.	C Milk. P.M.
Wallingford .... dep. 202R	—	8	1	—	7 8	8 5	8 32	9 5	10 22	11 35	12 28	1 15	1 56	2 52	3 50	4 58	6 8	6 42	7 14	7 48	8 15	9 0	9§45	10 V 0	2 45
Cholsey&M. ... arr	—	8	1	—	7 14	8 11	8 38	9 11	10 28	11 44	12 34	1 21	2 2	2 58	3 56	5 4	6 14	6 48	7 20	7 55	8 21	9 6	9§51	10 V 7	2 52

¶ From Reading. § To Reading. V Suspended.

1950 Working Timetable

Taken from original timetable

CHOLSEY & MOULSFORD and WALLINGFORD. (AUTO CAR.— ONE CLASS ONLY.)

SINGLE LINE worked by Train Staff and only one engine in steam at a time, or two coupled together. No Block Telegraph on this Line. Form of Staff, Square. Colour, Brown.

Week Days.

Down Trains

Distances.	Mile Post Mileage.	STATIONS.	Ruling Gradient 1 in	Point to poi't times. Mins.	Allow for Stop. Mins.	Allow for Start. Mins.	B Auto. Mixed a.m.	B Auto. a.m.	B Auto. a.m.	B Auto. a.m.	B Auto. a.m.	B Auto. Mixed a.m.	B Auto. p.m.	B Auto. p.m.	B Auto. Mixed SO p.m.	B Auto. p.m.	B Auto. p.m.	B Auto. p.m.	B Auto. p.m.	B Auto. p.m.	B Auto. p.m.	B Auto. p.m.	B Auto. p.m.	B Auto. SO p.m.	
— 48 37		Cholsey & M. dep.	—	—	—	—	7 25	8 15	8 55	9 35	10 15	11 20	1 0	2 15	3 15	4 15	5 15	5 45	6 10	7 5	7 35	8 40	10 0	11 20	....
2 52 51 8		Wallingford arr. 202 F.	—	8	1	1	7 34	8 21	9 1	9 41	10 21	11 29	1 6	2 21	3 24	4 21	5 21	5 51	6 16	7 11	7 41	8 46	10 6	11 26	....

Up Trains.

STATIONS.	Ruling Gradient 1 in	Point to poi't times. Mins.	Allow for Stop. Mins.	Allow for Start. Mins.	B Auto. a.m.	B Auto. a.m.	B Auto. a.m.	B Auto. a.m.	B Auto. a.m.	B Auto. Mixed SX a.m.	B Auto. Mixed SO a.m.	B Auto. p.m.	B Auto. p.m.	B Auto. p.m.	B Auto. Mixed SO p.m.	B Auto. p.m.	B Auto. p.m.	B Auto. p.m.	B Auto. p.m.	B Auto. p.m.	B Auto. p.m.	B Auto. SO p.m.	
Wallingford dep.	—	—	—	1	6 55	7 55	8 45	9 20	10 0	10 50	12 30	12 40	1 45	2 55	3 45	4 30	5 25	5 55	6 45	7 15	8 15	9 40	11 0	....
Cholsey & M. arr. 202 R.	—	8	1	1	7 1	8 1	8 51	9 26	10 6	10 59	12 39	12 46	1 51	3 1	3 51	4 39	5 31	6 1	6 51	7 21	8 21	9 46	11 6	....

SECTION.		Number of Wagons exclusive of Brake Van.														
		2-8-0			2-6-2 T			2-6-0			Ordinary Engines.					
											Tender.			Tank.		
From	To	Coal.	Goods.	Empties.	Coal.	Goods.	Empties.	Coal.	Goods.	Empties.	Coal.	Goods.	Empties.	Coal.	Goods.	Empties.
Wallingford Branch.																
Cholsey and Moulsford	Wallingford	...	...	...	...	...	...	...	...	...	...	...	...	20	30	40
Wallingford	Cholsey and Moulsford	...	...	...	...	...	...	...	...	...	...	...	...	17	25	34

Passenger tank engine.

Extract from G.W.R. "Maximum Loads" 1908

Early Plan

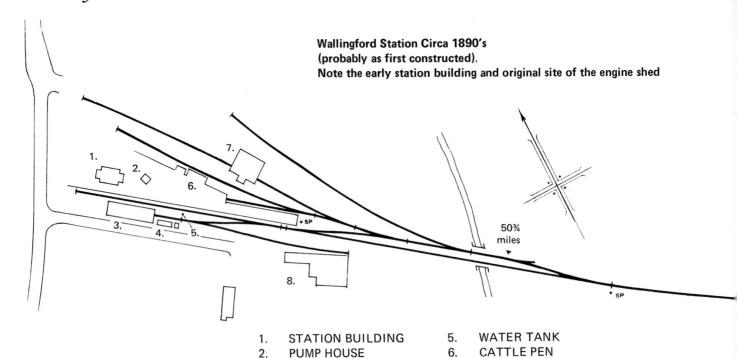

Wallingford Station Circa 1890's
(probably as first constructed).
Note the early station building and original site of the engine shed

50¾ miles

1. STATION BUILDING
2. PUMP HOUSE
3. ENGINE SHED
4. COAL STAGE
5. WATER TANK
6. CATTLE PEN
7. GOODS SHED
8. GAS WORKS

Intermediate Plan

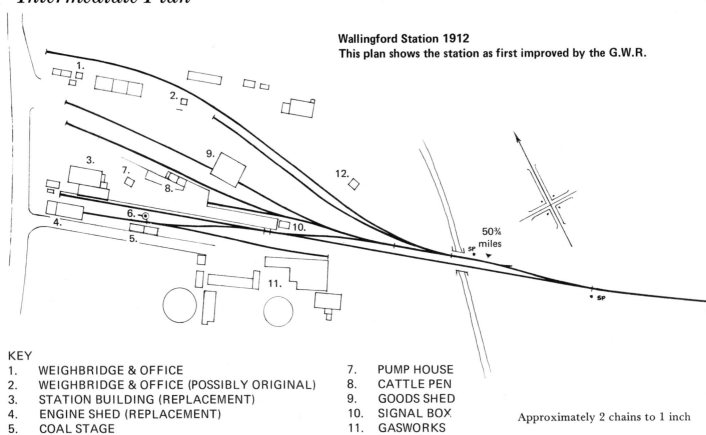

Wallingford Station 1912
This plan shows the station as first improved by the G.W.R.

50¾ miles

KEY
1. WEIGHBRIDGE & OFFICE
2. WEIGHBRIDGE & OFFICE (POSSIBLY ORIGINAL)
3. STATION BUILDING (REPLACEMENT)
4. ENGINE SHED (REPLACEMENT)
5. COAL STAGE
6. WATER TANK
7. PUMP HOUSE
8. CATTLE PEN
9. GOODS SHED
10. SIGNAL BOX
11. GASWORKS
12. P.W. HUT

Approximately 2 chains to 1 inch

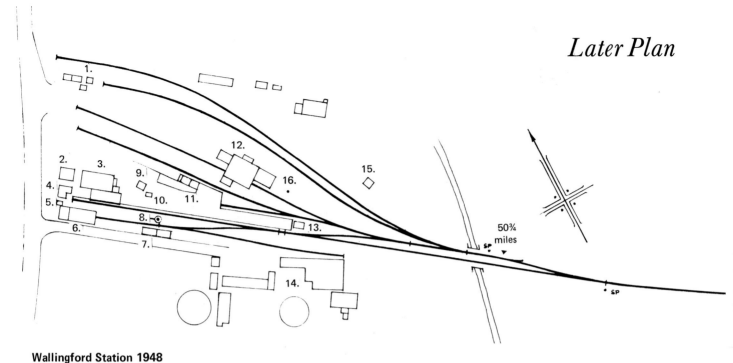

Wallingford Station 1948
(Back sidings sketched only).
This plan shows the station in its final form

KEY
1.	WEIGHBRIDGE & OFFICE	9.	PUMP HOUSE
2.	PARCELS OFFICE	10.	LAMP HUT
3.	STATION BUILDING	11.	CATTLE PEN
4.	BICYCLE SHED	12.	GOODS SHED
5.	LOCO DEPT. OIL SHED	13.	SIGNAL BOX
6.	ENGINE SHED	14.	GASWORKS
7.	COAL STAGE	15.	P.W. HUT
8.	WATER TANK (CONICAL)	16.	CRANE (6 TON)

A general view of the goods yard at Wallingford just prior to closure.   *O.P.C.*

Fig. WL4 A 517 class 0-4-2T, taking water at Wallingford in 1935.

F.M. Butterfield

Fig. WL5 *Photoscript — Deddington*

Fig. WL6 Wallingford Station Staff of 1925. From left to right:—
Standing — J. Peadle, C. Minty, Engine Drivers; unknown, E. Membury, Goods Porters; F. Jolly, Checker; F. Hadland, G. Fisher, Passenger Guards; W. Frewin, R. Frewin (brothers), Firemen; unknown loco cleaner and H. Keeley, Parcel Porter.
Seated — unknown Relief Clerk; Mr. Johnston, Chief Clerk; Mr. Cordery, Station Master; E. James, Booking Clerk; and R. Andrews, Goods Clerk.
Two members of the staff not available at the time were:—
A. Mann, Goods Porter and G. Heaven, Lad Porter.

Courtesy G.E. Membury

Fig. WL7 Wallingford Station forecourt in 1952 with the gasworks just visible beyond. The station was situated on the outskirts of the town, beside the A4130. The site was screened with large hoardings (see *Fig. WL19*) which ran alongside the pavement. The station buildings were constructed of red brick with a slate roof to a very plain design, almost completely unadorned with the exception of the incongruously ornate lintels. Early plans show a smaller building which may well have been constructed of timber.

M.J. Deane

Fig. WL8 A similar view of the forecourt taken after the withdrawal of passenger services. The smaller brick building to the right of the picture was a later addition, which was used as a parcels office.

K. Bowler

Fig. WL9 A closer view of the south end of the main station building showing the small brick extension which housed the gentlemen's lavatories. Notice in these views how the station canopy has been sited with a timber panel to screen this untidy arrangement. The wooden shed in the left hand foreground served as a pump house (see *Fig. WL12*).

M.J. Deane

Fig. WL10 The station buildings and platform in 1954. The double corrugated iron shed behind the buffer stop was used as a bicycle shed.

I.D. Beale

Fig. WL11 The road entrance to the gasworks, as seen in 1965 after closure showing the enginemen's mess room at the rear of the loco shed.

Author

Fig. WL12 No. 1444 waits in the station platform at Wallingford in 1952. The water supply for the conical topped tank came from a well opposite, situated immediately behind the station platform. A small steam engine (powered by steam from the branch locos) inside the wooden shed, illustrated in *Fig. WL9*, drove a three-cylinder water pump situated in the top of the well but was later replaced by an electric motor.

M.J. Deane

Fig. WL13 The loco shed was built by the GWR sometime around the turn of the century and was constructed of red brick with a slate roof. The original loco shed shown on early plans was sited a little further to the south (in front of this one) and may well have been a temporary affair constructed of timber. The small corrugated iron hut alongside the end of the building served as a loco dept. stores for oil and cotton waste etc.

I.D. Beale

Fig. WL14 An auto trailer at rest alongside the platform during shunting operations.

R.H.G. Simpson

Fig. WL15 Wallingford Station, looking towards the buffer stops in 1919, illustrating the original water tank which was replaced shortly after this date with an example of the familiar GWR conical topped tank of a larger capacity.

L. & G.R.P.

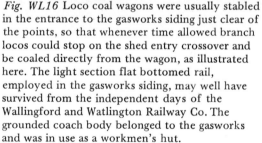

Fig. WL16 Loco coal wagons were usually stabled in the entrance to the gasworks siding just clear of the points, so that whenever time allowed branch locos could stop on the shed entry crossover and be coaled directly from the wagon, as illustrated here. The light section flat bottomed rail, employed in the gasworks siding, may well have survived from the independent days of the Wallingford and Watlington Railway Co. The grounded coach body belonged to the gasworks and was in use as a workmen's hut.

M.J. Deane

Fig. WL17 The station signal box was a trim little building, constructed of timber with a brick base and slate roof. The signalling at Wallingford survived until the early 1960's with the leading passenger porter doubling as signalman and the yard foreman manning the box during lengthy shunting operations.

C.F.D. Whetmath

Fig. WL18 The view of the gasworks from the station platform.

J.H. Moss

Fig. WL19 An overall view of the station and yard as seen from the gasworks sometime during the 1940's.

The first of the five sidings which served the yard terminated in an end loading dock at the end of the station platform, the next two served the cattle pen and goods shed respectively and the two rear sidings which were used for coal traffic and petrol tankers, served an area known as the 'Klondyke'! The station master's house can be seen beyond the buffer stops on the left of the picture.

Courtesy F. Bolton

Fig. WL20 Wallingford Station yard, looking towards the platform, in 1947, with a 14XX class 0-4-2T at work sorting wagons for the gasworks siding.

J.H. Russell

Fig. WL21 One of Messrs. Keen's trailers (which were built at Wallingford) being secured to a wagon in the yard during the 1940's. A large number of these trailers were often to be seen in the yard awaiting dispatch, as seen in Fig. WL19.

Courtesy F. Bolton

Fig. WL22 Wallingford goods shed as seen from the platform after closure. *Author*

Fig. WL23 The six-ton yard crane. *Author*

Fig. WL24 A view of the gasworks siding in 1952, looking towards the station. *M.J. Deane*

Fig. WL25 A busy scene at Wallingford in 1951, with No. 1447 sorting the yard.

The local coal merchant, H.W. Snow and Son, occupied a small office in the yard and at one time had their own wagons, but this company sold out to P.J. Ayres at some time during the 1950's.

R.H.G. Simpson

Fig. WL26 The goods shed was constructed of red brick with a slate roof, although the wall facing the passenger platform was composed of alternating courses of red and blue bricks. The office and loading bay extension were later additions and the building housed a small crane with a lifting capacity of 2 tons. The goods shed doors (just visible in *Fig. WL25*) date from the 1930's and replaced those destroyed in a shunting accident in which a wagon was mistakenly propelled through both pairs of closed doors.

Author

Fig. WL27 A closer view of the forecourt elevation of the goods shed.

K. Bowler

Fig. WL28 No 1447 leaving Wallingford with the 7.15 pm to Cholsey and Moulsford on 21st June, 1951.

The siding diverging on the left of this view was installed in 1933 to serve the C.W.S. Creamery. This siding was controlled by a ground frame which was unlocked by a key on the train staff. Milk was brought in by road from local farms, processed and dispatched each day at noon in tank wagons to Stewarts Lane.

Roye England

Fig. WL29 No. 1447 leaving Wallingford on 13th September, 1958.

R.M. Casserley

Fig. WL30 The C.W.S. Creamery at Wallingford.

A.E. Smith

Fig. WL31 A further view, this time looking from the station, of the road bridge illustrated in Fig WL29.

Author

Passenger services to Wallingford were withdrawn on 15th June, 1959 but the station remained open for goods traffic until 13th September, 1965.

The line is now truncated just short of the road bridge but remains in use to serve the Associated British Maltsters Mill which now occupies the site in the foreground of *Fig. WL29.* The road bridge has since been removed and the station has completely disappeared under a new housing development.

Further sources of reference:
Trains Illustrated Vol. 5 P257 1952

Fig. WL32 A.E. Smith

Fig. W1 0-6-0 Pannier tank No. 2098 awaiting departure from Watlington, 6th June, 1934. *F.M. Butterfield*

WATLINGTON

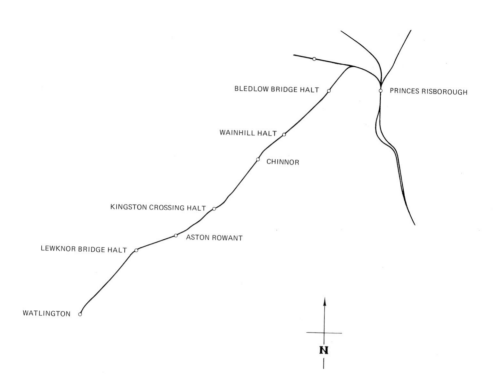

BLEDLOW BRIDGE HALT

PRINCES RISBOROUGH

WAINHILL HALT

CHINNOR

KINGSTON CROSSING HALT

ASTON ROWANT

LEWKNOR BRIDGE HALT

WATLINGTON

N

KEY FACTS

Company of Origin	Watlington & Princes Risborough Railway Co.
Date of Opening	15th August, 1872
Purchased by GWR	1st July, 1883
Date of Closure	1st July, 1957 Remaining open for goods traffic until 2nd January, 1961 Princes Risborough to Chinnor still open to serve Cement Works
Length of Branch	8 Miles 66 Chains
Ruling Gradient	1 in 60
Route Colour	Yellow
Overall Speed Restriction	30 mph
Single Line Worked by	Train Staff & One Engine in Steam or two coupled together

ORIGIN

The Watlington and Princes Risborough Railway was promoted largely by local land owners, following the failure of the Wallingford and Watlington Railway to reach Watlington. An Act of Parliament, on 26th July, 1869, authorised the construction of a Light Railway from the Great Western Railway Station at Princes Risborough, to a site some ¾ of a mile outside Watlington, a distance of 8 miles 66 chains with intermediate stations at Chinnor and Aston Rowant. The line was opened on 15th August, 1872 and immediately ran into financial difficulties. With expenditure exceeding income and rent owing to the GWR for the use of the junction at Princes Risborough, directors of the company soon found themselves running the line at their own expense. Having been offered the line on more than one occasion, the Great Western finally acquired the railway on 1st July, 1883 for the sum of £23,000, which was less than half the cost of its construction. The line was lightly constructed, following the contour of the land for much of its length, and was little improved under its new ownership, although additional rail level halts were opened at Bledlow Bridge, Kingston Crossing and Lewknor Bridge in 1906 and Wainhill Crossing in 1925.

Fig. W2 No. 4638 enjoys a tranquil moment at Watlington, 19th June, 1952.

H.C. Casserley

Early Plan (1)

Watlington Station Circa 1875, as first constructed by the Watlington & Princes Risborough Railway Co. The absence of the crossover near the engine shed (as seen on later plans) is almost certainly an error in the ordnance survey map on which this plan was based.

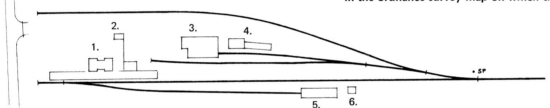

KEY

1. STATION BUILDING
2. COAL OFFICE
3. GOODS SHED
4. PROBABLY CATTLE PEN AND/OR LOADING DOCK
5. ENGINE SHED
6. WATER TANK

Early Plan (2)

Watlington Station Circa 1890's under early G.W.R. ownership

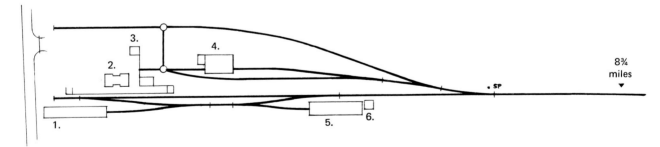

8¾ miles ▼

KEY

1. CARRIAGE SHED
2. STATION BUILDING
3. COAL OFFICE
4. GOODS SHED
5. ENGINE SHED
6. WATER TANK

Approximately 2 chains to 1 inch

Early Plan (3)

Watlington Station Circa 1911
Whether the point shown behind the cattle pen ever
replaced the turntable arrangement of the previous
plan is open to question, as there was hardly enough room
for a conventional point and headshunt, in fact at this
date the sidings may well have already been modified as shown
in the following plan.

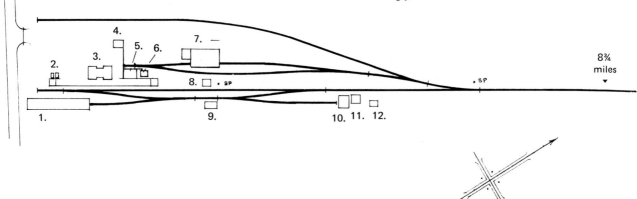

KEY

1.	CARRIAGE SHED	8.	SIGNAL BOX
2.	LAMP HUTS	9.	COAL STAGE
3.	STATION BUILDING	10.	PUMP HOUSE
4.	COAL OFFICE	11.	WATER TANK
5.	CATTLE PEN	12.	P.W. HUT
6.	COAL BUNKER		
7.	GOODS SHED		

Later Plan

Watlington Station 1948

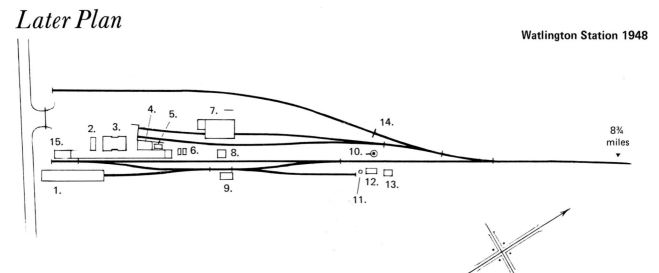

KEY

1.	CARRIAGE SHED	9.	COAL STAGE
2.	BICYCLE SHED	10.	WATER TANK (CONICAL)
3.	STATION BUILDING	11.	WELL COVER
4.	CATTLE PEN	12.	LOCO DEPT. STORES & MESS
5.	COAL BUNKER	13.	P.W. HUT
6.	LAMP HUTS	14.	LOADING GAUGE
7.	GOODS SHED	15.	TIMBER PLATFORM EXTENSION
8.	SIGNAL BOX		

Approximately 2 chains to 1 inch

Fig. W3 An unidentified 2021 class shunting a train of excursion stock at Watlington (circa 1936-37).
Mrs. Clarke & Mrs. Watts

OPERATION

The Watlington branch was operated on the 'One Engine in Steam' principle with a locomotive based at Watlington. The following notes apply to a typical weekday of 1937, at which time there were two drivers and three firemen resident at Watlington, providing a crew for each of the two shifts and a fireman for nights (the firemen worked the nightshift in rotation):

The locomotive was cleaned and prepared by the overnight fireman who was also responsible for unloading the loco coal wagon and pumping water to fill the conical tank. This was a grim duty, especially during the winter months as there was no shelter besides that afforded by the trees, since the loco shed was destroyed by fire at the beginning of the century.

The early turn crew booked on in time to work the 5.50 am goods, which ran engine and brake van to Princes Risborough in order to collect the branch goods. This first trip was tightly scheduled, for after shunting at Risborough a call was usually made at Aston Rowant and on returning to Watlington there was barely time to shunt the wagons (unsorted) into the long back siding, collect the auto trailer from the spare road, take water and pick up the waiting passengers for the 8.40 am which connected at Princes Risborough for London.

The yard was not sorted until 2.30 pm as between the return of the first passenger train and the departure of the 11.30 am the locomotive was required to pump water, the Chinnor goods was worked from Princes Risborough at 12.20 pm and the locomotive did not return to Watlington until 2.21 pm. After the arrival of the last passenger train at Watlington at 8.26 pm the auto trailer was replaced on the spare road leaving the run-round loop clear, and the yard was shunted for the 8.50 pm pick-up goods, which called at Aston Rowant and Chinnor as required. The locomotive and brake van returned to Watlington any time after 10.00 pm and sometimes very late.

There were no trains on Sundays other than the occasional 'Bluebell Excursion' from London in the Line's heyday which, it would seem, were essentially for ramblers as passengers were set down along the branch to explore the Roman Ridgeway. These trains are said to have consisted of three or four coaches together with the branch trailer to serve rail level halts (see *Fig. W3*).

The branch locomotive was changed each Monday morning at Princes Risborough, after the arrival of the 8.40 am from Watlington. The fresh locomotive was sent from Slough complete with a week's supply of pimps (firelighters) and cotton waste on board.

It is worth mentioning that locomotives usually faced down the branch towards Watlington, to ensure that the firebox crown remained covered whilst tackling the Chinnor bank.

As there were no Sunday services on the branch the locomotive at Watlington was 'lit-up' from cold each Monday morning. When the duty fireman had occasionally overslept and there was no hope of raising steam in time for the first passenger working, the fresh loco from Slough was sent on down the branch and the locomotives were exchanged at Watlington. The Slough crew remained at Watlington after the departure of the 8.40 am and returned with the branch loco to Slough later on.

Whilst push-pull passenger working was not employed on the branch, auto trailers were provided to serve the rail level halts and a standby four wheeled coach, which was kept in the carriage shed, was used to increase the accommodation as required.

During the final years of the line, owing to staff changes at Watlington, Slough loco crews were required to work the branch and loco's were no longer kept at Watlington, but journeyed to and from Slough each day. The branch locomotive left Slough at approximately 5.00 am and ran light engine to Watlington in order to work out the first train of the day. The early turn crew were relieved at Princes Risborough at mid-day and the late turn crew worked the loco back light engine to Slough in the evening, following the remainder of the day's services.

WATLINGTON BRANCH.

(Engine and Branch Car,)
One Class only.

SINGLE LINE.—Worked by Train Staff and only One Engine in Steam at a time, or two coupled together. Form of Staff, Round; Colour, Black.
Passenger Trains to carry "B" Head Lights.   Goods Trains to carry one Head Light in centre of buffer plank.

Week Days only.

Distance. M. C.	STATIONS.	Ruling Gradient 1 in	Point to point times. Mins.	Allow for stop. Mins.	Allow for start. Mins.	V Goods A.M.	Pass. A.M.	Goods P.M.	Pass. P.M.	Pass. K P.M.	Pass. P.M.	Pass. P.M.	Goods RR P.M.
—	Princes Risboro' .. .. dep.	—	—	—	1	7 0	10 6	12 20	1 55	3 55	5 45	8 0	10 † 0
1 52	Bledlow Bridge Halt .... ,,	107 F	—	—	—	....	10 11	—	2 0	4 0	5 50	8 5	—
2 75	Wainhill Halt .... ,,	68 R	—	—	—	....	10 14	—	2 3	4 3	5 53	8 8	—
3 57	Chinnor .... ,,	68 R	12	1	1	J 7 24 Q	10 17	12 34	2 6	4 6	5 56	8 11	—
5 17	Kingston Crossing Halt .. ,,	61 R	—	—	—	....	10 21	—	2 10	4 10	6 0	8 15	—
6 16	Aston Rowant .... ,,	116 R	8	1	1	8 8	10 24	—	2 13	4 13	6 3	8 18	—
7 —	Lewknor Bridge Halt .... ,,	117 F	8	—	—	....	10 27	—	2 16	4 16	6 6	8 21	—
8 7½	Watlington .... arr.	78 F	—	—	—	8 18	10 32	—	2 21	4 22	6 11	8 26	10†20

STATIONS.	Ruling Gradient 1 in	Point to point times. Mins.	Allow for stop. Mins.	Allow for start. Mins.	Goods. A.M.	Pass. K A.M.	Pass. A.M.	Goods P.M.	Pass. P.M.	Pass. P.M.	Pass. P.M.	Goods RR Z P.M.
Watlington .. ..dep.	—	—	—	1	5 50	8 40	11 30	—	3 0	4 33	6 50	8 50
Lewknor Bridge Halt ...... ,,	78 R	8	1	1	...	8 45	11 35	—	3 5	4 38	6 55	9 20
Aston Rowant .... ,,	117 R	—	—	—	Y	8§50	11 38	—	3 8	4 41	7 0	—
Kingston Crossing Halt...... ,,	116 F	—	—	—	—	8 53	11 41	—	3 11	4 44	7 3	—
Chinnor .... ,,	61 F	8	1	1	—	8§58	11 45	1 18	3 15	4 48	7 10	CR
Wainhill Halt .... ,,	68 F	—	—	—	...	9 1	11 48	—	3 18	4 51	7 13	—
Bledlow Bridge Halt .... ,,	68 F	—	—	—	...	9 4	11 51	—	3 21	4 54	7 16	—
Princes Risboro' ,,........ arr.	107 R	10	—	—	6 18	9 9	11 56	1 30	3 26	4 59	7 21	9 40

J Chinnor arrive 7.14 a.m. To call for S.T. purposes only.   **K** 8.40 a.m. Watlington stops at Shirburn Farm Occupation Crossing (near 8 m.p.) when required
to pick up passengers, and the 3.55 p.m. Princes Risboro' when required to set down.   **Q** Aston Rowant arrive 7.34 a.m.
V *Important this Goods trip works to time to enable 8.40 a.m. passenger from Watlington to start punctually.*
Y To run Engine and Van when necessary and arrive P. Risboro' 6.12 a.m.   **Z** Aston Rowant arrive 9.0 p.m.   § Aston Rowant arr. 8.47½, Chinnor arr. 8.56½.

PRINCES RISBOROUGH and WATLINGTON.

(ENGINE AND BRANCH CAR,
ONE CLASS ONLY.)

SINGLE LINE. Worked by Train Staff and only one engine in steam at a time, or two coupled together. Form of Staff, Round. Colour, Black.
Passenger Trains to carry "B" Head Code   Freight Trains to carry one Headlamp in centre of buffer plank.

Week Days only.

Down Trains.

Distance. M. C.	STATIONS.	Ruling Gradient 1 in	Point to point times. Mins.	Allow for Stop. Mins.	Allow for Start. Mins.	Freight K a.m.	Empty Auto. ¶ a.m.	Freight N RR a.m.	Passenger. a.m.	Freight p.m.	Passenger. p.m.	Passenger. p.m.	Freight SO p.m.	Passenger. p.m.	Passenger. p.m.	Freight p.m.
—	Princes Risborough .... dep.	—	—	—	1	5 30	7 57	9 20	10 22	12 20	12 40	1 54	3 55	5 48	8 20	10 15
1 52	Bledlow Bridge Halt .. ,,	107 F.	—	—	—	—	—	—	10 27	—	12 45	1 59	—	5 53	8 25	—
2 75	Wainhill Halt .. ,,	68R.	—	—	—	CR	CR	9 30	10 30	—	12 48	2 2	—	5 56	8 28	—
3 57	Chinnor .... ,,	68R.	12	1	1	Q			10 33	12 34	12 51	2 5	4 9	5 59	8 31	CR
5 17	Kingston Crossing Halt .. ,,	61 R.	—	—	—	—	—	—	10 37	—	12 55	2 9	—	6 3	8 35	—
6 16	Aston Rowant .. ,,	116 R.	8	1	1	6 35	CR	—	10 40	—	12 58	2 12	—	6 6	8 38	—
7 4	Lewknor Bridge Halt .... ,,	117 R.	8	1	—	—	—	—	10 43	—	1 1	2 15	—	6 9	8 41	—
8 75	Watlington .... arr.	78 F.	8	1	—	6 45	8 20	—	10 48	—	1 6	2 20	—	6 14	8 46	10 45

¶—May convey passengers from Princes Risborough when required.   **K**—Suspended.   **Q** Aston Rowant arrive 5.52 a.m.
N—Will run as " light engine " if required.

Up Trains.

STATIONS.	Ruling Gradient 1 in	Point to point times. Mins.	Allow for Stop. Mins.	Allow for Start. Mins.	Freight K a.m.	Passenger. a.m.	Passenger. a.m.	Engine and Van. V RR a.m.	Passenger. a.m.	Freight SX p.m.	Passenger. SO p.m.	Passenger. p.m.	Freight SO p.m.	Passenger. p.m.	Freight p.m.
Watlington .... dep.	—	—	—	1	4 20	7 25	...	11 30	...	...	1 15	3 10	...	7 15	9 0 Z
Lewknor Bridge Halt .. ,,	78 R.	—	—	—	—	7 30	8 47	11 35	...	...	1 20	3 15	...	7 20	9 25
Aston Rowant .... ,,	117 R.	8	1	1	7 33	8 52	11 38	...	...	1 23	3 18	...	7 23	—
Kingston Crossing Halt.. ,,	116 F.	—	—	—	—	7 36	8 55	11 41	...	...	1 26	3 21	...	7 26	—
Chinnor .... ,,	61 F.	8	1	1	CR	7 40	9 0	11 45	10†0	1 18	1 30	3 25	4 55	7 30	CR
Wainhill Halt .... ,,	68 F.	—	—	—	—	7 43	9 3	11 48	—	—	1 33	3 28	...	7 33	—
Bledlow Bridge Halt .. ,,	68 F.	—	—	—	—	7 46	9 6	11 51	—	—	1 36	3 31	...	7 36	—
Princes Risborough .... arr.	107 R.	10	1	—	4 48	7 51	9 11	11 56	10†15	1 30	1 41	3 36	5 5	7 41	9 45

K—Suspended.   **V**—Will run as " light engine " if required.   **Z**—Aston Rowant arrive 9.10 p.m.

Fig. W4 An unidentified 517 class 0-4-2T with a train of close coupled 'Holden' four-wheeled coaches at Watlington, probably just after the turn of the century.

Both the engine shed and the original timber built water tank are just visible behind the train.

Courtesy R.E. Gilbert

MOTIVE POWER

During the independent years of the line, locomotives and stock were hired from the specially formed Watlington Rolling Stock Company. There were two locomotives, a second hand Sharp Stewart 2-2-2 well tank and a 2-4-0 side tank by the same builder which became Watlington & Princes Risborough Rly. numbers 1 and 2 respectively.

No. 1 was scrapped when the GWR took over the line in 1883, but No. 2 was rebuilt, and subsequently despatched to work lightly laid branches in other parts of the country as GWR No. 1384 (see Lambourn Valley Railway Co.'s opening train).

Under the ownership of the GWR, Watlington became a sub-shed from Slough. 0-4-2 tank locomotives of the 517 class were officially listed for use on the branch, but these were succeeded by the Metro class 2-4-0 tanks and 2021 class 0-6-0 Saddle and Pannier tanks. Watlington's official allocation for 1920/21 is listed here as an example:—

2159	0-6-0 PT	Jan
2121	" ST	Feb - March
2137	" ST	April/Aug
2159	" PT	July/Dec
2121	" ST	Jan 1921
3584	2-4-0T	Jan 1921

The 2021 class came to be used almost exclusively on the line from the early 1920's until just after the Second World War when they were gradually superseded by the larger 57XX class Pannier tanks which worked the line until closure. No. 2112 was regularly allocated to Watlington since about 1930 and was still in service there in 1951.

Post-1939 allocations also included: Nos. 2055, 2078, 9789, 5755.

Other locomotives included 74XX class Pannier tanks No's 7441 and 7442 which appeared on the line during the early 1950's and it is said that one of the Collett 0-4-2 tanks ran to Watlington during the war.

SECTION		Number of Wagons exclusive of Brake Van.																	
		2-8-0			2-6-2 T			2-6-0			Ordinary Engines.								
											Tender.			Tank.				
From	To	Coal.	Goods.	Empties.	Coal.	Goods.	Empties.	Coal.	Goods.	Empties.	Coal.	Goods.	Empties.	Coal.	Goods.	Empties.		
Watlington Branch.																			
...ces Risboro ...	Watlington ...	...	...	...	...	...	...	...	...	...	...	...	...	13	20	27	Passenger tank engine, Swindon	
...tlington ...	Princes Risboro ...	...	...	...	...	...	...	...	...	...	...	...	...	14	22	28	make.	

Extract from G.W.R. "Maximum Loads" 1908

105

Watlington Station, G. W. R.

Fig. W5 Watlington Station circa 1905. This view taken from an old postcard, shows the engine shed, signalling and the original siting of the two corrugated iron lamp huts prior to the erection of the timber platform extension. Note the Saddle tank approaching the platform.

Courtesy B. Davis

Fig. W6 Watlington Station Staff of 1892. The gentleman third from the left is Robert Lett, Watlington's first station master. The loco just visible inside the shed appears to be either a '517' or 'Metro' class tank in original condition with smokebox wing plates.

Note the open 'porchway' of the station building (see *Fig. W11*). *Courtesy Pendon Museum*

Fig. W7 Watlington Station stood amidst fields some ¾ of a mile outside the town because the W & PR Rly. Co. were unable to purchase the remaining land that would have enabled the railway to have reached Watlington. Intending passengers could be seen at this point from the platform and the train would often be held until they reached the station!

H.C. Casserley

Fig. W8 Pyrton Farm Lane with the station entrance just visible on the left (beyond the car).
H.C. Casserley

Fig. W9 Watlington Station entrance in 1951. *R.H.G. Simpson*

Fig. W10 Similar to those at Aston Rowant and Chinnor, this attractively designed station building was constructed of brick and flint with a slate roof. The gable ends were enhanced by the shaped barge boards, Gothic style lintels and decorative ridge tiles being particularly worthy of note. The forecourt entrance to the building was rarely used, access being gained to the platform through the gateway to the right. The corrugated asbestos bicycle shed was erected on the site of the station garden during the Second World War.

J.H. Ahern FRPS

Fig. W11 The forecourt elevation of the station building circa 1936-37 with Station Master Pocock in the doorway. The timber panelling was an addition, sometime between 1892 and 1905 (see *Fig. W6*).

Mrs. Clarke & Mrs. Watts

Fig. W12 A variety of auto trailers were used on the branch over the years. This view shows an example of a 70′ corridor vehicle, stabled in the platform. The two corrugated iron huts in the foreground of this view can be seen in their original location in *Fig. W5*.

The nearer of the two huts was used as a lamp hut, the other being used for carriage cleaning equipment and even overnight storage of fish deliveries!

M.J. Deane

Fig. W13 Watlington carriage shed.

J.H. Ahern FRPS

Fig. W13a A detail view of the carriage shed interior. *Author*

Fig. W14 A closer view of the corrugated iron carriage shed which stood opposite the platform. There was insufficient clearance past the coal stage to enable the later designs of auto trailers to use the carriage shed but even earlier types are said to have been stabled on the spare road behind the signal box. A standby four-wheeled coach was kept in the shed during the line's heyday, but generally this siding was used for little else other than the loco coal wagons.

Auto trailers were usually cleaned in the platform on Sunday mornings using step ladders and planking which can be seen lying around in several views. *Author's collection*

Fig. W15 The station platform was barely long enough to accommodate two coaches. The timber extension at the far end was built during the late 1920's for milk traffic and electric lighting was installed in 1936, the two platform lamps utilising the original columns of the oil lamps.

The gates to the cattle pen opened across the platform to guide livestock into the pen on arrival, but outward bound cattle were usually loaded from the opposite entrance into waiting vehicles stabled in the dock behind (see *Fig. W20*).

J.H. Russell

Fig. W16 One of the smaller 850 class Pannier tanks No. 1969 makes a rare appearance at Watlington on 30th July, 1949.

J.H. Meredith

Fig. W17 The goods shed was a timber structure erected on a base of brick and flint. The weigh-house was incorporated within the main shell of the building and projected internally, the window of the same being just visible in this photograph at the far end of the shed. The 20 ton weighing machine situated just in front of the window, was installed around 1911 to replace a smaller cart machine. The goods shed housed the usual 1 ton crane, but there was no yard crane as such at Watlington and a travelling crane was sent from Reading as required for heavier loads. The ladder leaning against the wall was used for sheeting wagons and the empty fish boxes stacked against the shed (outside for obvious reasons) were left to accumulate until their quantity justified a wagon load.

J.H. Ahern FRPS

Fig. W18 Messrs. Tappin & Sons, local coal merchants, unloading a wagon in the yard at Watlington. Their predecessors, Messrs. Weedon Bros., occupied a small timber built coal office which had stood in the station forecourt, certainly since 1901, until its removal at the time of the Second World War. Weedon Bros. had their own wagons, which bore the names of the other depots at: Goring (where the company was based), Wallingford, Wantage, Wheatley and Watlington. The livery of the wagons is said to have been grey with white lettering, shaded black.

Courtesy Messrs. Tappin & Sons

Fig. W19 The original crane in the goods shed was replaced during the Second World War with a steel gantry crane of the same capacity which ran across the inside of the building. The vertical girder, that supported one end of the gantry, can be seen outside the wall of the building. The sliding door at this end of the goods shed replaced that visible in *Fig. W25* following a shunting accident.

M.J. Deane

Fig. W20 The cattle pen and double end loading bank. The sleeper built bunker, on the ramp to the pen, was used for the storage of station coal.

J.H. Ahern FRPS

Fig. W21 The sleeper built loco coaling stage with a stock of coal alongside which often totalled 80 tons or more.

J.H. Ahern FRPS

Fig. W22 No. 2112 resting in sylvan surroundings at Watlington one Sunday in May 1949, when the loco was not in steam.

J.H. Ahern FRPS

Fig. W23 Looking towards Princes Risborough from the end of the platform. Notice the gangers trolley stowed beside the coaling stage.   *J.H. Ahern FRPS*

Fig. W24 Signalling at Watlington disappeared in 1929 at the suggestion of the Station Master, who apparently pointed out the saving in labour and maintenance and was suitably commended for his observation. There were two signals, (one for each direction) a fixed distant which stood at Shirburn Crossing and ground lamps at several turnouts (see *Fig. W5*). The signal box illustrated here remained in use as a ground frame after the removal of the signalling. The little cabinet beside the door housed the key to the lever frame, which was later incorporated on the train staff.

M.J. Deane

Fig. W25 Watlington Station yard looking south west towards the buffer stops in 1947. The three sidings which served the yard were known as, from left to right, the 'Spare Road', Shed Road and Back Road. Note catch points incorporated in the pointwork from these sidings.

J.H. Russell

Fig. W26 0-6-0PT No. 9789 stands over the inspection pit at the site of the former loco shed, whilst pumping water from the well. The grounded horsebox body served as a loco stores mess, until it burned down in 1951, when some overalls which were drying over the stove caught light! The small cabinet, behind the loco, stood at the edge of the well and together with the similar example under the water tank, housed the switch gear for the electric pumps. Note the flexible pipe in the foreground, which is connected to one of the hydrants.

J.H. Russell

Fig. W27 The conical topped water tank which additionally supplied two hydrants alongside the loco siding and the 'NOT DRINKING WATER' supply to the station, followed a standard GWR design and was probably installed about 1920. The original wooden tank (just visible in *Fig. W4*) was rectangular in plan and mounted on timber trestles, with a leather bag for delivery. Early plans show a pump house beside the well, which would indicate a surface pumping engine, but this was later removed and water was subsequently raised by a steam pump inside the well. Two submergible electric pumps were also installed in the well in November 1935 but the steam equipment was retained and used during failures.

Steam for the pumping operation was provided by the branch locomotives. They were connected to the pump by means of two pipes; one was connected to the train heating pipe, which raised the water to ground level and the other was coupled in place of one of the whistles to feed the supply to the tank.

J.H. Russell

Fig. W29 Porter, Charlie Hopkins and Station Master R.H. Pocock, pose beside an unusually large walnut butt in the yard at Watlington about 1930. A travelling crane was sent to cope with this load which was apparently sent to London Docks for export.

Note the corrugated iron pump house (mentioned in *Fig. W27*) just visible on the extreme right of this view. *Courtesy Mrs. C. Hopkins*

Fig. W28 The yard throat, looking towards Princes Risborough in May, 1949.

The chimney stack, just visible behind the horsebox body, is all that remains of the platelayers hut illustrated in *Fig. W27*.

Note the new concrete bin under the conical tank; this was used for the storage of coal for the fire devil.

J.H. Ahern FRPS

Further sources of reference:
  Railway Magazine Vol. 73 *P157 1933*
  Model Railway News Vol. 26 *P144 1950*
  Railway Magazine Vol. 102 *P355 1956*
  Model Railway Construction Vol. 37 *P66 1970*
  The Watlington Branch by *J. Holden, O.P.C.*

ig. W30 The inspection pit in the foreground of this view is all that remained of the rmer loco shed (illustrated in *Fig. W4*) which was destroyed by fire soon after the turn the century. Loco's were thereafter stabled over this pit in the open, and continued to 'shedded' at Watlington up until the early 1950's.

The sleeper built hut in the background was installed in 1951, replacing both of those own in *Fig. W27*, but in the event, loco crews were provided with a 'toad' (brake van) nich was permanently stabled in the cattle dock (just visible in *Fig. W9*).

Photomatic

The Watlington branch was closed to passengers on 1st July, 1957, remaining open for goods traffic until 2nd January, 1961.

At the time of writing, the line remains intact as far as Chinnor and is still used to serve the cement works there. The course of the line beyond can still be followed in places, and much of Watlington Station remains, albeit derelict, overgrown and part of a very private estate.

Fig. W31   A.E. Smith

SCALE DRAWINGS OF BUILDINGS AT WATLINGTON

ELEVATION TO PLATFORM

Station Buildings

ELEVATION TO FORECOURT

0 Feet   10   20   30

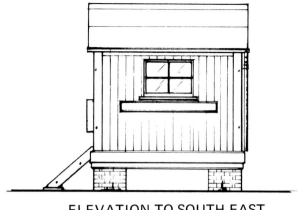

ELEVATION TO SOUTH EAST

END ELEVATION
FACING NORTH EAST

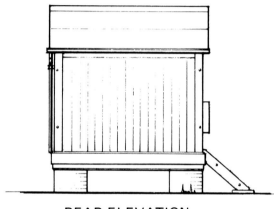

REAR ELEVATION

END ELEVATION
FACING SOUTH WEST

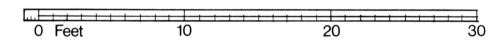

0 Feet   10   20   30

Signal Box

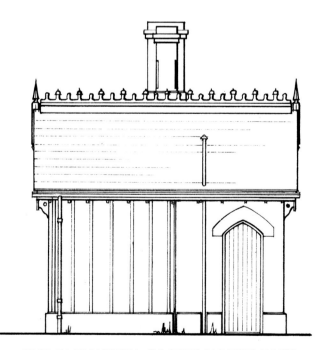

END ELEVATION FACING NORTH EAST

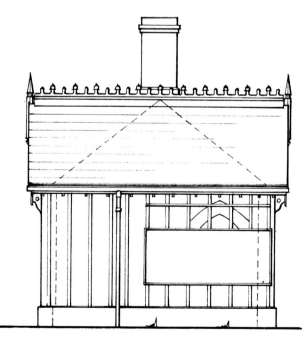

END ELEVATION FACING SOUTH WEST

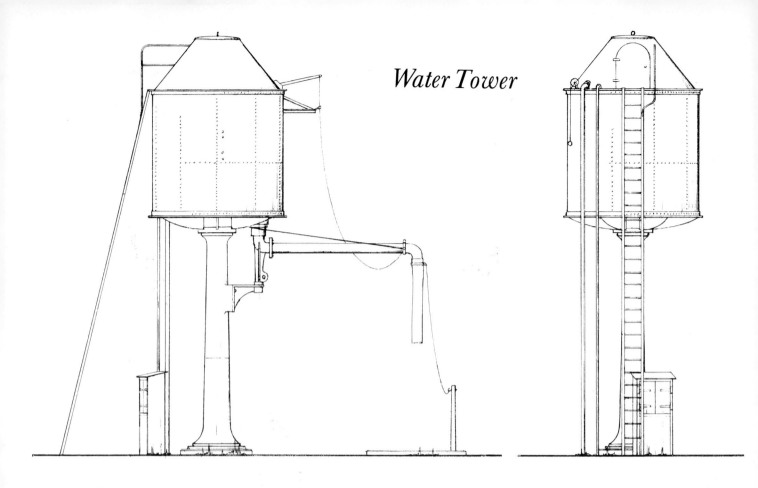

Water Tower

Watlington Platelayers Hut

Watlington Lamp Huts

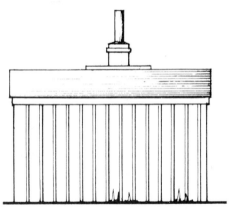

ELEVATION TO NORTH WEST

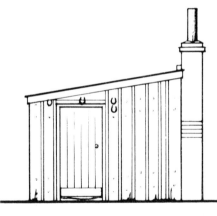

END ELEVATION
FACING SOUTH WEST

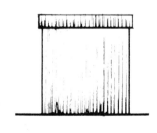

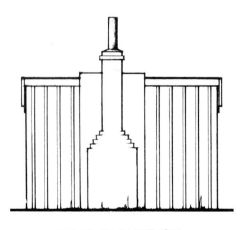

REAR ELEVATION

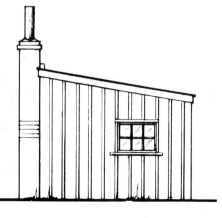

END ELEVATION
FACING NORTH EAST

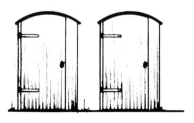

GREAT WESTERN BRANCH LINE TERMINI

Volume Two

ABBOTSBURY STATION.

GREAT WESTERN BRANCH LINE TERMINI

VOLUME TWO

by Paul Karau

FOR MYRTLE, A WEST COUNTRY GIRL.

A 517 class 0-4-2T at Ashburton circa 1930.

W. Becherlegge

Frontispiece — courtesy I.D. Beale.

Contents

Additional structure drawings (originally reproduced on fold-out sheets) pertaining to these stations appear in the supplementary section at the rear of this combined volume.

Introduction

At the time of writing little remains of the five west country stations that are featured in this second volume, so once again I have attempted to present a portrait of each location using a sequence of notes and photographs that is intended to give the reader some idea of how these stations once appeared and, where it has been possible, how each site had developed over the years.

My own drawings of the track plans and many of the buildings have once again been included, but following a number of enquiries for drawings of those buildings not included in the first volume, namely Wallingford station building and goods shed, perhaps I should explain that when I first surveyed the buildings at various stations the information collected was purely for my own use and not intended for publication. Naturally in retrospect I wish that I had made more exhaustive investigations at the time, but I have supplemented my own surveys wherever possible with information from official plans and taken every care to make each drawing as accurate as possible, as the completed structures all too often varied from the original architect's plans. It has not been possible to include drawings of any of the buildings at Hemyock or the station building and train shed at Moretonhampstead in this volume, but as my own interest in particular branch lines goes far beyond the production of these books, I would be pleased to hear from any reader who may have or knows of anyone with dimensions or additional photographic evidence of the various locations that form the subject of my research and in turn I will endeavour to publish such material in the future for the benefit of us all.

I sincerely hope that this book may enlighten those who have never had the opportunity of visiting these stations and perhaps restore a few memories to those who once knew them.

Paul Karau
1978

Moretonhampstead Station on the 25th July, 1957.

R.J. Sellick

Acknowledgements

I owe a great many thanks to so many people whose help and kindness and often new found friendship has enabled me to complete this volume, but I would particularly like to thank Bob Nicks, a retired Newton Abbot driver, and his wife, not only for insisting on helping me despite his serious ill health, but also for their kind hospitality and encouragement when the going was hard. I should also like to thank Tony Smith for always being on hand, Ivan Beale for so generously contributing so much of his own material for the Abbotsbury and Moretonhampstead chapters, and Pat Garland and Jim Russell for placing so much of their material at my disposal.

My thanks must also go to the following: Ron Aggett, Dr Ian C. Allen, A. Attewell, Mr Beame, Mr Bellamy, A.E. Bennett, W.A. Camwell, R.S. Carpenter, H.C. Casserley, Reg Clements, Brian and Eve Clist, D Collins, L.E. Copeland, N. de Courtais, E.T. Day, M.E.J. Deane, R.J. Doran, Fred Down, Roy Eadon, P.G.F. English, M.J. Esau, M.J. Fox, J.T. Fraser, C.J. Freezer (who also kindly allowed me to use the photos by the late S.R. Loxton), Jim French, R.G. Friend, S.M. Gill, J.E. Gready, John Harrison, Ron Hext, David Hyde, C.W. Judge, A.R. Kingdom, C.P. Legg, R.J. Leonard, L. Littleton, J.H. Lucking, J.H. Meredith, Keith Montague, J.H. Moss, M.J. Parsons, Mrs Perkins, Sidney Price, Harry Pursey, R.C. Riley, E.S. Russell, J.F. Russell Smith, E.G. Sambrook, R.J. Sellick, D. Thompson, M.B. Warburton, P.R.H. Webber, A. West, W.J. Westlake, J.H.W. Wood, Bristol Museum, British Railways, Lens of Sutton, Locomotive and General Railway Photographs, Real Photographs Co.

Finally I should like to thank my wife for her tolerance and all of the help and criticism that she has given me in compiling this book.

6

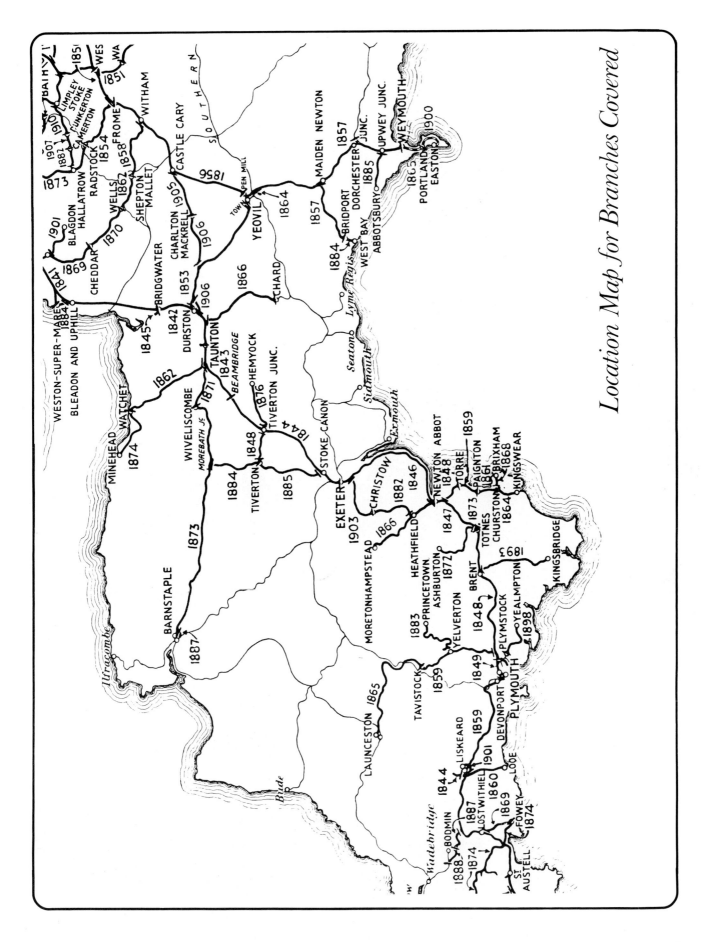

Location Map for Branches Covered

Fig. A1 Abbotsbury station circa 1935 with the original trackwork still in evidence and a camping coach just visible behind the platform.

D. Thompson

ABBOTSBURY

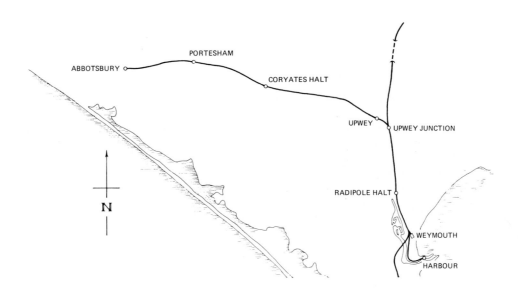

KEY FACTS

Company of Origin	Abbotsbury Railway Company
Date of Opening	9th November, 1885
Purchased by GWR	1st August, 1896
Length of Branch	6 miles 3 chains
Ruling Gradient	1 in 44
Route Colour	Uncoloured
Overall Speed Restriction	40 mph (25 mph Portesham stop board to Abbotsbury and 10 mph from 5m 60ch to Abbotsbury Station)
Single Line Worked by	Train staff and One Engine in Steam.

ORIGIN

Although Abbotsbury is situated on the beautiful Dorset coast the Abbotsbury railway was not promoted for access to the sea but to facilitate the commercial development of Iron Ore deposits at Abbotsbury and the Portland and Purbeck stone at Portesham. The line was promoted by local landowners and authorised by an Act of Parliament on the 6th August, 1877. The contract was placed for the line's construction in May 1879 but with the usual difficulties experienced in raising capital, money was soon owing to the contractor who finally ceased work in 1881 and sued the company for payment.

An Act of Parliament on the 19th May, 1882 granted an extension of time to complete the line and authorised deviations in the route to defeat the operations of a speculator who had bought the land and offered it to the Company at extortionate terms. Construction recommenced under a new contractor in October 1883, but opposing land owners delayed the completion of the line and the contractor's non-fulfilment of the terms of his agreement led the Company to threaten the cancellation of the contract, following which the contractor ceased work altogether and subsequently went bankrupt.

The Great Western Railway, who were to work and maintain the line after completion, advanced a sum of capital towards the line's completion and appointed one of their directors to the Abbotsbury Board. A third contractor was appointed and the railway was finally completed and opened on the 9th November, 1885.

The line extended westwards from Upwey, on the GW main line from Dorchester to Weymouth, a distance of 6 miles 3 chains to Abbotsbury with intermediate stations at Broadway and Portesham. The Great Western absorbed the Abbotsbury Railway Company on the 1st August, 1896 and later opened a new halt at Coryates in May 1906.

Fig. A2 The first train of the day at Abbotsbury in 1952.

I.D. Beale

OPERATION

Auto-fitted locomotives were usually provided from Weymouth for the branch services and normally faced towards Abbotsbury, but they only remained at the terminus for a few minutes before propelling their single auto trailers on the return journey.

In 1934 a Trowbridge man, Sidney Price, arrived at Abbotsbury to take charge of the station. He was a senior porter, grade one and remained here as the only member of the staff until closure!

The following notes apply to the weekday timetable of 1935 and describe a typical working day.

Mr Price arrived at 7.30 am to prepare for the 7.45 am from Weymouth which reached Abbotsbury at 8.09 am. This first train departed at 8.15 am with the local workmen and Grammar School children and Mr Price went home for breakfast. The second train conveyed a spare coach (usually an auto trailer), which was left outside the goods shed, and returned at 10.40 am. The locomotive then collected the branch goods and left Weymouth at 11.33 am calling at Upwey and Portesham and finally arriving at Abbotsbury at 12.30 pm. At this time wagons had also been collected from Upwey and Portesham on the down journey to save calling at these stations on return, but the excessive numbers of wagons that resulted at Abbotsbury provided shunting problems and, following the derailment of several

wagons on the engine release turnout at Abbotsbury (which isolated the engine), this practice was discontinued and wagons were thereafter picked up from the intermediate stations on the return journey. After the yard had been sorted at Abbotsbury the spare coach that had been left previously was attached to the train which then returned at 12.52 pm as a mixed working to Weymouth and Mr Price then went home for lunch.

During the holiday season the 2.50 pm from Weymouth usually arrived with a flood of visitors together with the station master from Upwey (who was in charge of the line) to collect the cash, this returned at 3.24 pm leaving Mr Price to continue with his bookwork. The 5.09 pm arrival sometimes conveyed the spare coach instead of the 10.12 am ex Weymouth the following day, and if this was the case then the coach was stabled on the run round loop opposite the platform before the train returned at 5.20 pm with the visitors that had arrived on the previous service. Mr Price then went home leaving the guard to attend to the passengers of the last two trains and lock up the station (putting the key under the door) before his final departure.

Although there had been a Sunday service during the early years of the line, that shown in the 1935 timetable had been introduced only since 1933 and is thought to have been short lived (there had been a special trip to Portesham on Sundays to collect milk).

SECTION.		Number of Wagons exclusive of Brake Van.															
		2-8-0			2-6-2 T			2-6-0			Ordinary Engines.							
											Tender.			Tank.			
From	To	Coal.	Goods.	Empties.	Coal.	Goods.	Empties.	Coal.	Goods.	Empties.	Coal.	Goods.	Empties.	Coal.	Goods.	Empties.	
Abbotsbury Branch.																	
Weymouth	Abbotsbury													6	9	12	Passenger tank engine
Abbotsbury	Weymouth																

Extract from GWR 'Maximum Loads' 1908.

ABBOTSBURY BRANCH.

Single Line, Upwey Junction to Abbotsbury, worked by Train Staff, and only one engine in steam at time, or two coupled.

DOWN TRAINS. — WEEK DAYS.

Mile Post Distances		STATIONS.	Ruling Gradient 1 in *	Point-to-Point Times.	Allow for Stop.	Allow for Start.	B Motor.	B Motor.	K Goods	B Motor.	B Motor.	B Motor. W	B Motor.	B Motor.
M.	C.			Mins.	Mins.	Mins.	a.m.	a.m.	a.m.	p.m.	p.m.	p.m.	p.m.	p.m.
2	22	WEYMOUTH .... dep.	—	—	—	1	*7 45	10 12	11 33	1 5	2 50	4 45	7 0	8 50
1	19	Radipole .... ,,	187 R.	—	—	—	7 49	10 16	SX	1 9	2 54	4 49	7 4	8 54
0	0	Upwey Junction .... ,,	74 R.	—	—	—	7 53	10 20		1 13	2 58	4 53	7 8	8 58
—	12	Stop Board ...... ,,	44 F.	7	1	1			11 P 42 SO					
—	35	Upwey .... ,,	44 F.	1	1	1	7 55	10 22	12 0	7 15	3 0 3 4	4 55	7 10	9 0
2	0	Friar Waddon .... ,,	190 R.	—	—	—	8 1	10 28		1 21	3 6	5 1	7 16	9 6
2	79	Coryates .... ,,	190 R.	—	—	—	8 3	10 32	12 15	1 25	3 5	5 5	7 20	9 10
4	47	Portesham ...... ,,	60 R.	—	—	—								
4	49	Stop Board ...... ,,	170 F.	13	1	1			12 P 25					
6	3	ABBOTSBURY .. arr.	60 F.	4	stop		8 9	10 36	12 30	1 29	3 14	5 9	7 24	9 14

UP TRAINS. — WEEK DAYS.

STATIONS.	Ruling Gradient 1 in *	Point-to-Point Times.	Allow for Stop.	Allow for Start.	B Motor.	B Motor.	B Mixed.	B Motor.		B Motor.	B Motor. W	B Motor.	B Motor.
		Mins.	Mins.	Mins.	a.m.	a.m.	p.m.	p.m.		p.m.	p.m.	p.m.	p.m.
ABBOTSBURY .... dep.	—	—	—	1	8 15	10 40	12 52	1 40		3 24	5 20	7 40	9 25
Portesham .... ,,	60 F.	4	1	2	8 19	10 44	1 2	1 44		3 28	5 25	7 44	9 29
Coryates .... ,,	60 F.	—	—	—	8 23	10 48	1 7	1 48		3 32	5 30	7 48	9 33
Friar Waddon . ,,	—	—	—	—	8 26						5 33		
Upwey .... ,,	190 F.	10	1	1	8 29	10 54	1 24	1 54		3 38	5 38	7 54	9 39
Upwey Jct. ... { arr.						10 55	1 27	SO			5 40		
{ dep.	44 R.	2	1	1	8 31	10 56	1 39	1 56		3 40	5 41	7 56	9 41
Stop Board .... ,,	50 F.	—	—	—			1 P 42						
Radipole ...... ,,	74 F.	—	—	—	8 35	11 0	SX	2 0		3 44	5 46	8 0	9 45
WEYMOUTH .. arr.	187 F.	6	1	—	8 39	11 4	1 45	2 4		3 48	5 50	8 4	9 49

W—Runs 7 minutes later on Saturdays.

DOWN TRAINS. — SUNDAYS.

STATIONS.	B Motor.			B Motor.			B Motor.			B Motor.
	p.m.			p.m.			p.m.			p.m.
WEYMOUTH .. dep.	2 40			4 15			8 45			8 7
Radipole ...... ,,	2 44			4 19			6 49			8 11
Upwey Jct. ...... ,,	2 48			4 23			6 53			8 15
Stop Board ...... ,,										
Upwey .... ,,	2 50			4 25			6 55			8 17
Friar Waddon .. ,,										
Coryates .... ,,	2 56			4 31			7 1			8 23
Portesham ...... ,,	3 0			4 35			7 5			8 27
Stop Board ...... ,,										
ABBOTSBURY .. arr.	3 4			4 39			7 9			8 31

UP TRAINS. — SUNDAYS.

STATIONS.	B Motor.			B Motor.			B Motor.			B Motor.
	p.m.			p.m.			p.m.			p.m.
ABBOTSBURY .. dep.	3 15			4 45			7 15			8 45
Portesham .... ,,	3 19			4 49			7 19			8 49
Coryates ...... ,,	3 23			4 53			7 23			8 53
Friar Waddon . ,,										
Upwey .... ,,	3 29			4 59			7 29			8 59
Upwey Jct. .. { arr.										9 1
{ dep.	3 31			5 1			7 31			
Stop Board ...... ,,										
Radipole ...... ,,	3 35			5 5			7 35			9 5
WEYMOUTH .. arr.	3 39			5 9			7 39			9 9

The Engineers will have absolute occupation of the Abbotsbury Branch daily from 5.0 a.m. until 15 minutes before first train is due to leave Upwey. See Special Instructions.

Taken from Original Timetables

WEYMOUTH AND ABBOTSBURY

Single Line, Upwey Junction to Abbotsbury, worked by Train Staff, and only one engine in steam at time, or two coupled.

DOWN TRAINS. — WEEK DAYS.

Mile Post Distances		STATIONS.	Ruling Gradient 1 in *	Point-to-Point Times.	Allow for Stop.	Allow for Start.	B Auto.	B Auto. SO	B Auto. SX	K Frght SX	B Auto. SO	B Auto.		B Auto.	B Auto.
M.	C.			Mins.	Mins.	Mins.	a.m.	a.m.	a.m	a.m.	p.m.	p.m.		p.m.	p.m.
2	31	WEYMOUTH ..dep.	—	—	—	1	7 28	9 40	9 57	11 38	1 5	4 55	....	6 20	8 25
1	28	Radipole ...... ,,	187 R.	—	—	—	7 32	9 44	10 1		1 9	4 59	..	6 24	8 29
0	0	Upwey Jct. Stn. ,,	74 R.	—	—	—	7 36	9 48	10 5	11 44	1 13	5 3	..	6 28	8 33
—	12	Stop Board .... ,,	44 F.	7	1	1				11 P 46					
—	35	Upwey .... ,,	44 F.	1	1	1	7 38	9 50	10 7	11 57	1 15	5 5	..	6 30	8 35
2	0	Friar Waddon .. ,,	190 R.	—	—	—	7 44	9 56	10 13		1 21	5 11	..	6 36	8 41
2	79	Coryates ...... ,,	190 R.	—	—	—	7 49	10 1	10 18	12 20	1 26	5 16	..	6 41	8 46
4	47	Portesham ...... ,,	60 R.	—	—	—				12 P 22					
4	49	Stop Board .... ,,	170 F.	13	1	1									
6	3	ABBOTSBURY arr.	60 F.	4	stop	—	7 54	10 6	10 23	12 27	1 31	5 21	..	6 46	8 51

UP TRAINS. — WEEK DAYS.

STATIONS.	Ruling Gradient 1 in *	Point-to-Point Times.	Allow for Stop.	Allow for Start.	B Auto.	B Auto. SO	B Auto. SX	B Mixed. SX	B Auto. SO	B Auto.		B Auto.	B Auto.
		Mins.	Mins.	Mins.	a.m.	a.m.	a.m.	p.m.	p.m.		p.m.		p.m.	p.m.
ABBOTSBURY .... dep.	60 R.	—	—	1	8 2	10 25	10 35	1 20	1 40	....	5 30	....	7 0	8 55
Portesham .... ,,	60 F.	4	1	2	8 6	10 30	10 40	1 28	1 45		5 36	..	7 6	9 0
Coryates ...... ,,	190 F.	—	—	—	8 10	10 35	10 45	1 33	1 50		5 41	..	7 11	9 5
Friar Waddon . ,,	190 F.	—	—	—										
Upwey .... ,,	190 F.	10	1	1	8 16	10 41	10 51	1 42	1 56		5 47	..	7 17	9 11
Upwey Jct. { arr.					8 17	10 42	10 52	1 45			5 49	..	7 18	9 12
{ dep.	44 R.	2	1	1	8 18	10 44	10 54	1 48	1 58		5 50	..	7 20	9 13
Stop Board .... ,,	50 F.	—	—	—										
Radipole ...... ,,	74 F.	—	—	—	8 21	10 48	10 58	1 52	2 1		5 55	..	7 24	9 16
WEYMOUTH .. arr.	187 F.	6	1	—	8 25	10 §53	11 2	1 56	2 5		5 59	..	7 28	9 20

The Engineers will have absolute occupation of the Abbotsbury Branch daily from 5.0 a.m. until 15 minutes before first train is due to leave Upwey. See Special Instructions.

§--Melcombe Regis Station.

Fig. A3 517 class 0-4-2T No. 1421 leaving Coryates Halt for Abbotsbury during January 1936.

Dr. Ian C. Allen

MOTIVE POWER

On 23rd January, 1894 Armstrong standard goods No. 52 was apparently in service on the line and became derailed on the curve near Upwey Junction station. Whether this was the branch loco at the time is not clear, but from the 16th January the following year six-coupled locos were no longer permitted on the branch, except in emergencies.

Although ex-Monmouthshire Railway & Canal Co. 4-4-0T No. 1304 was used on the line for a short period, the 517 class 0-4-2 tanks came to be used almost exclusively on branch services and were only replaced by the later

Collett 0-4-2T's during the final years.

The following locomotives are amongst those known to have worked the line:
517 class 0-4-2T's Nos. 202, 524, 531, 561, 563, 1163, 1421 and 1430; Collett 0-4-2T's Nos. 4803 (later as 1403), 4854 (later as 1454), 1453 and 1467 (No. 1453 was used on the last train).

Steam Railmotors Nos. 57, 65, 66, and Diesel railcars Nos. 20, 21 and 24 also saw some service on the line.

Fig. A4 Collett 0-4-2T No. 1454 at Abbotsbury in 1947.

J.H. Russell

Track Plan

Abbotsbury station circa 1904. The basic track layout
lasted until closure but the engine shed siding was removed
when the track was relaid in 1938 and the turnout replaced
with a catch point.

10.

9.

11.

8.

· SP

5.

7.

6.

· SP

4.

3.

1.

2.

KEY
1. STATION BUILDING
2. STATION COAL
3. WEIGHBRIDGE & OFFICE
4. CATTLE PEN
5. SIGNAL BOX
6. GOODS SHED
7. YARD CRANE
8. PROBABLY COAL STAGE AND/OR MESS
9. WATER TOWER
10. ENGINE SHED
11. P.W. HUT

Fig. A5 The foot of the station
approach road c.1910.
J.H. Lucking

Fig. A6 An early postcard view of the station forecourt shortly after the arrival of a steam railmotor with an early afternoon
service.

J.H. Lucking

THE STATION, ABBOTSBURY. 25.

Fig. A7 The station building was constructed to the same basic design as those at Portesham and Broadway, although Abbotsbury itself was slightly larger. The local stone employed in its construction was pale grey in colour and the roof was enhanced by the red and blue tiles which alternated every third row, the colour change being further emphasized with the use of decorative tiles, although weathering made this less obvious in later years.

The building is shown here on the 1st May, 1906 with the platform canopy in its original condition; this was later reduced in overhang and the valancing modified, probably during the 1920s.

I.D. Beale

Fig. A8 Looking east towards Weymouth in 1933 prior to the renewal of the original trackwork. The signal box is just visible on the left, almost opposite the goods shed, and smaller advertisement boards have replaced those illustrated in the previous figure.

L. & G.R.P.

Fig. A9 The line terminated in a shallow cutting just beyond the end of the platform and the engine release turnout was operated by a weighted hand lever alongside.

I.D. Beale

Fig. A10 No. 1403 at Abbotsbury on the 21st June, 1951. The station was oil lit throughout its life but it was not until after the Second World War that Mr Price finally acquired two tilley lamps, one of which was used in the office and the other on the station platform. The cast iron lamp in the foreground of *Fig. A1* was quite unique but had disappeared when the later posts shown here were installed.

E.S. Russell

Fig. A11 Two entrances in the far end of the building (see Fig. A10) served the gentlemen's lavatories and coal store whilst the remaining accommodation consisted of, from left to right: stores and lamp room, ladies' waiting room and lavatory and the general waiting room and booking hall, through which access was gained to the station office (the latter being situated at this end of the building behind the barred window). There was no drinking water at the station and the small gate alongside the building was the only entrance to the platform.

I.D. Beale

Fig. A12 A detail view of the canopy brackets showing the small shields which bore the initials of the Abbotsbury Railway.

I.D. Beale

Fig. A13 The rear of the station building. A sleeper-built coal pen once stood in the foreground of this view (see track plan) but was destroyed by fire one day when the gangers were burning the grass.

I.D. Beale

Fig. A14 Collett 0-4-2T No. 1467 at Abbotsbury on the 4th June, 1949 with trailer car No. 165.

J.H. Meredith

Fig. A15 There was little freight traffic at Abbotsbury, certainly since the 1930s, and on this occasion in 1947 there were no wagons at all at the terminus, although some were probably awaiting collection at Portesham and Upwey on the return journey.

J.H. Russell

Fig. A16 The same train with Collett 0-4-2T No. 1454 in charge. The end loading dock had not been used since the arrival of Mr Price's furniture in 1934 and the timber palings that originally extended along the rear of the station platform had been replaced with concrete posts and wire fencing by that time. Both Mr Price and his wife lovingly cared for the station gardens and often won prizes for them. There were roses along the platform fence and a number of vegetables around the station which included runner beans and new potatoes behind the station building.

J.H. Russell

Fig. A17 From 1935 to 1945 a camping coach was stabled on the siding behind the platform at Abbotsbury and another at Portesham. The first vehicle was a six wheeled clerestory with six berths, but this proved inadequate and was soon replaced with an eight berth bogie vehicle. This photograph shows a Bristol family on holiday there with members of a boys brigade camping party from Birmingham. Drinking water for the campers was sent from Portesham each day in churns and Mrs Price, who cleaned the vehicles on Saturday mornings, would often greet regular campers with a hot meal and a cup of tea on their arrival.

The coaches were taken away from the branch at the end of the war and believed to have been used in an ambulance train.

Courtesy S. Price

Figs. A18 & 19 Looking east and west respectively in 1947.

J.H. Russell

Fig. A20 517 class 0-4-2T No. 1430 on the yard entry cross-over with trailer No. 207 in June 1936, again featuring the original trackwork.

Dr. Ian C. Allen

Fig. A21 Signalling at Abbotsbury had originally consisted of home and starter signals, three revolving groundlamps and of course a fixed distant. The home and starter are believed to have been removed in 1904 but the signal box remained in use as a ground frame until the original track was renewed in 1938, at which time two separate ground frames were installed and the timber building sold off locally. The West ground frame illustrated here was situated at the foot of the platform, to control the yard and loop entry crossovers. (The original signalling equipment had been supplied by the Railway Signalling Company.)

A. West

Fig. A22 Looking east from the roof of the station building after closure showing the siding which served the cattle pen and end loading dock (cattle traffic had been lost to road transport during the 1930s).

Before the arrival of the camping coach the local coal merchant W.C. Hughes stored coal just beyond the cattle pen but N. Restorick, another coal merchant based at Upwey, succeeded him during the 1940s and thereafter only the occasional wagon of coal was sent through to Abbotsbury and this was unloaded by Mr Price! A weighbridge and an office which had been situated to the right of the pens was little used, except by local farmers, as corn or shingle from the beach was weighed at Weymouth. The weighbridge was removed about 1939 and the small creosoted timber office cut up for firewood.

I.D. Beale

Fig. A23 No. 1453 approaches the station on the 9th June, 1949.

A. West

Fig. A24 The spare coach was left each day for the midday goods which then returned to Weymouth as a mixed train.

J.H. Moss

Fig. A25 The goods shed was again constructed of local stone but with a slate roof and sliding doors. The building housed a small crane with a lifting capacity of 1 ton 10 cwt, but saw little use as goods were usually carried in the guard's van and dealt with at the station, any larger deliveries being sent from Weymouth by road! Incoming traffic included coal, potatoes, flour and paint, but with only one member of staff at the station outgoing corn, etc., was despatched in box vans to save sheeting open wagons. Before the 1930s locally caught mackerel had been sent out each morning but it seems that traffic was generally light. Mr Price bought himself a tradesman's bicycle with a rack and ran his own delivery service to and from the station.

The loading gauge hanging in the west doorway was the only one at the site.

J.H. Russell

Fig. A26 The forecourt and east elevations of the goods shed showing the sliding doors.

J.H. Russell

Fig. A27 This photograph shows the back siding, the location of which can be seen in the following view. This was used for the despatch or receipt of any loads that might be subject to delay in loading, thus leaving the goods loop free for shunting purposes. During the war wagonloads of ammunition from Weymouth were stored here away from the harbour. A 5 ton crane originally stood to the left of this view, the site of which can just be seen, but this had been removed by the 1930s, doubtless through lack of use!

The small corrugated iron shed in the foreground was installed during the final years (after 1947) and housed a hand pump for raising water from the well (mentioned in *Fig. A30*) to feed the 'NOT DRINKING WATER' supply at the station. (The water was stored in a tank in the station roof.)

I.D. Beale

Fig. A28 A general view of the site looking towards the buffers in 1947 with Abbotsbury East ground frame in the foreground. The line was on a falling gradient towards the buffer stops so wagons bound for the yard were often uncoupled here and allowed to run into the yard by gravity after the loco had run ahead and cleared the points.

J.H. Russell

Fig. A29 The water tower and crumbling remains of the engine shed in 1947.

J.H. Russell

Fig. A30 Because locos took water at Weymouth the water tower was seldom used for its prime purpose and although the short swivelling arm and delivery bag remained intact until the Second World War, for many years the tower was used solely to provide the station's water supply. The building housed a small steam pump for raising water from the well that was situated at the foot of the bank to the right of the upper view. The pump was powered by steam from the branch loco which stood on the running line alongside and was coupled to the pump by means of a flexible pipe connected in place of one of the whistles.

Just after the war the pumping engine was sent to Swindon for repair but never returned so Mr Price was left to replenish the tank using a hand pump in order to maintain the water supply at the station. A new hand pump was subsequently installed (as already mentioned in *Fig. A27*) to feed the station directly from the well and the water tower was finally abandoned.

I.D. Beale

A31 Looking east towards Weymouth from the water tower.

I.D. Beale

Fig. A32 The engine shed is believed to have been taken out of use when the GWR first acquired the line in 1896 and the doors subsequently removed to avoid liability for rates; the roof was also later removed before the early 1930's but there is some controversy over the date. It seems likely that the roof remained intact during the early 1920's as the GWR had considered the possibility of converting the building into living accommodation for the station master.

The shed siding remained overgrown for many years and was finally taken up when the branch track was renewed.

J.H. Russell

Fig. A33 The platelayers' hut at Abbotsbury was sleeper built with a slate roof and was situated on the embankment at the rear of the engine shed. Five men based at Upwey were responsible for the permanent way on the branch.

I.D. Beale

Fig. A34 A further view of the P.W. hut.

I.D. Beale

Fig. A35 A closer view of the canopy glazing.
I.D. Beale

Fig. A36 A detail view of the lavatory roof.
I.D. Beale

Fig. A37 The station after closure in 1960.

I.D. Beale

The Abbotsbury branch was closed to traffic on the 1st December, 1952 although the line remained open as far as Upwey for goods traffic until 1st January, 1962. A modern residence now occupies the site of the station building but the goods shed, engine shed and platelayers' hut remain standing.

Further sources of reference:
  Railways of Dorset *by J.H. Lucking published by*
    Railway Correspondence and Travel Society
  Railway Modeller *page 115 Vol. 6 No. 55 1955*

E.S. Russell

Fig. AN1 Collett 0-4-2T No. 1439 at Ashburton on the 18th September, 1952.

ASHBURTON

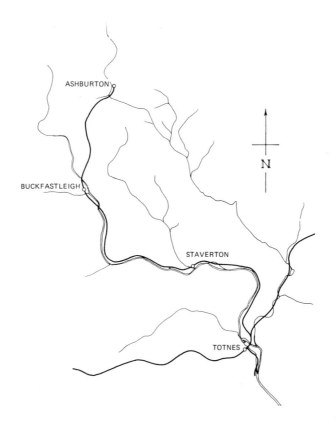

KEY FACTS

Company of Origin	Buckfastleigh, Totnes & South Devon Railway
Date of Opening	1st May 1872
Converted to Standard Gauge	21st–22nd May 1892
Purchased by GWR	28th August 1897
Length of Branch	9 miles 37 chains
Ruling Gradient	1 in 6
Route Colour	Uncoloured
Overall Speed Restriction	40 mph
Single Line Worked by	Block Telegraph and Train Staff and ticket, crossing stations at Buckfastleigh and Ashburton

ORIGIN

The Ashburton, Newton and South Devon Junction Railway was authorised on the 27th July, 1848 and was to have extended some 10½ miles from Newton Abbot, through Buckfastleigh to Ashburton. However, difficulty was experienced in raising the necessary capital and the company was dissolved in 1851 before any construction had begun.

Following later proposals in 1863 for the construction of a railway from Totnes, on the South Devon Railway, to Buckfastleigh, the Buckfastleigh, Totnes and South Devon Railway was authorised on the 25th June, 1864 and a second Act of Parliament on the 26th May, 1865 authorised an extension of the line to Ashburton. Construction came to a standstill by the end of 1867 pending negotiations with the contractor and only recommenced after a further Act of Parliament had granted an extension of time in which to complete the line and another contractor was appointed in 1868.

The railway was built to the broad gauge 7ft 0¼ inches, it was 9 miles 37 chains in length and was opened on the 1st May, 1872 with intermediate stations at Staverton and Buckfastleigh. The South Devon Railway worked the line until the 1st February, 1876 when the Great Western absorbed the SDR and inherited this responsibility. The branch was later converted to standard gauge on the 21st–22nd May, 1892 and finally passed into the hands of the GWR on the 28th August, 1897.

Fig. AN2 No. 4405 at Ashburton in 1952.
John Harrison

OPERATION

A locomotive from Newton Abbot was sub shedded at Ashburton to work the branch passenger services and had faced towards the terminus before the introduction of auto trailers to the branch (about 1930) after which locos faced 'up' the line and propelled the trailers to Ashburton.

There had been an overnight cleaner based at the shed who relieved the crew after the last train had arrived and remained with the engine until the morning. He began his duty by throwing out most of the fire and coaling the engine before moving it into the shed to rake out the ash-pan over the shed pit. During the night he cleaned the loco and kept warm on the footplate, to save lighting the fire in the cabin, where he was often joined by the local policeman! Before the driver arrived in the morning he would build up the fire, pump water to fill the tank outside, move the engine out to the coal stage ready for oiling and finish his duty by acting as fireman on the first return journey. After about 1930 the cleaner was taken away and the early turn fireman left to light up himself. The following notes describe a typical weekday of 1935:

The fireman booked on at 5.15 am to light up, although in practice the usual small fire was kept in at the back of the firebox and merely spread across the bars. The engine was cleaned, water was pumped and after moving the loco outside, ready for the driver to oil up, the fireman returned to shovel the ashes out of the shed pit. The driver arrived and the loco was backed over the engine release crossover and onto the auto trailer stabled in the platform; unless any tail traffic was conveyed the loco and trailer thereafter remained coupled together throughout the day's timetable. The first train departed with the local school children at 8.07 am returning from Totnes at 8.35 am but the 9.15 am didn't return until 10.35 am and the fireman would apparently take advantage of such time at Totnes to clean the loco, which of course saved time at the shed in the mornings. After the 11.10 am from Ashburton arrived at Totnes the branch goods from Newton Abbot left for Buckfastleigh and the auto train returned at 12.45 pm arriving at Ashburton at 1.07 pm. The loco and trailer ran over to the shed siding, and the early turn crew finished at 1.15 pm leaving the fresh crew to coal the engine and 'oil up'. The branch goods arrived from Buckfastleigh at 1.45 pm, the loco ran round its train, the branch auto ran over to the platform and the goods was set back into the run round loop to clear the running line for the auto train's departure at 2.00 pm. The goods loco took water at Ashburton and sorted the yard before taking the return goods to Buckfastleigh at 2.35 pm. The yard was again sorted at Buckfastleigh before the goods finally made its way back to Newton Abbot at 4.47 pm calling at Staverton

on the way. The branch auto train worked the 4.00 pm, which returned from Totnes with the school children, the 5.33 pm and 7.25 pm return services, the last train arriving back at Ashburton at 9.07 pm after which the trailer was left under the overall roof, beyond the release crossover, and the loco taken on shed for disposal. There was no Sunday service.

Cattle traffic was a regular source of income to the line but there were four main cattle fairs held at Ashburton each year from which cattle were sold to farmers from Cornwall and 'up country' as the opposite direction was known! The fairs often lasted until 9 or 10 pm and could require up to 90 wagons, which were brought to the larger yard at Buckfastleigh two or three days beforehand. During the fair the doors and windows of many of the buildings in St Lawrence Lane were boarded over for protection as cattle were held in the street prior to being taken into the pens, opposite the station, where the market was held. Then when they were sold drovers would bring them over to the station where they were loaded onto the train through the main pen, along the entire length of the loading bank opposite the platform. A locomotive was employed all day in bringing the empty wagons from Buckfastleigh into the terminus for loading and returning them to that station where they were held until they were sufficient in number to justify a trip to Totnes, after which the loco returned to continue the operation. Often the trains of empties taken to Ashburton were too long for the loco to run past on the run round loop (17 wagons are believed to have been maximum capacity of the loop), so the train was brought to a stand in the normal way just short of the engine release crossover. The loco then ran onto the loop alongside and, using the steel towing cable attached to the solebars of one of the wagons, the train was pulled further along to clear the loop entry point so that the loco could rejoin the other end to begin feeding the wagons to the pens for loading.

On the day of a cattle fair the branch goods only ran as far as Buckfastleigh where the wagons for Ashburton were left until the following day when, together with that day's wagons, two trips might be required to take them on to the terminus.

Of course the cattle workings were fitted in between passenger services, which were continued as usual by the branch crews, but the congested yard at Ashburton often prevented the auto train from running into the station any further than beyond the foot of the platform and during the final years the branch train terminated at Buckfastleigh on fair days and passengers were relayed to Ashburton by bus.

1935 Working Timetable

ASHBURTON BRANCH.

THE SPEED OF TRAINS OVER THE BRANCH MUST NOT EXCEED 40 MILES PER HOUR.

Single Line worked by South Devon Block Telegraph Instruments and Train Staff and Ticket. The Staff Stations are Totnes, Buckfastleigh and Ashburton. Staverton is an intermediate Block Post.

When absolutely necessary two Goods Trains, or a Passenger and a Goods Train, may cross at Buckfastleigh and Ashburton on the understanding that the Passenger Train is always kept on the Running Line, and if the Passenger Train has to stop at Buckfastleigh, it must stop at the Platform.

WEEK DAYS ONLY.

M.P. Mileage M/C	DOWN TRAINS.	Station No.	Ruling Gra-dient 1 in	Point to Point Times. Mins.	Allow for Stop. Mins.	Allow for Start. Mins.	Motor dep. A.M.	Motor SO dep. A.M.	Motor SX dep. A.M.	N'ton Abbot Goods. arr. A.M.	N'ton Abbot Goods. dep. A.M.	Motor SO dep.	Motor dep. P.M.	Motor SX dep. P.M.	Motor SO dep. P.M.	Motor SX dep. P.M.	Motor SO dep. P.M.	Motor dep. P.M.	Motor dep. P.M.	Motor dep. P.M.	Motor SO dep. P.M.
	Totnes	2001	—	—	—	1	8 35	10 30	10 35	11 14	11 35	12 5	12 45	1 30	2 42	4 30	5 0	6 37	8 45	10 45	
2/58	Staverton Crossing ..	2099					....														
3/25	Staverton	2100	536 R.	8	1	1	8 43	10 38	10 43	11 45	12 0	12 13	12 53	1 38	2 50	4 38	5 8	6 45	8 53	10 53	
6/75	Buckfastleigh	2101	110 R.	8	1	1	8 51	10 46	10 51	12 10	1 35	12 21	1 1	1 46	2 58	4 46	5 16	6 53	9 1	11 1	
9/37	Ashburton	2102	60 R.	8	1		8 57	10 52	10 57	1 45	—	12 27	1 7	1 52	3 4	4 52	5 22	6 59	9 7	11 7	

WEEK DAYS ONLY.

	UP TRAINS.	Ruling Gra-dient 1 in.	Point to Point Times. Mins.	Allow for Stop. Mins.	Allow for Start. Mins.	Motor dep. A.M.	Motor SO dep. A.M.	Motor dep. A.M.	Motor SO dep. A.M.	Motor dep. A.M.	N'ton Abbot Goods. SO arr. P.M.	N'ton Abbot Goods. SO dep. P.M.	N'ton Abbot Goods. SX arr. P.M.	N'ton Abbot Goods. SX dep. P.M.	Motor SX dep. P.M.	Motor SO dep. P.M.	Motor dep. P.M.	Motor dep. P.M.	Motor SO dep. P.M.
	Ashburton	—	—	—	1	8 7	9 15	11 10	12 40	2 0		2 35		2 35	4 0	4 15	7 25		9 40
	Buckfastleigh	60 F.	8	1	1	8 13	9 21	11 16	12 46	2 6	2 45	3 5	2 45	4 47	4 6	4 21	6 39	7 31	9 46
	Staverton	118 F.	8	1	1	8 22	9 30	11 25	12 55	2 15	3 15	3 25	4 57	5 10	4 15	4 30	5 48	7 40	9 55
	Staverton Crossing																		
	Totnes	536 F.	8	1	—	8 29	9 37	11 32	1 2	2 22	3 35	3 55	5 20	5 45	4 22	4 37	5 55	7 47	10 2

1948 Working Timetable

Taken from Original Timetables

TOTNES AND ASHBURTON.

THE SPEED OF TRAINS OVER THE BRANCH MUST NOT EXCEED 40 MILES PER HOUR.

Single Line worked by South Devon Block Telegraph Instruments and Train Staff and Ticket. The Staff Stations are Totnes, Buckfastleigh and Ashburton. Staverton is an intermediate Block Post.

When absolutely necessary two Freight Trains, or a Passenger and a Freight Train, may cross at Buckfastleigh and Ashburton on the understanding that the Passenger Train is always kept on the Running Line, and if the Passenger Train has to stop at Buckfastleigh, it must stop at the Platform.

Down Trains.   Week Days only.

M.P. Mileage M.	C.	STATIONS.	Ruling Gradient 1 in	Point to Point Times. Mins.	Allow for Stop. Mins.	Allow for Start. Mins.	Motor dep. a.m.	8.40 a.m. Newton Abbot Freight. arr. a.m.	8.40 a.m. Newton Abbot Freight. dep. a.m.	Motor dep. a.m.	Motor SO dep. a.m.	Motor SX dep. p.m.	Motor SO dep. p.m.	Motor SX dep. p.m.	Motor SO dep. p.m.	Motor SX dep. p.m.	Motor SO dep. p.m.	Motor SX dep. p.m.	Motor SO dep. p.m.	Motor dep. p.m.	Motor SO dep. p.m.
—	—	TOTNES	—	—	—	1	8 45	9 29	10 10	10 40	10 45	12 18	12 50	1 40	3 25	3 40	4 48	5 33	6 45	9 0	
2	56	Staverton Crossing	536 R.	—	—																
3	25	Staverton	536 R.	8	1	1	8 53	10 20	10 37	10 48	10 53	12 26	12 58	1 48	3 33	3 48	4 56	5 41	6 53	9 8	
6	75	Buckfastleigh	50 R.	8	1	1	9 1	1047	X11 35	10 50	11 1	12 34	1 6	1X56	3 41	3 56	5 4	5 49	7 1	9 16	
9	37	ASHBURTON	60 R	8	1	—	9 7	11 45	—	11 2	11 7	12 40	1 12	2 3	3 47	4 2	5 10	5 55	7 7	9 22	

Up Trains.   Week Days only.

STATIONS.	Ruling Gradient 1 in	Point to Point Times. Mins.	Allow for Stop. Mins.	Allow for Start. Mins.	Motor SO dep. a.m.	Motor SX dep. a.m.	Motor dep. a.m.	Motor dep. a.m.	Motor SO dep. p.m.	Newton Abbot Freight. SO arr. p.m.	Newton Abbot Freight. SO dep. p.m.	Newton Abbot Freight. SX arr. p.m.	Newton Abbot Freight. SX dep. p.m.	Motor SO dep. p.m.	Motor SX dep. p.m.	Motor SX dep. p.m.	Motor SO dep. p.m.	Motor SX dep. p.m.	Motor SO dep. p.m.	Motor SO dep. p.m.
ASHBURTON	60 F.	—	—	1	7 50	7 58	9 35	11 25	12 50	—	1 0	—	1 15	2 25	2 45	4 5	4 35	5 45	6 5	8 20
Buckfastleigh	50 F.	8	1	1	7 56	8 4	9 41	11X31	12 56	1 10	X1 59	1 25	2 15	2 31	2 51	4 11	4 41	5 51	6 11	8 26
Staverton	536 F.	8	1	1	8 5	8 12	9 49	11 39	1 5	2 9	2 26	2 25	2 45	2 40	2 59	4 19	4 49	5 59	6 19	8 35
Staverton Crossing	536 F.																			
TOTNES	536 F.	8	1	—	8 12	8 19	9 56	11 46	1 12	2 37	3 10	2 55	3 26	2 47	3 6	4 27	4 56	6 5	6 25	8 42

Number of Wagons exclusive of Brake Van.

SECTION.		2-8-0			2-6-2 T			2-6-0			Ordinary Engines. Tender.			Ordinary Engines. Tank.			
From	To	Coal.	Goods.	Emp-ties.	Coal.	Goods.	Emp-ties.	Coal.	Goods.	Emp-ties.	Coal.	Goods.	Emp-ties.	Coal.	Goods.	Emp-ties.	

Ashburton Branch.

Ashburton	Buckfastleigh ...													25	38	40	With two engines double loads may be taken, but no train must exceed 40 vehicles.
Buckfastleigh	Totnes													30	40	40	
Totnes	Buckfastleigh ...													25	38	40	
Buckfastleigh	Ashburton ...													13	25	30	

Extract from GWR 'Maximum Loads' 1908

MOTIVE POWER

Locomotives known to have worked the line during broad gauge days included South Devon Railway 0-6-0T *Taurus* and 2-4-0ST's *Melling* and *Cerebus*. However, after the line was converted to standard gauge in 1892 it would appear to have been worked almost exclusively by 517 class 0-4-2T's until the introduction of their successors, the 48XX class 0-4-2T's during the 1930s.

No. 571 is well remembered by one fireman and worked the line for some years around the time of the First World War with an open cab, copper capped chimney and polished brass dome.

The 1920 allocation to Ashburton was as follows:

Jan.—Feb.	571	517 class	0-4-2T
Feb.—March	1433	,, ,,	,,
March	217	,, ,,	,,
April—May	845	,, ,,	,,
June—Sept.	571	,, ,,	,,
Oct.—Jan. '21	845	,, ,,	,,

Nos. 1163 and 1165 also worked the line during the 1920s and No. 831 during the mid 1930s.

Other locomotives sent to Ashburton for a very short time during the mid-1930s included an 1854 class 0-6-0PT (number unconfirmed) and No. 1415, a Metro class 2-4-0T, but the new 48XX class Collett 0-4-2T's which were also tried at this time proved to be very popular with the branch crews and were thereafter used on the line until closure. No. 4870 came to be regarded as the branch loco, later renumbered 1470, and was treasured by the crews who even painted the screw reverser. The standby loco was No. 1466 and other members of the class known to have worked the line included Nos. 1427, 1429 and 1439.

The goods workings from Newton Abbot were generally hauled by 44XX class or 45XX class 2-6-2T's, but six coupled tanks had also performed this duty at one time.

Fig. AN4 An early view of an unidentified 517 class 0-4-2T at Ashburton, quite possibly No. 571.

S.M. Gill

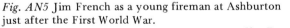
Fig. AN5 Jim French as a young fireman at Ashburton just after the First World War.

Jim French

Track Plans

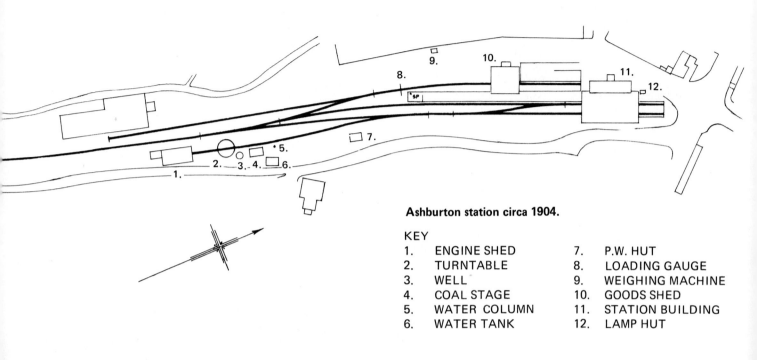

Ashburton station circa 1904.

KEY

1. ENGINE SHED
2. TURNTABLE
3. WELL
4. COAL STAGE
5. WATER COLUMN
6. WATER TANK
7. P.W. HUT
8. LOADING GAUGE
9. WEIGHING MACHINE
10. GOODS SHED
11. STATION BUILDING
12. LAMP HUT

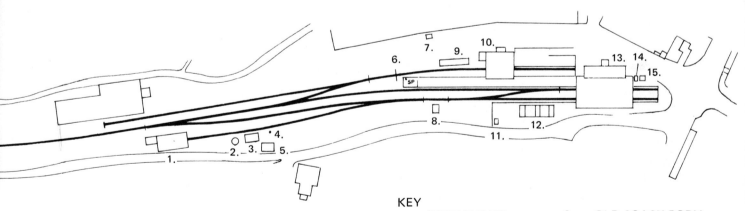

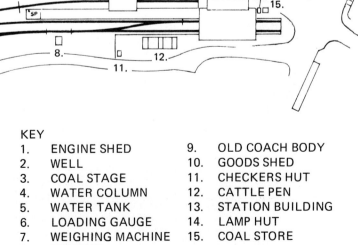

Ashburton station 1955. The basic layout remained
unchanged but the run round loop was extended, probably
in 1931. Modifications sketched only.

KEY

1. ENGINE SHED
2. WELL
3. COAL STAGE
4. WATER COLUMN
5. WATER TANK
6. LOADING GAUGE
7. WEIGHING MACHINE
8. P.W. HUT
9. OLD COACH BODY
10. GOODS SHED
11. CHECKERS HUT
12. CATTLE PEN
13. STATION BUILDING
14. LAMP HUT
15. COAL STORE

Fig. AN6 Ashburton station as seen from St Lawrence Lane in 1949 with the Station Hotel in the foreground and the yard entrance in the distant right of the picture.
Bristol Museum

Fig. AN7 An early comparison showing the unsightly screen alongside the station building and the original position of the corrugated iron lamp hut.

L. & G.R.P.

Fig. AN8 The station building was constructed of limestone, reddish-brown in colour, with blue quoins, red brick reveals to the door and window apertures and a slate roof. The design was almost identical, save for detail and minor dimensional differences to the one previously constructed at Moretonhampstead even to including a doorway (possibly two?) in the far end wall (visible in *Fig. AN26)* which may have served as a coal store but was bricked up by 1921 and the wall eventually painted black. Passengers entered the building through the main doorway, beneath the canopy, as the gated aperture at the far end of the train shed was only used by the staff for loading purposes. The canopy was removed about 1950. (Photo 1949)

C.J. Freezer

Fig. AN9 The lamp hut shown in *Fig. AN7* was turned through ninety degrees when the brick built coal store alongside was constructed during the 1920s. Both buildings are illustrated here in 1949.

C.J. Freezer

Fig. AN10 The platform elevation of the station building in 1962. Accommodation consisted of, from left to right, Parcels Office, Stationmaster's Office, Booking/Entrance Hall, ladies waiting room and lavatories and, through the aperture at this end of the train shed, the 'gents'.

P.G.F. English

Fig. AN11 The train shed was constructed of timber, braced with wrought iron tie rods and roofed with diagonal boarding clad with slates. The glazing from the eastern skylight (presuming that it was originally glazed) had been removed by the 1920s and the aperture left open. The roof differed from the one at Moretonhampstead in having a ventilation space in each gable.

J.T. Fraser

Figs. AN12 and 13 Detail views of the roof.

M.B. Warburton & P.G.F. English

Fig. AN14 Ashburton station in 1921. The cattle pens are not shown on the 1905 Ordnance Survey map so presumably date from after that time, but cattle facilities were improved in 1928 by continuing the loading platform through the train shed and removing the timber screen featured here. Cattle could then be loaded throughout the length of the loop siding, although still entering through the pens, using hurdles to guide them into the wagons. The new platform was constructed of concrete blocks and is clearly seen in *Fig. AN12*. The doors in the timber screens that partially enclosed the train shed were unused for many years and the one illustrated here was removed during the late 1940s. The station name is just apparent in the glass of the oil lamps along the platform.

L. & G.R.P.

Fig. AN15 The train shed as seen from behind the pens.

M.E.J. Deane

Fig. AN16 A 1950s comparison with *Fig. AN14*. The corrugated iron shed on the right was used as a checker's office during the cattle fairs, all the relevant paperwork being kept here together with the hose for washing down the pens. Coal for the gasworks beyond (built in 1840) was unloaded in the goods yard and taken over to the premises by the local carrier using a horse and cart, but the gas-works was closed just before the Second World War.

J.T. Fraser

Fig. AN17 No. 1439 shunting at Ashburton on the 18th September, 1952.

E.S. Russell

Fig. AN18 Looking towards Totnes from the station platform on the 22nd September, 1955. The engine release crossover was operated by padlocked yard levers and the starter signal at the foot of the platform was controlled by the signal lever just visible in *Fig. AN14* alongside the fence at the rear of the platform. The small timber built shed on the left served as a P.W. hut, replacing that shown in *Fig. AN26*.

M.B. Warburton

Fig. AN19 The branch goods awaiting departure in 1949.

R.J. Doran

Fig. AN20 A closer view of No. 4405 on the same occasion.

R.J. Doran

Fig. AN21 The loading bank on the left of the yard entrance was used for loading pit props and umber traffic. Umber was used as a pigment in paint manufacturing, it was dug locally and much of it was sent to Tamworth Paper Mills where it was used to colour brown paper (Date of Photo 1949).

Bristol Museum

Fig. AN22 Berry's the wool merchants were based at Buckfastleigh and, in this view, occupied the nearer of the warehouses that skirted the yard; the living accommodation at this end was occupied by one of their employees. Careful study of the photographs will reveal the small warehouse adjoining this first building which was occupied by Mr Mann, the local coal merchant, and the umber works beyond.

P.G.F. English

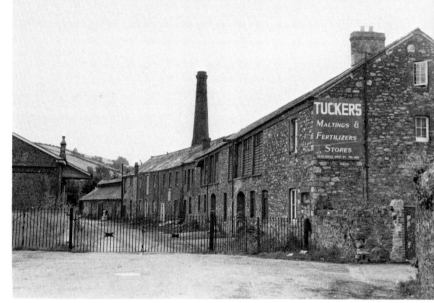

Fig. AN23 The GWR started a country lorry service at Ashburton about 1928, the driver was Sidney Baker, with L. Littleton, one of the porters, standing in as relief driver. The lorry was kept under the canopy of the goods shed each night and vehicles provided over the years included a Burford, Thornycroft and a Dennis. Bill Nicholls was a local carrier for the railway before the introduction of their own service and he had kept his lorry in the umber works. As many as 25 wagons of wool could be left at Totnes for Berry's and brought down to Ashburton as space would allow. The wool was transported in large bales which were unloaded by crane in the goods shed and onto the railway lorry which ferried them individually over to the warehouse whilst the next bale was being lifted from the wagon.

P.G.F. English

Figs. AN24 and 25 The goods shed was situated behind the station platform and was constructed of limestone with red brick arch lintels to the three main entrances and a slate roof. It was originally constructed with sliding doors to cover each entrance (see *Fig. AN26*) but the later addition of the wooden office that was built against the south facing wall required the replacement of the doors at that end of the building and the hinged doors shown below, mounted on upright lengths of bullhead rail, were subsequently fitted. (Photos 1949 and c. 1950.)

C.J. Freezer & M.E.J. Deane

STATION. ASHBURTON.

Q24

Fig. AN26 An early view of the site c. 1905—1910 showing the longitudinal track that remained at this time from the gauge conversion of 1892. The basic track layout remained unchanged but the run round loop was extended (probably in 1931) and the loop entry turnout eventually commenced from a point just south of the engine shed. The original P.W. hut, wooden loading gauge and sliding doors on the goods shed can all be seen.

Courtesy C.J. Freezer

Fig. AN27 A deserted yard scene, probably taken during the late 1920s, clearly illustrating the replacement loading gauge, wooden office and hinged doors. There was no yard crane at the terminus but the goods shed housed a light purpose crane with a lifting capacity of 2 tons. The 4 wheeled stock on the running line was typical of that used prior to the introduction of auto train working on the branch.

Real Photographs

Fig. AN28 This brick built office replaced the wooden one described during the early 1950s and still stands today.

P.G.F. English

Fig. AN29 The clerestory coach body, mounted on concrete blocks was installed during the final years for use as a store for Messrs Silcocks feed merchants.

P.G.F. English

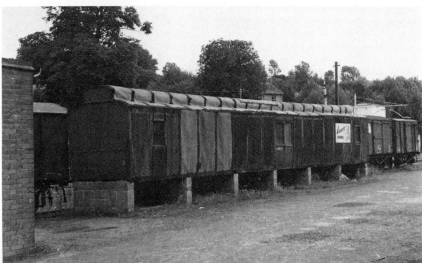

Fig. AN30 An early 1950s view of the site with the water tower in the foreground, alongside Parish Road.

M.E.J. Deane

Fig. AN31 No. 1470 departing with the branch train for Totnes on the 29th May, 1957.

R.J. Sellick

Fig. AN32 A stop board that was situated a short distance along the siding on the right of this view forbad locos to pass, as the far end of the siding was privately owned by Edwin Tucker & Sons, maltsters and seed merchants. Wagons for this siding were usually pulled in and out using the steel towing cable coupled to the locomotive on the running line alongside. When the wagon was moving the locomotive would ease the tension and the shunter released the cable, but all too frequently the cable ended up wrapped around the loading gauge and telegraph pole at the foot of the platform! The horse drawn cart belonged to the local coal merchant already mentioned, Mr Mann, but a Mr Tuxworth was another coal and grain merchant at Ashburton.

J.T. Fraser

Fig. AN33 The engine shed was again constructed of a reddish-brown limestone with red brick arch lintels and a slate roof with a central raised ventilator. The ground frame just outside the entrance was manned by a porter/signalman and used to control the loop and yard entry crossovers and the home signal.

W.A. Camwell

Fig. AN34 The water tower was supplied from a well that was situated alongside the coaling stage, to the right of the picture. Water was forced from the depths of the well and into the tank using steam from the branch loco, which stood inside the shed for the operation and was coupled to the apparatus by means of a flexible pipe at the far end of the building. Besides the water crane and the station lavatories, the tank also supplied a large standpipe at the cattle pens that was used for washing them out. Branch locos usually took water at Totnes to conserve the supply but the locomotive on the Newton Abbot goods took water during its stay here at lunchtime. On really hot summer days the crews had been known to climb into the water tower to cool off!

The coal stage was constructed of concrete blocks and replaced its sleeper built predecessor just before the Second World War. There was a shallow pit just in front of the structure which was used for 'oiling up' but there was also a deeper inspection pit inside the engine shed.

P.J. Garland

Fig. AN35 The well cover can be seen in the foreground of this photograph of No. 1470 alongside the coal stage on the 26th May, 1956.

M.E.J. Deane

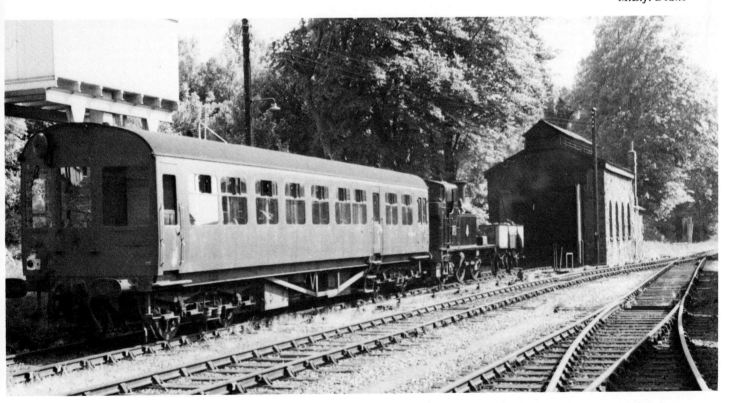

Fig. AN36 Loco coal wagons were kept in the loop siding until required and usually pulled into the shed siding using the steel towing cable. The late turn fireman had unloaded them in the morning before booking on duty but of course locos were coaled direct from the wagons whenever possible. No. 1470 is shown here on the shed siding at lunchtime on the 29th May, 1957 along with the branch trailer.

R.J. Sellick 49

Fig. AN37 Looking towards the buffer stops from the neck of the yard during the early 1950s with both the branch goods and the auto train at the station.

M.E.J. Deane

Fig. AN38 No. 1470 waits at the head of a cattle train whilst the fireman retrieves the staff on the 7th November, 1957.

M.B. Warburton

Fig. AN39 The same train shunting out past the crossing from West End and Stone Park.

M.B. Warburton

Fig. AN40 No. 1470 propels its single coach train past the home signal on its way into the terminus on the 26th May, 1956.

M.E.J. Deane

The Ashburton branch was closed to passengers on the 3rd November, 1958, the line remaining open for goods traffic only until the 7th September, 1962.

The Dart Valley Railway Company now operate steam hauled passenger services between Buckfastleigh and Totnes but the final section of the branch between Buckfastleigh and Ashburton was lost to the Company when part of the new A38 road from Exeter to Plymouth was built on the trackbed. The station building, goods shed, engine shed and even the checker's hut that was situated behind the cattle pens at Ashburton all remain standing although converted for various uses.

Further sources of reference:
The Ashburton Branch by *A.R. Kingdom OPC*
The Dart Valley Railway *Ian Allan*
Railway Modeller, *Vol. 12 Page 269, 1961*
Railway Modeller, *Vol. 15 Page 214, 1964*
Railway Modeller, *Vol. 19 Page 50, 1968*
Model Railway News *Vol. 41 Page 423, 1965*

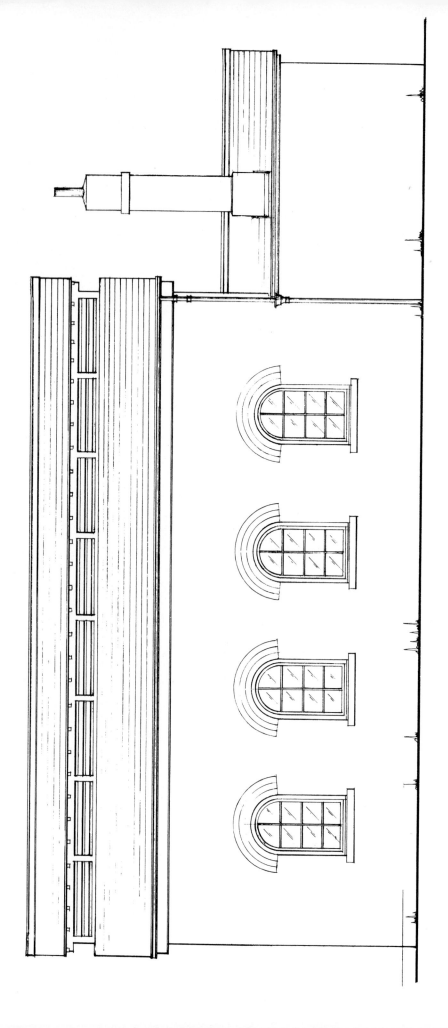

ASHBURTON ENGINE SHED

SIDE ELEVATION

52

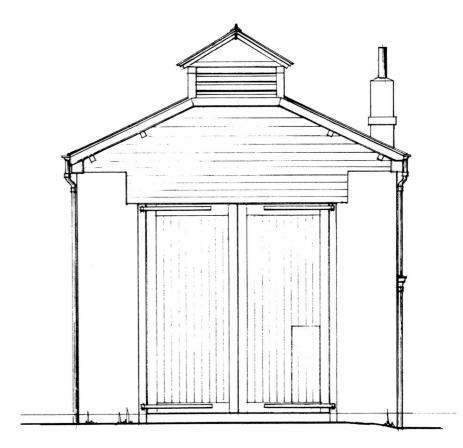

END ELEVATION TO THE NORTH

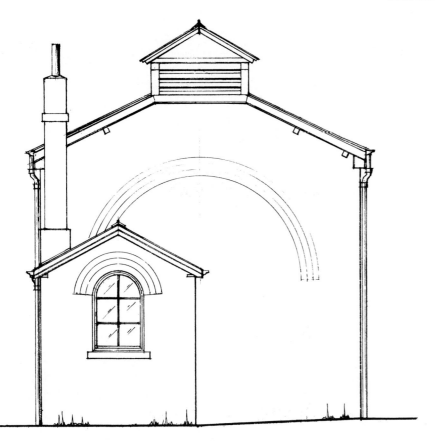

REAR ELEVATION

53

M.J. Fox

Fig. H1 A peaceful study showing the riverside location of Hemyock station in 1962.

HEMYOCK

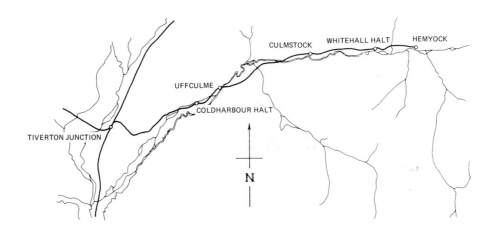

KEY FACTS

Company of Origin	Culm Valley Light Railway Co.
Date of Opening	29th May, 1876
Purchased by GWR	April 1880
Length of Branch	7 miles 33 chains
Ruling Gradient	1 in 67
Route Colour	Uncoloured
Overall Speed Restriction	15mph
Single Line Worked by	Train Staff and One Engine in Steam

ORIGIN

The Culm Valley Light Railway Company was a local enterprise which was formed in 1873 to build a standard gauge light railway from Tiverton Junction, on the then broad gauge Bristol and Exeter main line, 7½ miles to Hemyock with intermediate stations at Uffculme and Culmstock.

The Railway received Royal Assent on the 15th May, 1873 and construction began the following year, but progress was slow and the contract with the first builder was cancelled. Another builder was appointed but he met with problems, not the least of which was losing many of his workmen to the local farmers at harvest time; however, the line was eventually completed and finally opened on the 29th May, 1876 by which time the mixed gauge had reached Exeter and the regular working of standard gauge goods trains made through freight traffic possible.

The line was worked by the Great Western, this company having taken over the Bristol and Exeter Railway, who were to have worked the line, just prior to the opening of the CVR.

The line was lightly constructed and followed the banks of the river and existing land boundaries for most of its length, but the severe curves resulting imposed an overall speed restriction of 15 mph and seriously restricted the choice of motive power and rolling stock.

The railway soon ran into financial difficulties, passenger receipts dropped and the Great Western somewhat unwillingly purchased the line in April 1880, later opening halts at Coldharbour, 23rd February, 1929 and Whitehall, 27th February, 1933.

OPERATION

Before the engine shed at Hemyock was closed in 1929, two drivers and two firemen were based at the terminus; the early turn fireman lit up in the morning and the two drivers worked a midday train to help to balance the hours. Locomotives usually faced towards Hemyock and after the shed was closed, they were kept at Tiverton Junction which was itself a sub shed of Exeter.

The following notes describe the weekday timetable for 1948 at which time the terminus was staffed by a station master and two porters.

The early turn porter began at 7.00 am when the first train from Tiverton Junction arrived; this usually consisted of two coaches with a few wagons or empty milk tanks in tow. The loco ran round its train, detached the wagons, and departed again with the first passenger train at 7.30 am which conveyed the workmen and local school children for Tiverton. The 8.45 am from Tiverton Junction ran 'mixed' with the branch goods and one coach, dropping off wagons at intermediate stations as required. The yard at Hemyock was sorted on its arrival and the train returned as a passenger working at 10.30 am. The terminus was then quiet until the 1.35 pm ex Tiverton Junction arrived at 2.15 pm with more wagons in tow, as the 11.35 am from Tiverton Junction only ran as far as Uffculme. The 3.00 pm departed from Hemyock as a mixed train and the early turn porter finished at 3.30 pm, the late turn man having arrived at 12.00 midday. The school children returned on the 4.33 pm from the junction for which both coaches were again employed, one coach was detached and left at the terminus and the 5.55 pm ran 'mixed' with loaded milk tanks from the dairy. The last train from Tiverton Junction conveyed empty milk tanks and returned at 8.08 pm with the spare coach that had been left from the previous train, the late turn porter finishing his duty and locking the station after its departure.

There was no Sunday passenger service on the branch but the loco was still required to take empty tank wagons to the dairy in the morning and return for the loaded vehicles in the afternoon.

Fig. H2 Harold Pursey transferred from Dawlish in 1940 to become Hemyock's last station master.

Eve E. Clist

Fig. H3 No. 1451 at Hemyock on arrival with a farm removal train during the 1950s. The locomotive is said to have become derailed when running round this train and the livestock was stranded until a breakdown gang arrived from Exeter with the necessary jacks.

Courtesy H. Pursey

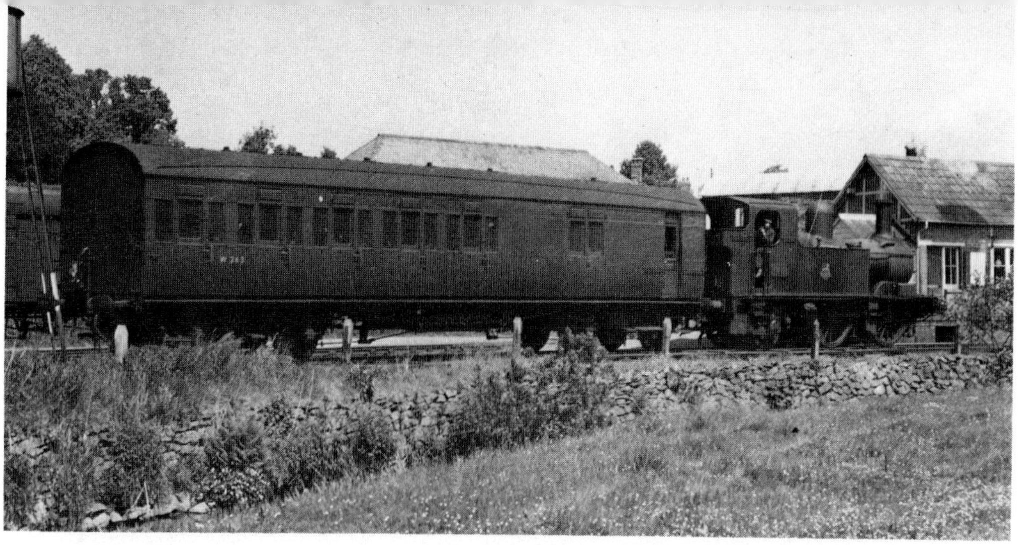

Fig. H4 No. 1451 at Hemyock with the branch train on the 25th May, 1952.

R.J. Sellick

1923 Working Timetable

CULM VALLEY BRANCH.

Single Line worked by Train Staff and only one Engine in Steam at a time. The Train Staff Stations are Tiverton Junction and Hemyock.

Distance M.	Distance C.	DOWN TRAINS. Week Days only.	Station No.	Ruling Gradient	1 B Mixed. arr.	1 B Mixed. dep.	2 B Mixed arr.	2 B Mixed dep.	3 B Mixed. R arr.	3 B Mixed. R dep.	4 B Mixed. R arr.	4 B Mixed. R dep.	5 B Passenger. arr.	5 B Passenger. dep.
					A.M.	A.M.	P.M.	noon	P.M.	P.M.	P.M.	P.M.	P.M.	P.M.
		Tiverton Junction	1538	—	—	**9 0**	—	**12 0**	—	**4 25**	—	*4 40*	—	**7 5**
2	14	Cold Harbour Siding	1610	67 R.	—	—	—	—	SX		SO		—	—
2	62	Uffculme	1611	105 R.	9 12	9 27	12 12	12 22	—	4 38	*4 52*	*4 53*	—	7 18
4	79	Culmstock	1612	68 R.	9 36	9 50	12 31	12 40	—	4 48	*5 2*	*5 3*	—	7 28
6	34	Whitehall Siding	1613	94 R.	C	R	—	—	—	—	—	—	—	—
7	27	**Hemyock**	1615	76 R.	**10 5**	—	**12 55**	....	**4 58**	—	*5 13*	—	**7 38**	—

UP TRAINS. Week Days only.	Ruling Gradient	1 B Mixed. arr.	1 B Mixed. dep.	2 B Mixed. arr.	2 B Mixed. dep.	3 B Mixed. arr.	3 B Mixed. dep.	4 B Passenger. arr	4 B Passenger. dep.
		A.M.	A.M.	A.M.	A.M.	P.M.	P.M.	P.M.	P.M.
Hemyock	—	—	**7 45**	—	**10 45**	—	**3 5**	—	**5 45**
Whitehall Siding	76 F.	—	—	—	—	—	—	—	—
Culmstock	94 F.	7 55	8 1	10 55	11 1	3 15	3 21	—	5 56
Uffculme	68 F.	8 10	8 18	11 10	11 18	3 30	3 38	6 5	6 7
Cold Harbour Sdg	150 F.	C	R	—	—	—	—	—	—
Tiverton Junct.	67 F.	**8 30**	—	**11 30**	—	**3 50**	—	**6 20**	—

Extract from the Regulations made by the Board of Trade for the working of the Culm Valley Light Railway:—

"This railway shall be worked between Tiverton Junction and Hemyock Station by means of one Engine in steam carrying the staff; that the rate of speed of the Trains shall not exceed fifteen miles an hour on any part of the said Railway; and that the Locomotive Engines, Carriages and Vehicles used on the Railway shall not have a greater weight than eight tons upon the rails on any one pair of wheels."

Long Round Timber.—Long Round Timber must not be accepted for transit at Uffculme, Culmstock or Hemyock.

R—Mixed Tiverton Junction and Hemyock only.

1948 Working Timetable

CULM VALLEY BRANCH.

Single Line worked by Train Staff and only one Engine in Steam at a time. The Train Staff Stations are Tiverton Junction and Hemyock.

DOWN TRAINS. — WEEK DAYS. / SUNDAYS.

M.P. Mileage M.	M.P. Mileage C.	STATIONS.	Ruling Gradient.	K Freight.§ arr.	K Freight.§ dep.	B Mixed. arr.	B Mixed. dep.	B Mixed. SX arr.	B Mixed. SX dep.	B Pass. SO arr.	B Pass. SO dep.	B Mixed arr.	B Mixed dep.	B Passenger. arr.	B Passenger. dep.	B Mixed. Y arr.	B Mixed. Y dep.				Sundays D Milk. Empties. arr.	Sundays D Milk. Empties. dep.	Sundays G Engine RR arr.	Sundays G Engine RR dep.
				a.m.	a.m.	a.m.	a.m.	a.m.	a.m.	a.m.	a.m.	p.m.	p.m.	p.m.	p.m.	p.m.	p.m.				a.m.	a.m.	p.m.	p.m.
—	—	**TIVERTON JUNCTION**	—	—	**5 50**	—	**8 45**	—	**11 35**	—	*11 35*	—	**1 35**	—	**4 33**	—	**7 10**	..	..	..	—	**8†15**	—	*2‖10*
2	20	**Coldharbour Halt**	67 R.	—	—	8 53½	8 54½	1143½	1144½	*1143½*	*1144½*	1 43½	1 44½	4 41½	4 42	7 18½	7 19½	....	....	....	—	—	—	—
2	68	**Uffculme**	150 R.	6 1	6 22	8 57	9 12	11 47	—	*11 47*	*12 0*	1 47	1 48	4 45	4 46	7 22	7 27	..	..	..	—	—	—	—
5	5	**Culmstock**	68 R.	6 31	6 41	9 21	9 30	▬	▬	*12 5*	—	1 59	2 0	4 55	4 56	7 36	7 37	....	....	....	—	—	—	—
6	40	**Whitehall Halt**	94 R.	C	R	9 36½	9 37½	..	..	▬	▬	2 8½	2 9½	5 2½	5 3½	7 43½	7 44½	..	..	..	—	—	—	—
7	33	**HEMYOCK**	76 R.	7 0	—	**9 42**	—	....	....	....	....	**2 15**	—	**5 8**	—	**7 49**	—	....	....	....	**9† 0**	—	*2‖55*	—

UP TRAINS. — WEEK DAYS. / SUNDAYS.

STATIONS.	Ruling Gradient.			B Passenger arr.	B Passenger dep.	B Passenger. arr.	B Passenger. dep.	B Mixed. SX arr.	B Mixed. SX dep.	B Passenger. SO arr.	B Passenger. SO dep.	B Mixed. arr.	B Mixed. dep.	B Mixed. arr.	B Mixed. dep.	B Mixed. Z arr.	B Mixed. Z dep.			Sundays G Engine RR arr.	Sundays G Engine RR dep.	Sundays C Milk. arr.	Sundays C Milk. dep.
				a.m.	a.m.	a.m.	a.m.	p.m.	p.m.	p.m.	p.m.	p.m.	p.m.	p.m.	p.m.	p.m.	p.m.			a.m.	a.m.	p.m.	p.m.
HEMYOCK	—	..	..	—	**7 30**	—	**10 30**	..	..	..	..	—	**3 0**	—	**5 55**	—	**8 8**	..	..	—	*9‖20*	—	**3 40**
Whitehall Halt	76 F.	....	....	7 34½	7 35	1034½	1035½	....	....	....	....	3 5	3 6	5 59½	6 0½	8 12½	8 13	....	....	—	—	—	—
Culmstock	94 F.	..	..	7 41½	7 42	10 42	10 44	..	V	—	*12 10*	3 13	3 15	6 7	6 9	8 19½	8 20½	..	..	—	—	—	—
Uffculme	68 F.	....	....	7 50	7 51	10 53	10 54	—	12 10	*12 19*	*12 20*	3 24	3 27	6 18	6 19	8 29½	8 30½	....	....	—	—	—	—
Coldharbour Halt	150 F.	..	..	7 53½	7 54	1056½	1057½	1212½	1219½	*1222½*	*1224½*	3 30	3 31	6 21½	6 22½	8 33	8 33½	..	..	—	—	—	—
Stopboard 0m. 23½c.	—	....	....	—	P	—	P	—	P	—	P	—	P	—	P	—	P	....	....	—	P	—	P
TIVERTON JUNCTION	67 F.	..	..	**8 2**	—	**11 7**	—	**12 28**	—	*12 33*	—	**3 41**	—	**6 33**	—	**8 42**	—	..	..	*10† 5*	—	**4 25**	—

The Branch is worked between Tiverton Junction and Hemyock stations by means of one engine in steam carrying a staff. The speed of trains must not exceed fifteen miles per hour on any part of the Branch. The Locomotive Engines, Carriages, and Vehicles used must not have a greater weight than thirteen tons eighteen cwts. on any one pair of wheels. Special 8-wheel Passenger Coaches are provided to work on the Branch. Ordinary 8-wheel stock for passenger use, vehicles over 60-ft. in length, and also 6-wheel Stock (with the exception of 6-wheel Milk Tanks) are prohibited. The Branch is worked by engines of the 0–4–2 Tank type. The engine is prohibited from using :—

Uffculme.—Loading Bank Siding, and Small's Siding. **Whitehall.**—Siding. **Culmstock.**—Loading Bank—not to approach within thirty yards of dead end.

The W.R. Standard Load Gauge applies over the Branch. **Hemyock.**—Private Siding not protected by Level Crossing Gates.

Long Round Timber.—Long Round Timber must not be accepted for transit at Uffculme, Culmstock, or Hemyock

V—Not to convey wagons from Uffculme for Tiverton Junction. **Y**—Wagons not to be detached or attached at Culmstock and not to convey more than two wagons for Hemyock. To convey cattle traffic for Uffculme as necessary. **Z**—Will convey goods wagons from Hemyock only. §—Runs as a Mixed Train, Uffculme to Culmstock.

Trainmen to open and close Crossing Gates as shown below:—

- 5.50 a.m. Tiverton Junction to Hemyock—Cold Harbour and Uffculme
- 7.10 p.m. Tiverton Junction to Hemyock—Whitehall
- 5.55 p.m. Hemyock to Tiverton Junction—Whitehall
- 8. 8 p.m. Hemyock to Tiverton Junction—Whitehall

} Fireman to open gates on arrival of train, and guard to close gates across the line after train has drawn clear of crossings.

Taken from Original Timetables

Fig. H5 A Collett 0-4-2T with a mixed train at Hemyock during April 1938.

Dr. Ian C. Allen

Fig. H6 No. 1429 in charge of a mixed train at the terminus on the 19th September, 1955.

M.B. Warburton

MOTIVE POWER

The Bristol and Exeter Railway built two 0-6-0 tank locomotives for the line which later became GWR Nos 1376 and 1377. They were constructed in 1874 and 1875 respectively but despite their short wheelbase and 3′ 6″ diameter driving wheels, they proved unsuited to the sharp curves on the branch and were subsequently transferred to Oswestry and Weymouth in 1881.

Three 2-4-0 tank locomotives, under construction for the broad gauge at Newton Abbot when the South Devon Railway was absorbed by the GWR in 1876, were completed at Swindon as standard gauge locos in 1878 and numbered 1298 to 1300. No. 1299 was completed as a crane loco but Nos. 1298 and 1300 were sent to work the CVR. The gradients of the line severely taxed their efforts, one in particular situated on a curve between Uffculme and Culmstock would often defeat them and wagons were detached at Uffculme for collection on the following trip. No. 1298 was scrapped in 1926 but No. 1300 remained in service on the line until it was finally withdrawn in 1934.

The 1920 allocation was as follows:

Jan.—Feb.	1298
March	1300
April	1298
May	1300
June	1298
July—Dec.	1300
Jan. '21	1298

Other locomotives employed on the branch included GWR No. 1384 ex-Watlington & Princes Risborough Railway 2-4-0T, which saw considerable service on the line before being sold to the Weston, Clevedon & Portishead Light Railway in 1911; No. 1192 ex-Cambrian Railways 2-4-0T in 1928 and ex-Liskeard & Looe Railway 2-4-0T No. 1308, *Lady Margaret* in 1929.

The new and larger Collett 0-4-2T's made less difficulty of the gradients and soon came to be used exclusively on the branch from the time of their introduction until the end of steam services. No. 5812 was employed for several years from the time of its construction in 1933 and subsequent locomotives included Nos. 1405, 1429, 1435, 1440, 1449, 1450, 1451, 1468, 1471.

Fig. H7 No. 1451 shunting milk tank wagons at Hemyock about 1959.

E.G. Sambrook

Track Plans

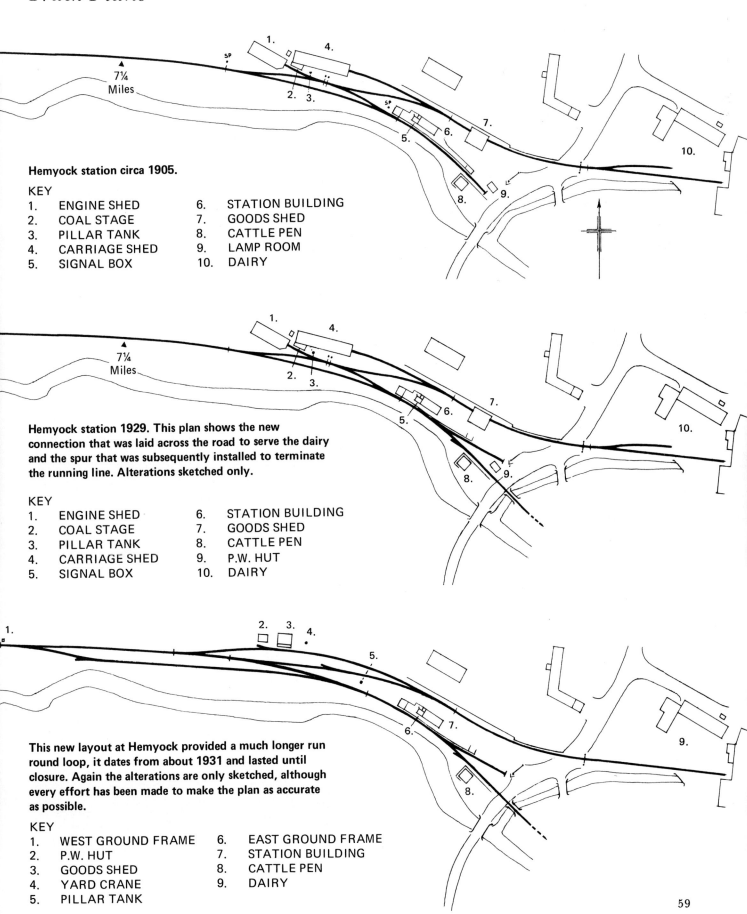

Hemyock station circa 1905.

KEY

1. ENGINE SHED
2. COAL STAGE
3. PILLAR TANK
4. CARRIAGE SHED
5. SIGNAL BOX
6. STATION BUILDING
7. GOODS SHED
8. CATTLE PEN
9. LAMP ROOM
10. DAIRY

Hemyock station 1929. This plan shows the new connection that was laid across the road to serve the dairy and the spur that was subsequently installed to terminate the running line. Alterations sketched only.

KEY

1. ENGINE SHED
2. COAL STAGE
3. PILLAR TANK
4. CARRIAGE SHED
5. SIGNAL BOX
6. STATION BUILDING
7. GOODS SHED
8. CATTLE PEN
9. P.W. HUT
10. DAIRY

This new layout at Hemyock provided a much longer run round loop, it dates from about 1931 and lasted until closure. Again the alterations are only sketched, although every effort has been made to make the plan as accurate as possible.

KEY

1. WEST GROUND FRAME
2. P.W. HUT
3. GOODS SHED
4. YARD CRANE
5. PILLAR TANK
6. EAST GROUND FRAME
7. STATION BUILDING
8. CATTLE PEN
9. DAIRY

Fig. H7a Hemyock station was situated to the north of the town, on the north bank of the River Culm at Millhayes. This picturesque view shows No. 1300 with a train of early four wheeled coaches at Hemyock, probably just after the turn of the century, before removal of the trees that once overshadowed the station. The original station nameboard is illustrated here and the roof of the first goods shed can be seen in the background.

Lens of Sutton

Fig. H8 This old postcard view dates from about 1912, after the removal of the signals. The double doors of the main entrance to the station building at this time led into the booking hall and ladies' lavatory whilst the large sliding door at this end served the parcels and stationmaster's offices.

Courtesy of R. S. Carpenter

Fig. H9 No. 1384 at Hemyock at some time between 1900 and 1910. The small gateway on the river bank gave access to the rear of the cattle pen, which drained directly into the river and periodically required shovelling out by one of the porters! Both the pen itself and the station platform were washed down with endless buckets of water collected from the river. There had been considerable horse and cattle traffic at one time and a large number of pigs were sent by rail, mainly to South Wales, from a pig market that was held at Hemyock until 1932.

L. & G.R.P.

Fig. H10 A contemporary view looking east along the station platform. The oil lamps illustrated here bore the station name in the glass but were later replaced with Tilley lamp posts.

L. & G.R.P.

Fig. H11 A passenger's viewpoint, looking eastwards along the railway and the river.

G.N. Southerden—Courtesy Railway
Magazine

Fig. H12 The first major alteration at Hemyock was carried out during the late 1920s when the original track was extended beyond the platform and across the road to provide a second connection to the dairy. The platform was reconstructed, a new spur subsequently laid in place to terminate the running line and the station building extended and modified as described in *Fig. H22.* The home and starter signals originally provided had disappeared by 1912 but the signal box was manned by a porter/signalman as required and retained this nameplate until the layout revision c. 1930. Both this and the previous photograph are believed to have been taken about 1929-30.

G.N. Southerden—Courtesy Railway
Magazine

Fig. H13 Ex-South Devon Railway 2-4-0T No. 1300 awaiting departure with a mixed train on the 25th May, 1929. The wooden shed alongside the cattle pen may well have once served as a lamp hut but was at this time in use as a platelayers cabin.

H.C. Casserley

Fig. H14 A closer look at the wooden carriage shed with No. 1384 posed for the photographer c. 1905. The short run-round loop is particularly evident here, being situated on the north side of the running line at this time.

Courtesy R.S. Carpenter

Fig. H15 No. 1300 again alongside the water column on the 25th May, 1929. The engine shed behind was constructed of timber to a very unusual design, measuring some 55′ x 18′ and was closed on the 21st October the same year.

H.C. Casserley

In 1929 the GWR announced that 'improvements were to be made on the CVR to afford standard clearance and to allow of the unrestricted running of ordinary stock'. At Hemyock, during the Autumn of 1930, additional land was purchased behind the carriage shed and alongside the river bank. The goods shed, carriage shed and engine shed were then removed and a new track layout adopted in which the run-round loop was changed to the south side of the running line and substantially lengthened. The work is thought to have been completed by about 1932.

Fig. H16 A similar view to *Fig. H10* showing the reconstructed platform. The gateway alongside the station building was only used by the staff for loading, the platform ramp providing passenger access to the station.

Lens of Sutton

Fig. H17 No. 1451 at Hemyock with mixed train in 1962.

M.J. Fox

Fig. H18 The station entrance during the early 1950s.

R.G. Nelson

Fig. H19 The sliding door in the rear of the station building served the parcels office, which housed a 20cwt weighing machine.

I.D. Beale

Fig. H20 Another view of the rear of the station with the line to the dairy skirting the foreground.

P.G.F. English

Fig. H21 No. 1451 propels its single coach train back into the loop prior to running round.

E.G. Sambrook

Fig. H22 The station building was constructed of red brick with half timbering and a red tiled roof. The doorway at the far end was converted from a window and the centre window replaced the double doorway featured in *Fig. H8* during the late 1920s when the platform was reconstructed as previously described. The extension at this end of the building was added at the same time, and constructed of concrete blocks with a flat roof and looked quite out of keeping. Subsequently accommodation was as follows: a gentlemen's lavatory was tucked away behind the signal box at the far end of the building, the ladies' lavatory and booking office were entered by the first door, the adjoining station office was entered via the parcels office through the sliding door and the new extension served as a waiting room and stationery store. There was no drinking water at the site so the station staff filled their kettle at the dairy!

E.G. Sambrook

Fig. H23 The platform elevation again after closure to passengers.

I.D. Beale

Fig. H24 No. 1451 alongside the platform with one of the ex-Barry Railway coaches No. W263 on the 25th May, 1952.

R.J. Sellick

Fig. H25 The station again from the south bank of the river.

I.D. Beale

Fig. H26 The little wooden signal box had a slate roof and is shown here with the replacement nameplate.

E.G. Sambrook

Fig. H27 The course of the original running line can be seen extending past the cattle pen, through the gates and across the road to the dairy. This siding was used for the delivery of coal to the dairy and consignments of empty tins for powdered milk etc. Coal had been unloaded by hand until after the Second World War when a conveyor was installed and deliveries thereafter made in bottom door wagons. This was of course a private siding but it was often used by the railway during the day to ease the congestion in the tiny yard.

R.G. Nelson

Fig. H28 The concrete posted cattle pen was constructed during the late 1920s to replace the one illustrated in *Fig. H9* but during and after the war most of the cattle from Taunton market were delivered by road. Station coal had been kept alongside the pen, but the wagon containing the coal was left to serve each of the branch stations in turn, and by the time it reached Hemyock almost a week later barely enough remained and a further supply was required for the terminus!

E.G. Sambrook

Fig. H29 The narrow yard access behind the station building is apparent in this 1950s view.

R.G. Nelson

Fig. H30 The milk depot and creamery was opened by the Culm Valley Dairy Company in 1886 and taken over by the Wilts United Dairy Ltd in 1916. Of course milk had originally been collected from the local farms by horse and cart, but the depot's eventual fleet of 12 or 14 motor lorries was not always able to cope and local lorry owners were often hired to help out with collections. A bulk supply of pasteurised milk was sent to London each day (Wood Lane, Vauxhall and Ilford) and provided a major source of income to the line with usually six, and occasionally up to twelve, 3,000 gallon tank wagons being despatched in any one day. Dried milk, ice cream powder and cream for butter making were also produced and before the 1920s butter, cheese and condensed milk.

Locomotives were not permitted across this road crossing so empty tank wagons were left at the gateway each night and pulled over by the factory staff in the morning using a winch and wire cable. Two flagmen were posted in the road to warn any traffic and, using the gradient, loaded wagons were returned by gravity having first summoned one of the railway porters (usually by banging a spanner on the buffers) to accept them.

The building on the left of this view was occupied by G. Small & Son, poultry and cattle feed merchants with their own mill at Uffculme. Coal was stored in the extension at this end of the building as this firm were also local coal merchants. Feedstuffs also came in by rail for another local merchant, T. Hine who had his own mill in Hemyock.

P.G.F. English

Fig. H31 No. 1405 with the 5.55 pm to Tiverton Junction on the 21st June, 1957.

J.E. Gready

Fig. H32 Looking west from the foot of the platform during the late 1950s.

R.G. Nelson

Fig. H33 Looking south east over the station on the 24th August, 1950. The short length of flat bottomed track in the goods siding survived until the late 1950s.

R.J. Sellick

Fig. H34 Another rural scene from the south bank of the River Culm in 1962. The dairy owned the tanks of the 6 wheeled milk tank wagons and were charged only for the loaded journey to their destination. The railway owned and maintained the chassis, the axleboxes being topped up at Exeter for the high speed journey to London. However, during the final years this was carried out at Hemyock each day, a drum of oil for this purpose being kept in the gateway on the platform as seen in *Fig. H19*.

M.J. Fox

Fig. H35 The pillar tank at Hemyock had originally stood alongside the carriage shed as seen in *Fig. H15* and was resited during the layout revision. The tank was gravity fed via a small reservoir that was situated in the garden of a farm on the hill to the north of the site, the supply pipe continuing across the road bridge to serve a farm on the south bank of the river. The tank additionally supplied the station lavatories and the portable steps in the foreground were used for boarding the passenger coach when a lengthy train prevented it from standing alongside the platform.

E.G. Sambrook

Fig. H36 No. 1451 again shunting at Hemyock on the 25th May, 1952.

R.J. Sellick

Figs. H37 and 38 The goods shed was constructed of corrugated iron with an asbestos roof and surmounted on a timber platform which was served by pre-cast concrete steps. There were sliding doors in front and behind and a skylight in the north pitch of the roof. The building, which was additionally used to store lamp oil, replaced the goods shed that had stood in the station forecourt of which no photograph has so far been discovered. There was no weighbridge at the terminus and the local deliveries were made by a railway lorry based at Cullompton that called at each station daily.

J.H. Moss & E.G. Sambrook

Fig. H39 In 1930 a 3 ton fixed hand crane was provided at Hemyock (also Uffculme and Culmstock), the 20cwt or 30cwt crane housed in the original goods shed having previously been the only one at the site. This photograph was taken after the removal of the lifting chain.

E.G. Sambrook

Fig. H40 Looking back at the site showing the platelayers' hut that was erected alongside the goods shed during the final years.

P.G.F. English

Fig. H41 The old sleepers behind the goods shed were awaiting disposal, but all the sleepers used on the branch were second hand ones that had been used on the main line for ten years or so. (Photo 19th September, 1955.)

M.B. Warburton

Fig. H42 A final look back at the site from the disused occupation crossing with the West ground frame in the foreground and the longer run-round loop illustrated to the right of the running line.

P.G.F. English

Fig. H43 From the same spot but this time looking west towards Tiverton Junction.

P.G.F. English

The Hemyock branch was closed to passengers on the 9th September, 1963 but the line remained open to serve the milk depot until the 31st October, 1975.

Further sources of reference:
The Culm Valley Railway by Crombleholme, Stuckey & Whetmath. Published by Branch Line Handbooks.
Railway Magazine *Vol. 78 Page 117 1936*
Railway Magazine *Vol. 78 Page 423 1936*
Railway World *Vol. 14 Page 38 1953*
Railway World *Vol. 23 Page 369 1962*
Railway World *Vol. 37 Page 106 1976*

Fig. M1 Collett 0-4-2T No. 1466 at Moretonhampstead on the 20th September, 1955.

M.B. Warburton

MORETONHAMPSTEAD

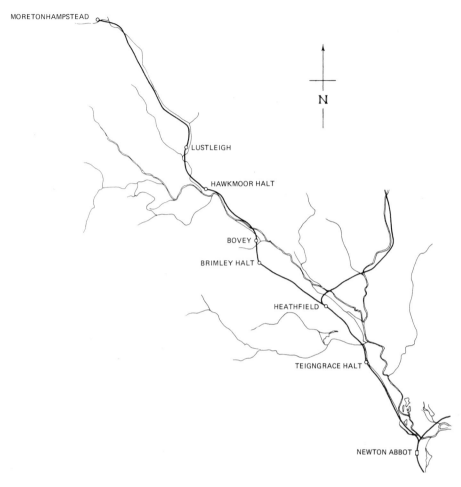

KEY FACTS

Company of Origin	Moretonhampstead and South Devon Railway Company
Date of Opening	4th July, 1866
Purchased by SDR	1872
Purchased by GWR	1877
Conversion to Standard Gauge	20th–23rd May, 1892
Length of Branch	12 miles 28 chains from Newton Abbot
Ruling Gradient	1 in 49
Route Colour	Yellow
Overall Speed Restriction	. . .
Single Line Worked by	Electric Train Staff (crossing stations Heathfield and Bovey)

ORIGIN

The Newton and Moretonhampstead Railway Company was incorporated in 1858 to promote a railway from Newton Abbot, on the South Devon Railway, a distance of some 12¼ miles to Moretonhampstead up the valleys of the Teign and Bovey rivers. The company was reconstituted by the Earl of Devon to form the Moretonhampstead and South Devon Railway and the line was authorised on the 7th July, 1862. The South Devon Railway had a controlling interest and subscribed £500 to the scheme, which was to have cost £88,500 but eventually totalled £155,000. Despite difficulties in raising the required capital the line was finally opened on the 4th July, 1866 and operated by the SDR in return for 50% of the gross receipts.

The single line was constructed to broad gauge (7' 0¼") and climbed some 500ft to the terminus at Moretonhampstead with intermediate stations at Teigngrace (1867), Chudleigh Road (1874—later renamed Heathfield), Bovey and Lustleigh. All of the bridges had been constructed to take double track at the insistence of the South Devon Railway in case of later doubling, but this was never done.

The M&SDR was absorbed by the South Devon Railway in 1872 and later became one of the many branch lines owned by the Great Western when the SDR was absorbed by this Company in 1877.

The line was converted to standard gauge in 1892 and new halts were later opened at Brimley in 1928 and Hawkmoor in 1931.

124

MORETONHAMPSTEAD BRANCH.

Single Line, worked by Electric Train Staff. Heathfield and Bovey are Crossing Stations. The Staff Stations are Newton Abbot, Heathfield, Bovey, and Moretonhampstead.

DOWN TRAINS. **WEEK DAYS.**

M.P. Mlieage M.	C.	STATIONS.	Ruling Gradient.	Time Allowances for Ordinary Freight Trains, see page 2. Point-to-Point Times.	Allow for Stop.	Allow for Start.	K Trusham Goods. arr.	dep.	B 7.25 a.m. Totnes Passenger. arr.	dep.	B 8.10 a.m. Paignton Passenger. arr.	dep.	B Auto. arr.	dep.	B 9.55 a.m. Kingswear Passenger. ‡ arr.	dep.	B Auto. arr.	dep.	K Goods. arr.	dep.	B Motor. arr.	dep.	B Auto. arr.	dep.
				Mins.	Mins.	Mins.	a.m.	a.m.	a.m.	a.m.	a.m.	a.m.	a.m.	a.m.	a.m.	a.m.	a.m.	a.m.	a.m.	a.m.	p.m.	p.m.	p.m.	p.m.
—	—	NEWTON ABBOT	—	—	—	1	—	7 0	7 40	7 55	8 32	8 55	—	9 52	10‡35	X1040	—	11 30	—	10 48	..	..	—	12 20
1	43	Teign Bridge Siding	100 R.	4	1	1	7 6	7 25	—	—	—	—	—	—	— •	—	—	—	C	R	SU	S-	—	—
1	51	Teign Bridge Level C.	—	—	—	—	—	—	—	—	—	—	—	—	—	—	—	—	—	—	PEN	DED	—	—
2	28	Teigngrace	100 R.	—	—	—	—	—	7 59	8 0	8 59	9 0	9 56	9 56½	—	—	11 34	1134½	—	—	....	....	12 24	1224½
3	70	HEATHFIELD	70 R.	5	1	1	7 32	8 40	8 3½	8 4½	9 3½	X9 9	10 0	10 1	10 46	10 47	11 38	11 39	11 0	X11 15	—	X12 0	12 28	X1232
5	6	Granite Siding	69 R.	—	—	—			—	—	—	—	—	—	—	—	—	—	C	R	—	—	—	—
5	19	Pottery Siding	53 R.	—	—	—	Goods Brake Van to be sent Heathfield on this train daily.		—	—	—	—	—	—	—	—	—	—	C	R	—	—	—	—
5	46	Brimley Halt	53 R.	—	—	—			8 8	8 9	9 12½	9 13½	10 4½	10 5½	1050½	1051½	11 42	1143½	—	—	12 4½	12 5	1235½	1236½
6	6	Bovey	66 F.	5	2	2			8 10½	X8 14	9 15	9 16	10 7	X10 8	10 53	X1054	11 45	—	11 23•	X12 25	12 7	—	12 38	—
7	61	Hawkmoor Halt	—	—	—	—			—	8 19	—	9 21	—	—	—	10 59			—	—				
8	66	Lustleigh	50 R.	11	1	2			8 22	8 23	9 24	9 26	10 15	10 17	11 2	11 5	..	..	CR	ST	..	..	..	..
12	28	MORETONHAMPSTEAD	49 R.	14	1	—			8 34	—	9 37	—	10 28	—	11 16	—	....	....	12 52	—	....	....	....	....

DOWN TRAINS. **WEEK DAYS**—continued.

STATIONS.	B 12.20 p.m. Paignton Passenger. arr.	dep.	B Auto. arr.	dep.	B Passenger. arr.	dep.	B 2.0 p.m. Kingswear Passenger. ‡ arr.	dep.	B Auto. arr.	dep.	B Auto. arr.	dep.	G Engine arr.	dep.	B Auto. arr.	dep.	B 3.45 p.m. Kingswear Passenger.‡ arr.	dep.	B 5.35 p.m. Paignton Passenger. arr.	dep.	B Auto. arr.	dep.	B Motor. arr.	dep.
	p.m.	p.m.	p.m.	p.m.	p.m.	p.m.	p.m.	p.m.	p.m.	p.m.	p.m.	p.m.	p.m.	p.m.	p.m.	p.m.	p.m.	p.m.	p.m.	p.m.	p.m.	p.m.	p.m.	p.m.
NEWTON ABBOT	12 43	12 50	—	2 15	—	2 15	2‡47	X2 53	—	3 5	—	3 14	—	X 3 50	—	4 10	4‡35	5 2	5 57	X6 8	—	6 35	....	....
Teign Bridge Siding	—	—	—	—	SU	S-	—	—	—	—	SU	S-	—	—	—	—	—	—	—	—	—	—	SU	S-
Teign Bridge Level C.	—	—	—	—	PEN	DED	—	—	—	—	PEN	DED	—	—	—	—	—	—	—	—	—	—	PEN	DED
Teigngrace	—	—	2 19	2 19½	—	—	—	—	3 9	3 9½	3 18	3 19	—	—	4 14	4 14½	5 6	5 7	—	—	6 39	6 39½	..	..
HEATHFIELD	1256X	12 57	2 23	2 24	2 21½	2 22½	2 59	3 0	3 13	3 14	3 22½	3X23½	4‖ 0	—	4 18	X4 21	5 10½	5 11½	6 14	X6 17	6 43	6 44	-- X	7 26
Granite Siding	—	—	—	—	—	—	—	—	—	—	—	—			—	—	—	—	—	—	—	—	—	—
Pottery Siding	—	—	—	—	—	—	—	—	—	—	—	—	..	..	—	—	—	—	—	—	—	—	—	—
Brimley Halt	1 0½	1 1½	2 27½	2 28½	2 26	2 27	3 3½	3 4½	3 17½	3 18½	3 27	3 28	....	....	4 24½	4 25½	5 15	5 16	6 20½	6 21½	6 47½	6 48½	7 29½	7 30
Bovey	1 3	1 4	2 30	—	2 28½	X2 30	3 6	X3 7	3 20	—	3 29½	X3 32	..	..	4 27	4 28	5 17½	X5 19	6 23	6 24	6 50	—	7 32	—
Hawkmoor Halt	—	1 9			—	2 35	—	3 12			—	3 37	....	....	—	4 33	—	5 24	—	6 29				
Lustleigh	1 12	1 15	..	..	2 38	2 40	3 15	3 18	..	..	3 40	3 42	..	..	4 36	4 38	5 27	5 29	6 32	6 34	..	..	..	..
MORETONHAMPSTEAD	1 26	—	....	....	2 51	—	3 29	—	....	....	3 53	—	....	....	4 49	—	5 40	—	6 45	—	....	....	....	....

‡ Starts from Newton Abbot on Saturdays.

No. 5.

Moretonhampstead Branch—*continued.*

UP TRAINS. **WEEK DAYS**—continued.

STATIONS.	Ruling Gradient.	Time Allowances for Ordinary Freight Trains, see page 2. Point-to-Point Times.	Allow for Stop.	Allow for Start.	B Passenger. arr.	dep.	B Passenger arr.	dep.	B Passenger. arr.	dep.	B Auto. arr.	dep.	B Auto. arr.	dep.	B Auto. arr.	dep.	B Passenger. arr.	dep.	B Motor. arr.	dep.	K Trusham Goods. arr.	dep.	B Auto. arr.	dep.
		Mins.	Mins.	Mins.	a.m.	a.m.	a.m.	a.m.	a.m.	a.m.	a.m.	a.m.	a.m.	a.m.	a.m.	a.m.	p.m.	p.m.	p.m.	p.m.	p.m.	p.m.	p.m.	p.m.
MORETONHAMPSTEAD	—	—	—	1	—	7 55	—	8 45	—	9 51	—	10 37	....	....	—	11 35	—	12 5	....	....	....	....	....	....
Stop Board 12mp.	L.	—	1	1	—	—	—	—	—	—	—	—	..	..	—	—	—	—	..	..	..	..	..	..
Lustleigh	49 F.	10	1	1	8 3	8 4	8 53	8 54	9 59	10 0	10 45	10 46	....	....	11 43	11 44	12 13	12 14	SU	S-	....	....	....	....
Hawkmoor Halt	—	—	—	—	—	8 6	—	8 56	—	10 2	—	10 48	..	..	—	11 46	—	12 16	PEN	DED	..	..	..	..
Stop Board 6m. 15½c.	50 F.	—	—	—	—	—	—	—	—	—	—	—	....	....	—	—	—	—	....	....	....	....	....	....
Bovey	50 F.	8	2	2	8 10	X8 13	9 0	9 1	10 6	X1014	10 52	X10 55	—	11 50	11 50	X11 52	12 20	X1221	—	12 40	..	..	—	12 48
Brimley Halt	66 R.	—	—	—	8 15	8 16	9 3	9 4	10 16	10 17	10 57	10 58	11 52	11 53	11 54	11 55	12 23	12 24	12 42	12 43	....	....	12 50	12 51
Pottery Siding	53 F.	2	2	2	—	—	—	—	—	—	—	—	—	—	—	—	—	—	—	—	..	..	—	—
Granite Siding	53 F.	1	1	1	—	—	—	—	—	—	—	—	—	—	—	—	—	—	—	—	....	....	—	—
HEATHFIELD	69 F.	3	1	1	8 20	8 21	9 8	X9 10	10 21	10 22	11 2X	11 3	11 57	11 58	11 59	X12 0	12 28½	X12 31	12 47	X —	12 3	1 10	12 55	X1258
Teigngrace	70 F.	—	—	—	8 24	8 25	9 13	9 14	10 25	10 26	—	—	12 1	12 2	12 3	12 4	—	—			—	—	1 1	1 2
Teign Bridge Level C.	—	—	—	—	—	—	—	—	—	—	—	—	—	—	SU	S-	—	—	....	....	—	—	—	—
Teign Bridge Siding	100 F.	6	1	1	—	—	—	—	—	—	—	—	—	—	PEN	DED	—	—	..	..	C	R	—	—
NEWTON ABBOT	132 R.	4	1	—	8 30	—	9 19	—	10 31	X —	11 10	—	12 7	—	12 9	—	12 38	‡	....	....	1 20	—	1 7	—

UP TRAINS. **WEEK DAYS**—continued.

STATIONS.	B Passenger. arr.	dep.	B Auto. arr.	dep.	B Motor. WSO arr.	dep.	B Auto. arr.	dep.	B Passenger. arr.	dep.	K Goods. arr.	dep.	B Passenger. arr.	dep.	B Auto. arr.	dep.	K Goods. arr.	dep.	B Passenger. arr.	dep.	B Auto. arr.	dep.	B Passenger. arr.	dep.
	p.m.	p.m.	p.m.	p.m.	p.m.	p.m.	p.m.	p.m.	p.m.	p.m.	p.m.	p.m.	p.m.	p.m.	p.m.	p.m.	p.m.	p.m.	p.m.	p.m.	p.m.	p.m.	p.m.	p.m.
MORETONHAMPSTEAD	—	1 35	....	....	....	....	....	....	—	3 15	—	2 5	—	3 55	—	5 0	....	....	—	5 50	....	....	—	7 0
Stop Board 12mp.	—	—	..	..	SU	S-	..	..	—	—	2 6	P2 8	—	—	—	—	..	..	—	—	..	..	—	—
Lustleigh	1 43	1 44	....	....	PEN	DED	....	....	3 23	3 24	2 17	2 25	4 3	4 4	5 8	5 9	....	....	5 58	5 59	....	....	7 8	7 9
Hawkmoor Halt	—	1 46	..	..	..	..	..	..	—	3 26	—	—	—	4 6	—	5 11	..	..	—	6 1	..	..	—	7 11
Stop Board 6m. 15½c.	—	—	....	....	....	....	....	....	—	—	2 33	P2 35	—	—	—	—	....	....	—	—	....	....	—	—
Bovey	1 50	1 51	—	2 35	..	..	—	3 30	3 30	X3 34	2 36•	X 3 40	4 10	4 12	5 15	X5 20	..	..	6 5	6 6	—	6 55	7 15	7 17
Brimley Halt	1 53	1 54	2 37	2 38	....	....	3 32	3 33	3 36	3 37	—	—	4 14	4 15	5 22	5 23	....	....	6 8	6 9	6 57	6 58	7 19	7 20
Pottery Siding	—	—	—	—	..	..	—	—	SU	S-	C	R	—	—	—	—	..	..	—	—	—	—	—	—
Granite Siding	—	—	—	—	....	....	—	—	PEN	DED	C	R	—	—	—	—	....	....	—	—	—	—	—	—
HEATHFIELD	1 58	1 59	2 42	2 43	—	*2 40*	3 37	3 38	3 41	3 43	4 10	•X4 30	4 19	X4 20	5 27	5 28	—	5 38	6 13X	6 16	7 2	7 3	7 24	7 25
Teigngrace	2 2	2 3	—	—	—	—	3 41	3 42	3 46	3 47	—	—	4 23	4 24	5 31	5 32	—	—	—	—	7 6	7 7	—	—
Teign Bridge Level C.	—	—	—	—	—	—	—	—	—	—	—	—	—	—	—	—	—	—	—	—	—	—	—	—
Teign Bridge Siding	—	—	—	—	—	—	—	—	—	—	—	—	—	—	—	—	5 44	6 0	—	—	—	—	—	—
NEWTON ABBOT	2 8	—	2 50	X —	*2 47*	—	3 47	X —	3 52	X —	4 40	—	4 29	—	5 37	—	6 5	X —	6 23	—	7 12	—	7 32	X —

‡—Forms 12.45 p.m. to Kingswear, Saturdays excepted

No. 5.

125

Taken from Original Timetable

Moretonhampstead Branch—*continued.*

126

No. 5.

DOWN TRAINS. WEEK DAYS—continued.

STATIONS.	B Auto. arr.	dep.	B Passenger. arr.	dep.	B Auto. arr.	dep.	B Passenger. arr.	dep.
	p.m.	p.m.	p.m.	p.m.	p.m.	p.m.	p.m.	p.m.
NEWTON ABBOT	—	X7 33	—	7 53	—	X9 10	—	9 47
Teign Bridge Siding	—	—	—	—	—	—	—	—
Teign Bridge Level C.	—	—	—	—	—	—	—	—
Teigngrace	7 37	7 37½	—	—	9 14	9 14½	—	—
HEATHFIELD	7 41	7 42	7 59	8 0	9 18	9 19	9 53	X9 54
Granite Siding	—	—	—	—	—	—	—	—
Pottery Siding	--	—	—	—	—	—	—	—
Brimley Halt	7 45½	7 46½	8 3½	8 4½	9 22½	9 23½	9 57½	9 58½
Bovey	7 48	—	8 6	X8 7	9 25	—	10 0	10 1
Hawkmoor Halt	▬▬	▬▬	—	8 12	▬▬	▬▬	10 5	10 7
Lustleigh	..	..	8 15	8 17	..	..	10 10	10 12
MORETONHAMPSTEAD	....	....	8 28	—	....	....	10 23	—

DOWN TRAINS. SUNDAYS.

STATIONS.	B Passenger. arr.	dep.	B Passenger. arr.	dep.	B Passenger. arr.	dep.	B Passenger. arr.	dep.
	a.m.	a.m.	a.m.	a.m.	p.m.	p.m.	p.m.	p.m.
NEWTON ABBOT	—	9 30	— X	10 50	—	2 19	—	3 26
Teign Bridge Siding	—	—	—	—	—	—	—	—
Teign Bridge Level C.	—	—	—	—	—	—	—	—
Teigngrace	—	—	—	—	—	—	—	—
HEATHFIELD	9 37	9 38	10 57	10 58	2 26	2 27	3 33	3 34
Granite Siding	—	—	—	—	—	—	—	—
Pottery Siding	—	—	—	—	—	—	—	—
Brimley Halt	9 41½	9 42½	11 1½	11 2½	2 30½	2 31½	3 37½	2 38½
Bovey	9 44	9 45	11 4	11 5	2 33X	2 36	3 40	—
Hawkmoor Halt	—	9 50	—	11 10	—	2 41	▬▬	▬▬
Lustleigh	9 53	9 55	11 13	11 15	2 44	2 46	..	..
MORETONHAMPSTEAD	10 6	—	11 26	—	2 57	—	....	....

STATIONS.	B Passenger. arr.	dep.	B Passenger. arr.	dep.	B Passenger. arr.	dep.	B Passenger. arr.	dep.
	p.m.	p.m.	p.m.	p.m.	p.m.	p.m.	p.m.	p.m.
NEWTON ABBOT	—	4 15	—	6 2	—	7 40	—	9 10
Teign Bridge Siding	—	—	—	—	—	—	—	—
Teign Bridge Level C.	—	—	—	—	—	—	—	—
Teigngrace	—	—	—	—	—	—	—	—
HEATHFIELD	4 22	4 23	6 9	6 10	7 47	7 48	9 17	9 18
Granite Siding	—	—	—	—	—	—	—	—
Pottery Siding	—	—	—	—	—	—	—	—
Brimley Halt	4 26½	4 27½	6 13½	6 14½	7 51½	7 52½	9 21½	9 22½
Bovey	4 29	X4 32	6 16	6 17	7 54	7 55	9 24	9 25
Hawkmoor Halt	—	4 37	—	6 22	—	8 0	—	9 30
Lustleigh	4 39	4 42	6 25	6 27	8 3	8 5	9 33	9 35
MORETONHAMPSTEAD	4 53	—	6 38	—	8 16	—	9 46	—

UP TRAINS. WEEK DAYS—*continued.*

STATIONS.	B Motor. arr.	dep.	B Auto. arr.	dep.	B Paignton Passenger. arr.	dep.	B Auto. arr.	dep.
	p.m.	p.m.	p.m.	p.m.	p.m.	p.m.	p.m.	p.m.
MORETONHAMPSTEAD	....	....	....	....	—	8 36	....	....
Stop Board 12mp.	SUS	S-	..	..	—	—	..	..
Lustleigh	PEN	DED	....	....	8 44	8 45	....	....
Hawkmoor Halt	..	..	..	..	—	8 47	..	..
Stop Board 6m. 15½c.	....	....	....	....	—	—	....	....
Bovey	—	7 45	—	X8 10	8 51	8 52	—	9 45
Brimley Halt	7 47	7 48	8 12	8 13	8 54	8 55	9 47	9 48
Pottery Siding	—	—	—	—	—	—	—	—
Granite Siding	—	—	—	—	—	—	—	—
HEATHFIELD	7 52	X —	8 17	8 18	8 59	9 0	9 52	X9 55
Teigngrace	▬▬	▬▬	8 21	8 22	—	—	—	—
Teign Bridge Level C.	..	..	—	—	—	—	—	—
Teign Bridge Siding	....	....	—	—	—	—	—	—
NEWTON ABBOT	..	..	8 27	—	9 7	X9 10	10 2	—

UP TRAINS. SUNDAYS.

STATIONS.	B Passenger. arr.	dep.	B Passenger. arr.	dep.	B Passenger. arr.	dep.	B Passenger. arr.	dep.
	a.m.	a.m.	a.m.	a.m.	p.m.	p.m.	p.m.	p.m.
MORETONHAMPSTEAD	—	10 15	—	11 38	—	2 20	....	....
Stop Board 12mp.	—	—	—	—	—	—	..	..
Lustleigh	10 23	10 24	11 46	11 47	2 28	2 29	....	....
Hawkmoor Halt	—	10 26	—	11 49	—	—	..	..
Stop Board 6m. 15½c.	—	—	—	—	—	—	....	....
Bovey	10 30	10 31	11 53	11 54	2 34	X2 35	—	3 45
Brimley Halt	10 33	10 34	11 56	11 57	2 37	2 38	3 47	3 48
Pottery Siding	—	—	—	—	—	—	—	—
Granite Siding	—	—	—	—	—	—	—	—
HEATHFIELD	10 38	10 39	12 1	12 2	2 42	2 43	3 52	3 53
Teigngrace	—	—	—	—	—	—	—	—
Teign Bridge Level C.	—	—	—	—	—	—	—	—
Teign Bridge Siding	—	—	—	—	—	—	—	—
NEWTON ABBOT	10 47	X —	12 9	—	2 50	—	4 0	—

STATIONS.	B Passenger. arr.	dep.	B Passenger. arr.	dep.	B Passenger. arr.	dep.	B Passenger. arr.	dep.
	p.m.	p.m.	p.m.	p.m.	p.m.	p.m.	p.m.	p.m.
MORETONHAMPSTEAD	—	4 15	—	5 22	—	6 50	—	8 25
Stop Board 12mp.	—	—	—	—	—	—	—	—
Lustleigh	4 23	4 24	5 30	5 31	6 58	6 59	8 33	8 34
Hawkmoor Halt	—	4 26	—	5 33	—	7 1	—	8 36
Stop Board 6m. 15½c.	—	—	—	—	—	—	—	—
Bovey	4 30	X4 31	5 37	5 38	7 5	7 6	8 40	8 41
Brimley Halt	4 33	4 34	5 40	5 41	7 8	7 9	8 43	8 44
Pottery Siding	—	—	—	—	—	—	—	—
Granite Siding	—	—	—	—	—	—	—	—
HEATHFIELD	4 38	4 39	5 45	5 46	7 13	7 14	8 48	8 49
Teigngrace	—	—	—	—	—	—	—	—
Teign Bridge Level C.	—	—	—	—	—	—	—	—
Teign Bridge Siding	—	—	—	—	—	—	—	—
NEWTON ABBOT	4 47	—	5 54	—	7 22	—	8 57	—

OPERATION

Branch locomotives usually faced towards Moretonhampstead and were often sub-shedded there for lengthy periods, only returning to Newton Abbot perhaps overnight for boiler washouts. A cleaner, upgraded to fireman, to work the last train out to Moretonhampstead each day, remained there all night to cover the shed duties and worked the first train in to Newton Abbot in the morning, where he was relieved by a fireman from that depot. This arrangement was apparently because there was only one fireman at Moretonhampstead before the introduction of the 8 hour day (during the 1920s), when a second fireman and an overnight shedman were stationed there. The shedman remained at Moretonhampstead until 1945/6 after which the firemen were left to prepare the loco themselves.

The early turn fireman arrived at 4 am to light up and prepare the loco, then in fine weather, when there was sufficient steam pressure he would move it outside the shed to finish his cleaning. The driver arrived about 6.30 am and oiled up, then the two coaches were collected from the train shed and taken over to the platform to commence the day's services.

The engine shed at Moretonhampstead was closed after the winter workings of 1947 and whilst the timings remained almost identical, the following notes apply to the working timetable of 1948 at which time the branch locomotive ran light engine to Moretonhampstead to begin the day's services returning to Newton Abbot after the last train.

Services not extending beyond Heathfield have been omitted for clarity.

The 7.50 am from Moretonhampstead reached Newton Abbot at 8.25 am and before the branch shed had been closed was taken on shed there for coal and water before continuing on to Paignton, often with a third trailer car (the Moretonhampstead men had worked the 'Torbay Express' from Kingswear to Paignton before the bridges on that line were strengthened to take the larger 4-6-0's). The first train crossed at Bovey with the 7.25 am from Totnes which subsequently worked the 8.40 am and 10.15 am services from Moretonhampstead. The branch train left Paignton at 10.05 am arriving back at Moretonhampstead at 11.11 am and thereafter remaining on the branch to work the 11.35 am, 1.55 pm, 3.55 pm, 5.20 pm and 7.00 pm services. The last train left Newton Abbot at 8.10 pm arriving at the terminus at 8.47 pm, the coaches were stabled on the loop siding and at 9.00 pm the loco finally returned light engine to Newton Abbot. On Saturdays a late service was provided to Newton Abbot at 9.05 pm, returning therefrom at 10.00 pm, the loco leaving for the shed from Moretonhampstead at 10.50 pm.

The branch goods was worked by Newton Abbot men and left Kingsteignton yard each day at 11.15 am, first calling at Teignbridge sidings to drop off empties and then Heathfield. Wagons for Bovey Granite and Pottery sidings were taken on to Bovey where they were left until the return journey as the connections to these sidings only allowed them to be served by 'up trains'. Having sorted the yard at Bovey the train continued past Lustleigh, which again could only be served on the return journey, and arrived at Moretonhampstead at 12.55 pm. The yard was shunted and the return train was formed in the siding behind the platform, then water was taken and if there was time the crew would eat their lunch before departing at 2.25 pm. Of course, if traffic was heavy they might not finish in time and would have to wait until the 3.05 pm auto train from Newton Abbot had arrived and departed again at 3.55 pm, the goods would then follow when the section was clear. Lustleigh was the first call on the return journey, then Bovey to collect the wagons for Pottery and Granite sidings and finally Teignbridge sidings where loaded wagons of stone and clay were collected. The resulting train which often totalled some 60 wagons arrived back at Newton Abbot at about 5.30 pm and the crew returned the locomotive to the depot and booked off.

A Sunday service from Newton Abbot was introduced on the 3rd June, 1923 with two trains for Moretonhampstead departing at 10.40 am and 7.15 pm returning at 11.50 am and 8.15 pm respectively with a return trip to Bovey only at 2.15 pm. As seen in the 1935 timetable the Sunday service had increased to eight return trips by this time but they are thought to have finished for the Second World War and not resumed.

MORETONHAMPSTEAD BRANCH—continued.

UP TRAINS. WEEK DAYS.

STATIONS.	Ruling Gradient.	Point-to-Point Times. (Time Allowances for Ordinary Freight Trains see page 2.)	Allow for Stop.	Allow for Start.	B Auto. arr.	dep.	B Auto. arr.	dep.	B Auto. arr.	dep.	arr.	dep.	arr.	dep.	B Auto. arr.	dep.	K Christow Freight. arr.	dep.	B 12.50 p.m. Exeter Auto. SX arr.	dep.	B 1.0 p.m. Exeter Auto. SO arr.	dep.	arr.	dep.
		Mins.	Mins.	Mins.	a.m.	a.m.	a.m.	a.m.	a.m.	a.m.					a.m.	a.m.	p.m.	p.m.	p.m.	p.m.	p.m.	p.m.		
MORETONHAMPSTEAD	—	—	—	1	—	7 50	—	8 40	—	10 15	..	..	..	..	—	11 35	..	..	..	..	..	..	..	..
Stop Board 12mp.	L.	—	1	1	—	—	—	—	—	—	..	..	..	..	—	—	..	..	..	..	..	..	..	..
Lustleigh	49 F.	10	1	1	7 58	7 59	8 48	8 48½	10 23	1023½	..	..	..	..	11 43	11 44	..	..	..	..	..	..	..	..
Hawkmoor Halt	—	—	—	—	—	8 1	—	8 50	—	10 26	..	..	..	..	—	11 46	..	..	..	..	..	..	..	..
Stop Board 6m. 15½c.	50 F.	—	—	—	—	—	—	—	—	—	..	..	..	..	—	—	..	..	..	..	..	..	..	..
Bovey	50 F.	8	2	2	8 5	X8 8	8 54	8 55	10 30	10 32	..	..	..	..	11 50	11 52	..	..	..	..	..	..	..	..
Brimley Halt	66 R.	—	—	—	8 10	8 11	8 57	8 58	10 34	10 35	..	..	..	..	11 54	11 55	..	..	..	..	..	..	..	..
Pottery Siding	53 F.	2	2	2	—	—	—	—	—	—	..	..	..	..	—	—	..	..	..	..	..	..	..	..
Granite Siding	53 F.	1	1	1	—	—	—	—	—	—	..	..	..	..	—	—	..	..	..	..	..	..	..	..
HEATHFIELD	69 F.	3	1	1	8 15	8 16	9 2	9 3	10 39	X1042	..	..	..	..	11 59	12 0	12 22	1 3	1 52	1 55	2 2	2 5	..	..
Teigngrace Halt	70 F.	—	—	—	8 19	8 20	9 6	9 7	10 45	1045½	..	..	..	..	12 3	12 4	C	R	1 59	2 0	2 9	2 10	..	..
Teign Bridge Level C.	—	—	—	—	—	—	—	—	—	—	..	..	..	..	—	—	—	—	—	—	—	—	..	..
Teign Bridge Siding	100 F.	6	1	1	—	—	—	—	—	—	..	..	..	..	—	—	C	R	—	—	—	—	..	..
NEWTON ABBOT	132 R.	4	1	—	8 25	—	9 12	—	10 50	—	..	..	..	..	12 9	—	1 21	—	2 5	—	2 15	—	..	..

UP TRAINS. WEEK DAYS—continued.

STATIONS.	B Auto. arr.	dep.	K 1.55 p.m. Exeter Freight. SX arr.	dep.	B Auto. arr.	dep.	K Freight. arr.	dep.	B Auto. arr.	dep.	arr.	dep.	arr.	dep.	B Auto. arr.	dep.	G Engine. SX arr.	dep.	arr.	dep.	B Auto. SO arr.	dep.	G Engine SO arr.	dep.
	p.m.	p.m.	p.m.	p.m.	p.m.	p.m.	p.m.	p.m.	p.m.	p.m.					p.m.	p.m.	p.m.	p.m.			p.m.	p.m.	p.m.	p.m.
MORETONHAMPSTEAD	—	1 55	..	..	—	3 55	—	2 25	—	5 20	..	..	..	..	—	7 0	—	9‖0	..	..	—	9 5	—	10‖50
Stop Board 12mp.	—	—	..	..	—	—	2 26	P2 27	—	—	..	..	..	..	—	—	—	—	..	..	—	—	—	—
Lustleigh	2 3	2 4	..	..	4 3	4 4	2 38	2 45	5 28	5 28½	..	..	..	..	7 8	7 9	—	—	..	..	9 13	9 14	—	—
Hawkmoor Halt	—	2 6	..	..	—	4 6	—	—	—	5 30½	..	..	..	..	—	7 11	—	—	..	..	—	9 16	—	—
Stop Board 6m. 15½c.	—	—	..	..	—	—	2 53	P2 54	—	—	..	..	..	..	—	—	—	—	..	..	—	—	—	—
Bovey	2 10	2 12	..	..	4 10	4 12	2 56	3 25	5 34½	5 35½	..	..	..	..	7 15	7 17	C	S	..	..	9 20	9 21	C	S
Brimley Halt	2 14	2 15	..	..	4 14	4 15	—	—	5 37½	5 38	..	..	..	..	7 19	7 20	—	—	..	..	9 23	9 24	—	—
Pottery Siding	—	—	..	..	—	—	C	R	—	—	..	..	..	..	—	—	—	—	..	..	—	—	—	—
Granite Siding	—	—	..	..	—	—	C	R	—	—	..	..	..	..	—	—	—	—	..	..	—	—	—	—
HEATHFIELD	2 19	2 21	3 20	X 3 30	4 19	4 21	3 55	●5 5	5 42	5 43	..	..	..	..	7 24	7 25	C	S	..	..	9 28	9 29	C	S
Teigngrace Halt	2 24	2 25	—	—	4 24	4 25	—	—	5 46	5 46½	..	..	..	..	7 28	7 29	—	—	..	..	9 32	9 33	—	—
Teign Bridge Level C.	—	—	—	—	—	—	—	—	—	—	..	..	..	..	—	—	—	—	..	..	—	—	—	—
Teign Bridge Siding	—	—	—	—	—	—	5 13	●5 24	—	—	..	..	..	..	—	—	—	—	..	..	—	—	—	—
NEWTON ABBOT	2 30	—	3 42	—	4 30	—	5 30	—	5 51	—	..	..	..	..	7 34	—	9‖35	—	..	..	9 38	—	11‖25	—

MORETONHAMPSTEAD BRANCH.

Single Line, worked by Electric Token or Train Staff. Auxiliary Token instruments on Platforms Nos. 5 and 9 at Newton Abbot. Intermediate Token instrument at Newton Abbot end of the Up Loop at Heathfield. Heathfield and Bovey are Crossing Stations. The Token or Staff Stations are Newton Abbot, Heathfield, Bovey and Moretonhampstead.

DOWN TRAINS. WEEK DAYS.

M.P. Mileage M.	C.	STATIONS.	Ruling Gradient.	Point-to-Point Times. (Time Allowances for Ordinary Freight Trains, see page 2.)	Allow for Stop.	Allow for Start.	G Engine. arr.	dep.	K Christow Freight. arr.	dep.	B 7.25 a.m. Totnes Auto. arr.	dep.	B Auto. arr.	dep.	K Exeter Freight. arr.	dep.	B 10.5 a.m. Paignton Auto. W arr.	dep.	K Freight. arr.	dep.	B Auto. arr.	dep.	arr.	dep.
				Mins.	Mins.	Mins.	a.m.	a.m.	a.m.	a.m.	a.m.	a.m.	a.m.	a.m.	a.m.	a.m.	a.m.	a.m.	a.m.	a.m.	p.m.	p.m.		
—	—	**NEWTON ABBOT**	—	—	—	1	—	6‖55	—	7 0	7 41	7 50	—	9 20	—	9 30	10 27	10 32	—	11 15	—	12 50	..	..
1	43	Teign Bridge Siding	100 R.	4	1	1	—	—	7 6	7 20	—	—	—	—	—	—	—	—	C	R	—	—	..	..
1	51	Teign Bridge Level C.	—	—	—	—	—	—	—	—	—	—	—	—	—	—	—	—	—	—	—	—	..	..
2	28	Teigngrace Halt	100 R.	—	—	—	—	—	—	—	7 54	7 55	9 24	9 25	—	—	10 36	1036½	—	—	12 54	1254½	..	..
3	70	**HEATHFIELD**	70 R.	5	1	1	C	S	7 27	8 40	7 58½	8 0	9 28½	9 30	9 41	●10 9	10 40	X1043	11 25	11 40	12 58	12 59	..	..
5	6	Granite Siding	69 R.	—	—	—	—	—	▬	▬	—	—	—	—	▬	▬	—	—	C	R	—	—	..	..
5	19	Pottery Siding	53 R	—	—	—	—	—	..	..	—	—	—	—	..	..	—	—	C	R	—	—	..	..
5	46	Brimley Halt	53 R.	—	—	—	—	—	..	..	8 3½	8 4½	9 33½	9 34	..	..	1046½	1047½	—	—	1 2½	1 3½	..	..
6	6	Bovey	66 F.	5	2	2	C	S	..	..	8 6	X8 11	9 36	9 37	..	..	10 49	10 51	11 47●	12 20	1 5	1 6	..	..
7	61	Hawkmoor Halt	—	—	—	—	—	—	..	..	—	8 16	—	9 42	..	..	—	10 56	—	—	—	1 11	..	..
8	65	Lustleigh	50 R.	11	1	2	—	—	..	..	8 19	8 20	9 45	9 46	..	..	10 59	11 0	1233 S	T1238	1 14	1 15	..	..
12	28	**MORETONHAMPSTEAD**	49 R.	14	1	—	7‖30	—	..	..	8 31	—	9 57	—	..	..	11 11	—	12 55	—	1 26	—	..	..

DOWN TRAINS. WEEK DAYS—continued.

STATIONS.	B Exeter Auto. arr.	dep.	arr.	dep.	B Auto. arr.	dep.	arr.	dep.	B Auto. arr.	dep.	arr.	dep.	B Auto. arr.	dep.	arr.	dep.	arr.	dep.	B Auto. arr.	dep.	arr.	dep.	B Auto. SO arr.	dep.
	p.m.	p.m.			p.m.	p.m.			p.m.	p.m.			p.m.	p.m.					p.m.	p.m.			p.m.	p.m.
NEWTON ABBOT	—	2 55	..	..	—	3 5	..	..	—	4 38	..	..	—	6 10	..	..	..	..	—	8 10	..	..	—	10 0
Teign Bridge Siding	—	—	..	..	—	—	..	..	—	—	..	..	—	—	..	..	..	..	—	—	..	..	—	—
Teign Bridge Level C.	—	—	..	..	—	—	..	..	—	—	..	..	—	—	..	..	..	..	—	—	..	..	—	—
Teigngrace Halt	2 59	3 0	..	..	3 9	3 9½	..	..	4 42	4 42½	..	..	6 14	6 14½	..	..	..	..	8 14	8 15	..	..	10 4	10 5
HEATHFIELD	3 4	3 25	..	..	3 13	3 14	..	..	4 46	4 47	..	..	6 18	6 19	..	..	..	..	8 18½	8 19½	..	..	10 8½	10 9
Granite Siding	▬	▬	..	..	—	—	..	..	—	—	..	..	—	—	..	..	..	..	—	—	..	..	—	—
Pottery Siding	..	..	..	..	—	—	..	..	—	—	..	..	—	—	..	..	..	..	—	—	..	..	—	—
Brimley Halt	..	..	..	..	3 17½	3 18	..	..	4 50½	4 51½	..	..	6 22½	6 23½	..	..	..	..	8 23	8 24	..	..	10 13	10 14
Bovey	..	..	..	..	3 20	3 21	..	..	4 53	4 54	..	..	6 25	6 26	..	..	..	..	8 25½	8 27	..	..	1015½	10 16
Hawkmoor Halt	..	..	..	..	—	3 26	..	..	—	4 59	..	..	—	6 31	..	..	..	..	—	8 32	..	..	—	10 21
Lustleigh	..	..	..	..	3 29	3 30	..	..	5 2	5 3	..	..	6 34	6 35	..	..	..	..	8 35	8 36	..	..	10 24	10 25
MORETONHAMPSTEAD	..	..	..	..	3 41	—	..	..	5 14	—	..	..	6 46	—	..	..	..	..	8 47	—	..	..	10 36	—

W Starts from Newton Abbot on Saturdays.

Taken from Original Timetable

Fig. M2 No. 5533 takes water before rejoining its train in the platform.

M.J. Esau

MOTIVE POWER

A Hawthorn class 2-4-0ST *Penn* was amongst the loco-motives that worked the line in Broad Gauge days, but no further evidence of this period has been found.

Standard gauge 0-6-0 saddle tanks, '517' and 'Metro' classes were employed on the line since the turn of the century and locomotives allocated to Moretonhampstead between 1912 and the 1930s included: 571, 517 class 0-4-2T; 737 and 1650, 1076 class 0-6-0; 2179 2-6-2T; 3590 Metro class 2-4-0T; various 27XX class 0-6-0ST's.

Since their introduction in 1906, the 45XX class 2-6-2T's (originally numbered 2161-90) came to be used on the branch and gradually replaced the smaller loco's listed above, the 1920 allocation is given here as an example:

Jan.—Feb.	4524
March	4529
April—Jan. '21	4538

Other small 'prairies' allocated to Moretonhampstead between 1924 and 1945 included Nos. 4582, 4587, 5571 and 5572.

After the war Collett 0-4-2T's were used on the branch services, particularly No. 4827 which of course later became No. 1427, also Nos. 1439, 1466 and 1470.

Other locomotives included Nos. 4179, 4406, 4516, 4518, 4526, 4547, 5551, 5567 and during the final years No. 82039.

Fig. M3 No. 1427 takes water at Moretonhampstead on the 7th June, 1958.

M.B. Warburton

SECTION.		Number of Wagons exclusive of Brake Van.									Ordinary Engines.						
		2-8-0			2-6-2 T			2-6-0			Tender.			Tank.			
From	To	Coal.	Goods.	Empties.	Coal.	Goods.	Empties.	Coal.	Goods.	Empties.	Coal.	Goods.	Empties.	Coal.	Goods.	Empties.	
Moretonhampstead Branch.																	
Newton Abbot … …	Bovey … …													22	35	44	6-wheel coupled. With two engines double loads may be taken, but no train must exceed 45 vehicles.
Bovey … …	Moretonhampstead …													12	20	25	
Moretonhampstead …	Bovey … …													26	35	45	
Bovey … …	Newton Abbot … …													26	35	45	

Extract from GWR 'Maximum Loads' 1908

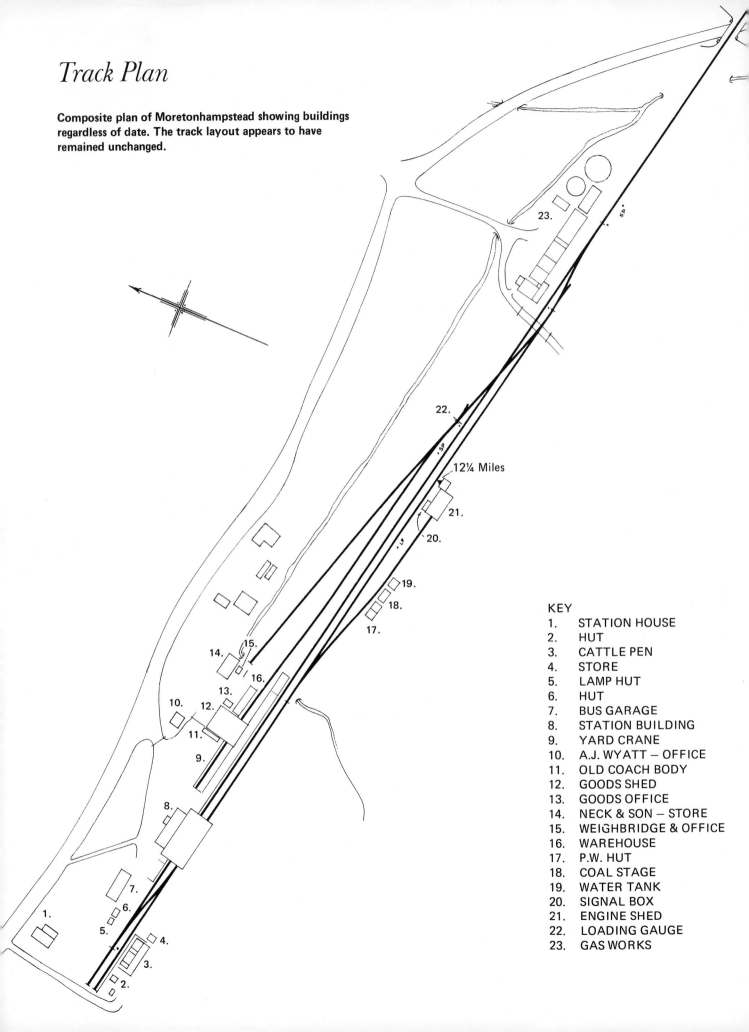

Track Plan

Composite plan of Moretonhampstead showing buildings regardless of date. The track layout appears to have remained unchanged.

23.

22.

12¼ Miles

21.

20.

19.

18.

17.

15.

14.

16.

13.

10.

12.

11.

9.

8.

7.

6.

5.

1.

4.

3.

2.

KEY
1. STATION HOUSE
2. HUT
3. CATTLE PEN
4. STORE
5. LAMP HUT
6. HUT
7. BUS GARAGE
8. STATION BUILDING
9. YARD CRANE
10. A.J. WYATT – OFFICE
11. OLD COACH BODY
12. GOODS SHED
13. GOODS OFFICE
14. NECK & SON – STORE
15. WEIGHBRIDGE & OFFICE
16. WAREHOUSE
17. P.W. HUT
18. COAL STAGE
19. WATER TANK
20. SIGNAL BOX
21. ENGINE SHED
22. LOADING GAUGE
23. GAS WORKS

Fig. M4 An early view of the station in broad gauge days.

Courtesy R.G. Friend

Fig. M5 The station at Moretonhampstead was situated to the south east and just below the town, alongside the A382 to Newton Abbot. The path in the foreground was used for passenger access, the main entrance being situated further down the hill as seen overleaf

A.E. Bennett

Fig. M6 This photograph clearly shows the location of the site, the land in the foreground had been used as garden allotments by the staff.

A. Attewell

Fig. M7 The station building and train shed as viewed from the road.

I.D. Beale

Fig. M8 The main entrance 1957.

A. Attewell

Fig. M9 An early view of the station c. 1907-9 showing the original slate roof and glazed skylights of the train shed and the small canopy that protected the main doorway. The GWR provided a motor bus service from Moretonhampstead to Chagford which commenced in 1906 and a further service to Princetown in 1909. There were two vehicles kept at the terminus in the wooden garage featured in *Fig. M17* but the services were taken over by the Western National Omnibus Co. in 1929. A Mr Grey ran a Hackney carriage to and from the station about 1910 but it has not been established for how long this service continued.

L. & G.R.P.

Fig. M10 The station building and overall roof varied only in detail from those which were subsequently erected at Ashburton. The main building was constructed of local stone with a slate roof whilst the train shed was built entirely of timber and braced with wrought iron tie rods. By the late 1940s the original skylights had fallen into disrepair to the extent that all the glazing was removed about 1950 and the resulting aperture later covered with corrugated iron, leaving a ventilation gap either side of the ridge. The canopy over the main entrance was also removed at this time and the slate roof of the train shed was replaced with roofing felt and battens. The station was gas lit and supplied by the local gasworks that was situated at the neck of the yard and the only sources of drinking water at the site were the standpipe housed in the small wooden cabinet near the 'gents' and a tap inside the office.

I.D. Beale

Fig. M11 The platform elevation of the station building.

I.D. Beale

Fig. M12 The first door on the left served both the parcels office and the adjoining station office, the second door had served the station office but was at this time unused, the main double doorway led into the booking hall and waiting room through which access was gained to the ladies lavatories and the last opening led to the 'gents' which was situated at the far end of the building.

I.D. Beale

Fig. M13 No. 4587 backs over the release crossover to run past its train on the 25th July, 1957.

R.J. Sellick

Fig. M14 A final interior view of the train shed showing the screen and timber support columns.

I.D. Beale

89

Fig. M15 The cattle pens were situated beyond the end of the run-round loop and constructed of bridge rail, measuring some 46′ by 23′. The small brick building alongside was used to store bales of hay, for feed, and sawdust which was spread in the pens to prevent the animals from slipping. There had been a considerable amount of pony traffic at one time but this seems to have almost finished after the Second World War.

I.D. Beale

Fig. M16 Access to the pens was by means of a narrow lane which ran from the main road across the end of the buffer stops and finished at the white gate on the right. The vertical posts were used to suspend Hurricane lamps after the removal of the lamp featured in the next view.

I.D. Beale

Fig. M17 The cattle pens again, but this time in 1921. The timber buildings on the left served as a garage to house the company's motor buses, but they are believed to have been let for other purposes from 1927 onwards and finally removed in 1947, at which time or thereabouts one of the pair of corrugated iron huts alongside the headshunt was removed, leaving the other in use as a lamp hut. The practice of whitewashing pens and cattle vehicles was later abandoned, apparently having merely provided a false impression of hygiene.

L. & G.R.P.

Fig. M18 The branch coaches were stabled in the loop siding at the end of each day's services and the points set for the loco shed to safeguard the running line. The sleeper built lock-up behind the lamp hut was used to store station coal and the land on the right, together with that either side of the station approach path, was used as garden allotments by the staff, who also kept chickens at the site. (Date 18th July, 1949.)

J.H. Meredith

Fig. M19 No. 1439 at Moretonhampstead on the 1.35 pm to Newton Abbot on the 14th October, 1950, with trailer cars Nos. W148 and W104.

W.A. Camwell

Fig. M20 The train shed from the south.
I.D. Beale

Fig. M21 A midday auto train at Moretonhampstead.

Real Photographs

Fig. M22 Moretonhampstead, perhaps 1907-9, showing the longitudinal sleepered track that remained from the gauge conversion and the original station nameboard mounted on the south wall of the goods shed. The station lamp further along the platform may have been oil lit and the iron railing fence has replaced the timber palings featured in *Fig. M4*.
L. & G.R.P.

Fig. M23 A complementary photograph of the terminus, taken in 1909 before the construction of the station house and featuring one of the 'new' small 'prairie' tanks at the head of a train of assorted passenger stock.

Chapman & Son, Courtesy A.R. Kingdom

Fig. M24 A similar view in 1955 clearly showing some of the garden allotments.

M.B. Warburton

Fig. M25 Messrs. Neck & Son were established coal merchants in Moretonhampstead and occupied the building at the end of the back siding, storing coal in the basement and iron ore (used for dye pigment) in the loft. The corrugated iron weighhouse and weighing machine in front of this were installed in 1910. The corrugated iron warehouse alongside the goods shed dates from about the time of the Second World War, it was constructed to a standard GWR design and occupied by Bibby's agricultural feed merchants. In 1956 the warehouse was extended by its own length again to accommodate another feed merchant, Messrs Silcocks who had occupied the grounded van body at the opposite end of the goods shed. The warehouse was in fact extended again during the final years before closure and totalled some 164 feet in length. (Photo, 1955.)

I.D. Beale

Fig. M26 The goods shed was constructed of local stone with a slate roof and sliding doors which opened to reveal curved entrances as seen in *Fig. M24*. The roof was replaced with corrugated iron, probably about 1950, before which time roses had graced the wall of the building growing from a small garden that was situated at the rear of the station platform.

I.D. Beale

Fig. M28 The forecourt elevation of the goods shed showing the corrugated iron goods office that was constructed in 1910 to ease the office accommodation. There had been a horse drawn freight delivery service at Moretonhampstead but motor lorries are believed to have taken over by 1920, one local carrier being J. Osborne from Chagford who had his own lorry and made deliveries to and from the railway.

The small wooden hut in the foreground of this view housed the meter for the station's gas supply but a larger building which had stood at this site, visible in *Fig. M17*, was occupied by A.J. Wyatt, a local corn and seed merchant who used the building as an office and store.

I.D. Beale

Fig. M27 The 6 ton crane illustrated here was used mainly for loading locally cut timber (much of which was used for pit props) and replaced the original 4 ton crane sometime after 1912. The goods shed housed a 2 ton crane. Messrs. Leavers, another feed merchant, later occupied the grounded van body when Silcocks had moved into the new warehouse already described. Notice the doorway connecting the goods shed and van body.

I.D. Beale

Fig. M29 The branch goods waits behind the platform for the arrival and departure of the mid afternoon auto train from Newton Abbot.

J.H. Moss

Fig. M30 The auto train arrives.

J.H. Moss

Fig. M31 The water tower was gravity fed from the nearby Budleigh Farm, the supply being checked through a meter that was situated in a manhole at the occupation crossing by the gasworks. The tank was equipped with a water crane and additionally supplied another alongside the running line together with the station's requirements. The coal stage alongside measured 20 feet long by 10 feet 4 inches wide and was taken out of use when the shed was closed. Coal wagons were unloaded by the shedman and during the war a reserve stock of coal was stored on the north of the siding just outside the engine shed; however, certainly in later years branch locos were coaled at Newton Abbot after their arrival with the first train. The whitewashed building served as a platelayers' hut with the wooden extension at this end being used for the storage of tools and equipment.

A. Attewell

Fig. M32 The engine shed was again of stone construction and very similar to that which was subsequently built at Ashburton, although the enginemen's cabin at the rear of the building was offset to one side of the rear 'entrance'. Sliding doors were an unusual feature on such a small building and very much gave the appearance of being an afterthought. (Photo 12th April, 1936.)

W.A. Camwell

Fig. M33 Another unusual feature was the signal box which was built onto the side of the engine shed (probably by the GWR on their acquisition of the line), which, unlike the other stations featured in this volume, was manned by a full time signalman.

I.D. Beale

Fig. M34 A further view of the building from the north east.

I.D. Beale

Fig. M35 Whilst a yard lamp stood beside the shed siding and the enginemen's cabin was gas lit, branch crews were left to manage with flare lamps as the shed itself had no lighting at all. The panelling that enclosed the rear 'entrance' to the shed was erected during the 1930s following a mishap when the branch locomotive ran through the rear wall! Whether, as with Ashburton, the aperture was previously sealed with stonework has not been established.

I.D. Beale

Fig. M36 The south wall of the building, clearly showing the corrugated iron that replaced the original slate roof on the ventilator during the early '50s.

I.D. Beale

Fig. M37 The engine shed was closed in 1947/48 after which branch locomotives travelled light engine to and from Newton Abbot each day. The sliding doors were removed about 1949 and the building was let to the Newton Abbot Co-op for use as a coal depot. Road access was made by means of a new road crossing featured below and brick built coal bunkers were constructed alongside the shed siding.

M.E.J. Deane

Fig. M38 A comparatively deserted yard scene of 1955 showing the 'back siding' which was used for mileage traffic. Albert Yea was a paraffin distributor for Moretonhampstead and the surrounding district and his premises are featured on the right of this view. The paraffin came in tankers by rail and each winter Mr Yea, who was also a rabbit trapper for the local farmers, would send rabbits by rail to London, Manchester and Birmingham.

I.D. Beale

Fig. M39 Looking towards Newton Abbot showing the lattice post starter signal and railbuilt loading gauge. The whitewashed house on the left was occupied by the manager of the gasworks beyond.

I.D. Beale

Fig. M40 It had been standard railway practice to avoid facing points wherever possible on running lines and the yard entry crossover at Moretonhampstead remained such an example until closure. At the beginning of the day's services the locomotive would often collect the two coaches from the train shed and wait at this end of the loop until the signalman arrived. (Photo, 1955.)

I.D. Beale

Fig. M41 Looking east from the occupation crossing during the early 1950s.

M.E.J. Deane

Fig. M42 A further view of the neck of the yard (taken in 1955), featuring the concrete posted home signal and another glimpse of the gasworks.

I.D. Beale

Figs. M43 and 44 The line left Moretonhampstead on an embankment and was carried over the A382 on the plate girder bridge illustrated here; it then plunged into the cutting illustrated on the left, past the advanced starter (tubular steel) and on to Newton Abbot.

A. Attewell & I.D. Beale

Fig. M45 This commemorative stone, situated alongside the station approach path, recorded the opening of the Moretonhampstead and South Devon Railway Company and the names of the original directors. The stone was erected by Mr Cumings' son in 1924 and is seen here suitably amended on the occasion of the line's closure to passenger traffic on the 2nd March, 1959.

R.J. Leonard

The branch was closed to goods traffic on the 6th April, 1964 but at the time of writing the line remains in use as far as Heathfield to serve an oil terminal and a haulage firm now occupies the station site at Moreton-hampstead, where the goods shed, engine shed, warehouse and platelayers' hut remain standing.

Further source of reference
   The Haytor Granite Tramway & Stover Canal *by*
   M.C. Evans published by David & Charles

Fig. P1 44XX class 2-6-2T No. 4401 rests alongside the platform with the branch train at Princetown during the August of 1953.

PRINCETOWN

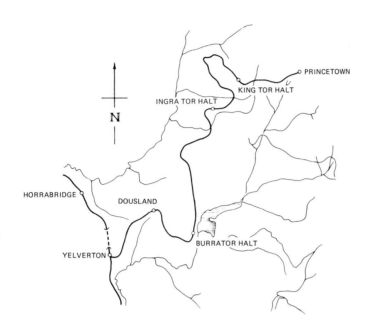

KEY FACTS

Company of Origin	Princetown Railway Company
Date of Opening	11th August, 1883
Purchased by GWR	31st December, 1921
Length of Branch	10 miles 39 chains
Ruling Gradient	1 in 40
Route Colour	Yellow
Overall Speed Restriction	20 mph
Single Line Worked by	Electric Train Staff (No intermediate crossings)

ORIGIN

The village of Princetown was founded at the beginning of the 19th Century by Thomas Tyrwhitt, a member of Parliament for Okehampton, who subsequently persuaded the Government to build a prison there to house captives from the Napoleonic Wars. The prison was opened in 1809 but after 1816 it stood empty for a while and was even used as a Naphtha factory.

In 1818 Sir Thomas Tyrwhitt, as he had become, was serving as an MP for Plymouth and proposed that a railway be built to link Princetown with Plymouth. The line was to extend some 24½ miles from Laira to Princetown via Yelverton and Dousland. No time was wasted and the Plymouth and Dartmoor Railway Company was incorporated and the line authorised by an Act of Parliament on the 2nd July, 1819. The line was constructed and opened as far as King Tor on the 26th September, 1823 and the remaining section to Princetown in December 1826. (The terminus here was situated behind the present Devils Elbow Inn.) The railway was horse drawn and carried passengers and large quantities of granite from the moor.

The Great Western Railway had considered the construction of a branch line from the Tavistock Railway to Princetown providing that land owners readily came forward and that the Government undertook to construct the first three miles from Princetown using convict labour, but this scheme was abandoned when the Plymouth & Dartmoor Co. offered their railway from Yelverton to Princetown in return for shares in a new company which became the Princetown Railway Co.

The new line received Royal Assent on the 13th August, 1878 and was financed by the GWR. It was constructed to standard gauge and ran from a point just south of Roborough Tunnel, on the Tavistock Branch, a distance of 10 miles 23 chains to a new terminus on the western edge of Princetown with one intermediate station at Dousland. The single line was built almost entirely on the course of the P&D Rly and was opened on the 11th August, 1883. The Great Western worked the railway and branch trains ran through to Horrabridge (over mixed gauge) until a new passenger station was constructed at the junction at Yelverton and opened on the 1st May 1885, after which branch trains terminated here.

The Princetown Railway remained independent until the 1st January, 1922 when it was absorbed by the GWR. Halts were later opened at Burrator, 14th February, 1924; King Tor, 2nd April, 1928 and Ingra Tor, 2nd March 1936.

Fig. P2 2-6-2T No. 4410 near Sheepstor and Burrator Halt on the 5th July, 1955.

R.J. Doran

OPERATION

The following description applies to the weekday time-table of 1948.

Locomotives for the branch were provided from Laira shed and sub-shedded at Princetown, where the water supply enabled them to be kept for up to eight weeks between boiler washouts. In normal circumstances locos always faced Princetown, thus keeping the firebox crown covered on the steep gradients.

There were two drivers and two firemen at Princetown which provided the necessary crews for each shift but no overnight cleaner, so the early turn fireman booked on duty at 4 am, raked out the ashpan and lit the fire. In practice a small fire was packed under the firehole doors each night during the week which saved lighting up, as this would usually hold until the morning when it could be spread across the bars and slowly built up. Of course with no Sunday service the Monday morning light up was always from cold.

The fireman would generally clean and prepare the loco whilst he was waiting for it to 'come round' then at 6.30 am the driver arrived and oiled up before moving off shed. Water might be taken but if the tanks were half full, this was sufficient to make it to Yelverton where the water supply was gravity fed, thus saving the more valuable Princetown supply which the crews had to pump from the well.

At 7.00 am one of the coaches was collected from beyond the platform together with the goods brake and set back into the platform. The first train left at 7.35 am and conveyed the workmen and local school children from the village, this returned as a mixed train, having collected a few wagons from Yelverton and arrived back at Princetown at 9.30 am. The wagons were placed in the yard, water might have to be taken and the driver went off for breakfast leaving the fireman to cook his 'on the shovel'.

The second departure at 10.30 am ran passenger only to Yelverton arriving back at 12.01 pm. The fireman booked off and the late turn driver acted as fireman for the following trip. On Mondays, Wednesdays and Fridays, the yard was sorted and the branch goods, together with an empty coach, departed at 12.55 pm, calling at Swell Tor quarry, Dousland, Yelverton and working on through to Horra-bridge. Swell Tor could only be served on the descent to

Yelverton when the siding connection became a trailing crossover, so that empties had first to be taken to Prince-town. The branch goods was collected from Horrabridge and the train returned as a mixed working from Yelverton calling at Dousland, putting off wagons there as required and finally arriving back at Princetown at 3.32 pm. It was this mixed working that would be particularly heavy going in bad weather, especially with any number of loaded coal wagons in tow, and excessive slipping could often bring the train to a stand on the banks to the extent that the loco-motive might have to leave the train at Ingra Tor and run on to Princetown for sand and water.

Tuesdays and Thursdays differed in that the 12.08 pm from Princetown ran mixed to Yelverton (one coach and the goods brake) and then on to Horrabridge to collect the branch goods as described.

After 3.32 pm the 'early' driver finished and the late turn fireman came on duty, the wagons were detached from the train and placed in the yard and the locomotive rejoined its single coach train for the 3.55 pm passenger working, which returned with the school children. The 6.00 pm, which was the last train of the day, arrived back at Princetown at 7.41 pm, the coach was stabled beyond the platform and the loco was taken over to the shed for disposal. On Tuesday and Thursday evenings the loco-motive was often used to pump water to replenish the tank at the shed.

On Wednesdays and Saturdays before the war, there was an additional return trip which left Princetown at 8.00 pm and arrived back at 10.20 pm, this was known as the 'Woolworth Special' because cheap tickets were issued for the 4 pm for which both coaches were then used and passengers returned on this last train. During the heavy snowfalls on Dartmoor small 19XX class tank locomotives fitted with snowploughs were run up and down the branch between trains, often backed with a rough 45XX that was due for overhaul at Swindon. 0-6-0 tank locomotives were used as they could be turned at either end of the journey to face into the snow, using the 23′ 6″ diameter turntables pro-vided at Yelverton and Princetown. In really bad conditions passenger services were stopped altogether and the Navy were often called in to dig out the road crossings etc.

1935 Working Timetable

PRINCETOWN BRANCH.

Single Line; worked by Electric Train Staff.   **No Intermediate Crossing Place.**
Dousland is a Block Post.
DOWN TRAINS.   Speed of Trains on this Branch not to exceed 20 miles an hour.
A—Trains call at Burrator Halt during the hours of daylight only.

M.P. Mileage		Distances from Yelverton		STATIONS.	Station No.	Ruling Gradient 1 in	Point to point times.	Allow for stop.	Allow for start.	B Mixed	B Pass.	B Mixed	B Pass.	B Pass.	B Pass. WSO
M	C	M	C				Mins.	Mins.	Mins	dep. A.M.	dep. A.M.	dep. P.M.	dep. P.M.	dep. P.M.	dep. P.M.
0	0	—	47	**Yelverton ..**	2114	40 R	5	—	1	8 36	11 23	2 50	5 12	6 55	9 47
1	47	1	47	Dousland	2125	42 R	5	1	1	8 48	11 29	2 56	5 18	7 1	9 53
2	1	2	1	Prowse's Crsg.	2126	—	—	—	—						
2	72	2	70	Burrator Platfm	2127	40 R	—	—	—	8A54	11 35	3 2	5A24	7A7	
3	58	3	58	Lowry Road Cg.	2127	40 R	—	—	—						
7	63	7	63	Swell Tor Siding	2129	41 R	—	—	—						
8	74	9	0	King Tor Halt			—	—	—	9 20	11 56	3 23	5 45	7 28	10 14
10	37	10	39	**Princetown**	2130	47 R	30	1	—	9 29	12 3	3 30	5 51	7 34	10 20

UP TRAINS.   WEEK DAYS ONLY.

Distance from Princetown.		STATIONS.	Ruling Gradient 1 in	Point to point times.	Allow for stop.	Allow for start.	B Pass.	B Pass.	B Mixed TTh SO	K Goods. TThSX		B Pass.	B Pass.	B Passr. WSO
M	C			Mins.	Mins.	Mins.	dep. A.M.	dep. A.M.	dep. P.M.	arr. P.M.	dep. P.M.	dep. P.M.	dep. P.M.	dep P.M.
—	—	**Princetown**	L	—	—	1	7 30	10 30	12 14	—	12 55	4 0	6 0	8 0
—	11	Stop Board		1	1	1				P				
		King Tor Halt					7 36	10 36	12 21		—	4 6	6 6	8 6
2	56	Swell Tor Sidi'g	47 F	8	1	1	—	—	—	1 5C	R1 20	—	—	—
6	58	Stop Board	47 R	4	1	1				P				
6	61	Lowry Rd. C'sg.	—	—	—	—	—	—	—			—	—	—
7	49	Burrator Platfm	—	—	—	—	7A57	10 57	12 43	—		4A27	6A26	8A27
8	38	Prowse's Crosi'g	40 F	—	—	—	—	—	—			—	—	—
8	72	Dousland	42 F	5	1	1	8 3	11 3	12 50	1 43		4 33	6 32	8 33
9	3	Stop Board	50 F	1	1	1				P	1 55			
10	39	**Yelverton**	40 F	3	2		8 8	11 8	12 54	2 2		4 38	6 37	8 38

1948 Working Timetable

YELVERTON AND PRINCETOWN.

Single Line, worked by Electric Train Staff.   **No Intermediate Crossing Place.**
Dousland is a Block Post.
SPEED OF TRAINS ON THIS BRANCH NOT TO EXCEED 20 MILES AN HOUR.

Down Trains.   Week Days only.

M.P. Mileage		Distances from Yelverton		STATIONS.	Ruling Gradient 1 in	Point to point times.	Allow for Stop.	Allow for Start.	B Mixed.	B Pass.	B Pass. SO	B Mixed.	B Pass.	B Pass.
M	C	M	C			Mins.	Mins.	Mins.	dep. a.m.	dep. a.m.	dep. p.m.	dep. p.m.	dep. p.m.	dep. p.m.
0	0	—	0	**YELVERTON .. ....**	40 R	5	1	1	8 36	11 20	1 22	2 51	4 51	7 0
1	47	1	17	Dousland	40 R	—	—	—	8 48	11 26	1 28	2 57	4 57	7 6
2	1	2	1	Prowse's Crossing	45 R	—	—	—						
2	72	2	72	Burrator Halt.	40 R	—	—	—	8 54	11 32	1 34	3 3	5 3	7 12
3	58	3	58	Lowry Road Crossing	40 R	—	—	—						
6	20	6	20	Ingra Tor	42 F	—	—	—	9 9	11 44	1 46	3 15	5 15	7 24
7	63	7	63	Swell Tor Siding	41 R	—	—	—						
8	74	8	74	King Tor Halt	55 R	—	—	—	9 22	11 55	1 57	3 26	5 26	7 35
10	43	10	43	**PRINCETOWN** arr.	47 R	30	1		9 30	12 1	2 3	3 32	5 32	7 41

Up Trains.   Week Days only.

Distance from Princetown.		STATIONS.	Ruling Gradient 1 in	Point to point times.	Allow for Stop.	Allow for Start.	B Pass.	B Pass.	B Mixed TTh Pass. SO	K Freight. MWFO SO		D Pass.	B Pass.	B Pass.
M	C			Mins.	Mins.	Mins.	dep. a.m.	dep. a.m.	dep. p.m.	arr. p.m.	dep. p.m.	dep. p.m.	dep. p.m.	dep. p.m.
—		**PRINCETOWN .. ....**	L	—	—	1	7 35	10 30	12 8	—	12 55	2 10	3 55	8 0
—	11	Stop Board	47 F	1	1	1				P				
1	52	King Tor Halt	55 F	—	—	—	7 40½	10 36	12 14			2 15½	4 1	6 6
2	60	Swell Tor Siding	41 F	8	1	1	7 49½	10 45	12 23	1 5C	R1 20	2 24½	4 10	6 15
4	23	Ingra Tor	42 R	—	—	—				P				
6	58	Stop Board	42 R	4	1	1								
6	65	Lowry Road Crossing	40 F	—	—	—	8 1	10 57	12 35			2 36	4 22	6 27
7	51	Burrator Halt.	40 R	—	—	—								
8	42	Prowse's Crossing	42 F	—	—	—								
8	76	Dousland	42 F	5	1	1	8 6	11 3	12 41	1 48	1 55	2 41	4 28	6 33
9	3	Stop Board	50 F	1	1	1				—	P			
10	43	**YELVERTON** arr.	40 F	3	2		8 11	11 8	12 46	2 5		2 46	4 33	6 38

Taken from Original Timetables

Fig. P3 No. 4407 passes the starter signal as it leaves Princetown with a single coach train for Yelverton in April 1951.

MOTIVE POWER

Two former Llynvi and Ogmore Railway 0-6-0 side tank locomotives that had since become GWR Nos. 919 and 923, were employed on the branch when it first opened in 1883 and are thought to have remained in use there until they were withdrawn in 1892 and 1888 respectively.

517 class 0-4-2T's and 19XX 0-6-0T's then worked the line until the introduction of the Churchward 44XX class 2-6-2T's in 1905 (then numbered 3101-10). This new class had a high tractive effort with its 4′ 1½″ diameter driving wheels and proved to be ideally suited to the steep gradients and sharp curves of the line, so much so that they came to be Princetown's almost exclusive allocation.

The 1920 allocation was as follows:—

Jan.—Mar.	4403
April	4404
May—Aug.	4410
Sept.	4404
Oct.—Jan '21	4410

In 1931 an experimental wheel flange lubrication system was fitted to No. 4402, in which oil was sprayed onto the driving wheel flanges, (powered by a Westinghouse pump) in an attempt to reduce the friction caused by the severe curvature of the line. However, this was found to cause excessive slipping and was later abandoned as was a gravity fed system which was also tried on No. 4407*. Nos. 4402 and 4410 were subsequently fitted with a new or perhaps modified system that remained in use until their withdrawal. Very briefly, in the adopted system a coolant was sprayed under steam pressure, onto the rail surface close to the leading pony wheels, which in the case of No. 4402 had special tyres with a wider tread. The coolant was a white fluid similar to that used in machine cutting diluted with ten parts water and used to fill the two reservoirs alongside the smokebox each morning. The apparatus was only employed on the ascent to Princetown and was controlled by the leading pony truck reins to feed the outer rail on each curve and cut off on the straight. Simple lubricators were also fitted to each side of the loco (see *Fig. P5*) and fed neat fluid onto the rear driving wheel flanges to help reduce the friction when running bunker first on the descent to Yelverton.

No. 4402 came to be regarded as the branch locomotive, with No. 4410 standing in during boiler washouts etc. During the later years one fireman carried out any maintenance possible at Princetown on Sundays in order to keep No. 4402 on the branch until she was finally withdrawn in 1949.

19XX class 0-6-0 saddle and pannier tanks fitted with snowploughs were frequently used to clear the line during the winter months and the larger wheeled 45XX 2-6-2T's were occasionally to be seen at Princetown and regularly worked the branch services during the 1950's, taking over completely when No. 4410 was withdrawn in 1955. Nos. 4534, 4549, 4568 and 4583 were amongst those known to have worked the line.

* Information up to this point about flange lubrication given in Locomotives of GWR Part 9

Fig. P4 Driver Gough replenishes the flange lubrication apparatus on No. 4410 during the afternoon of the 5th July, 1955.

R.J. Doran

Fig. P5 A close up of the rear flange lubricators on No. 4410.
R.J. Doran

Track Plans

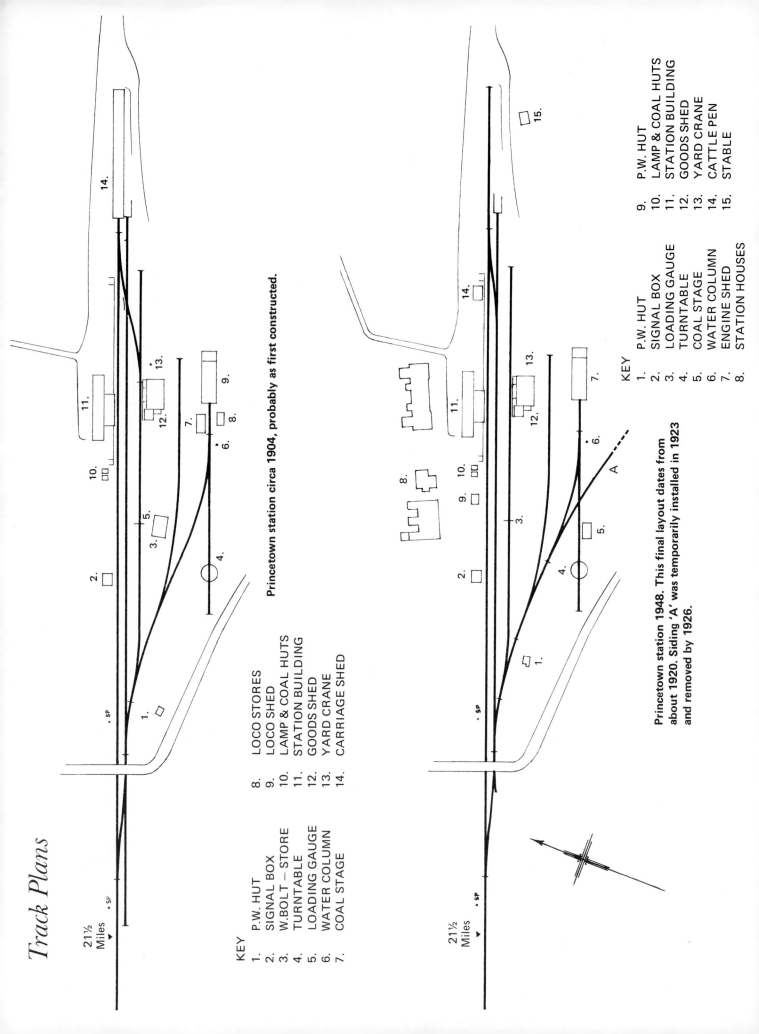

21½ Miles

Princetown station circa 1904, probably as first constructed.

KEY
1. P.W. HUT
2. SIGNAL BOX
3. W.BOLT – STORE
4. TURNTABLE
5. LOADING GAUGE
6. WATER COLUMN
7. COAL STAGE
8. LOCO STORES
9. LOCO SHED
10. LAMP & COAL HUTS
11. STATION BUILDING
12. GOODS SHED
13. YARD CRANE
14. CARRIAGE SHED

21½ Miles

Princetown station 1948. This final layout dates from about 1920. Siding 'A' was temporarily installed in 1923 and removed by 1926.

KEY
1. P.W. HUT
2. SIGNAL BOX
3. LOADING GAUGE
4. TURNTABLE
5. COAL STAGE
6. WATER COLUMN
7. ENGINE SHED
8. STATION HOUSES
9. P.W. HUT
10. LAMP & COAL HUTS
11. STATION BUILDING
12. GOODS SHED
13. YARD CRANE
14. CATTLE PEN
15. STABLE

Figs. P6 and P7 Winter scenes at Princetown taken on the 25th February, 1956.

R.J. Sellick

Fig. P8 Princetown station c. 1905. There were no doorways in this side of the building and the gateway at the end of the path from the village was the only entrance to the platform.

L. & G.R.P.

Fig. P9 This view was taken from the end loading bank looking towards Yelverton during the construction of the first three of the station houses again—about 1905. The original track layout featured here is thought to have been altered in 1920 when the single slip and crossover to the goods shed were removed. The headshunt just beyond the bridge was also removed, possibly at the same time.

L. & G.R.P.

Fig. P10 An interesting comparison with *Fig. P9*, taken on the 23rd September, 1948 but this time showing the end loading bank. The original cattle pen can be seen here, although the date of origin is unknown and much of the timber palings at the rear of the platform remain albeit in a somewhat dilapidated condition. The yard crane had replaced the 2 ton crane shown in *Fig. P9* by 1912 and had a lifting capacity of 5 tons, this apparently saw most use in handling farm machinery and container traffic (provisions) for the prison.

The terrace of four station houses on the right were a later addition, authorised in 1907 but not built until about 1925. The first of the three beyond them was detached and occupied by the Station Master and the semi-detached pair at the far end were situated just outside the parish boundary.

L.E. Copeland

Fig. P11 An eight berth clerestory camping coach was stabled at Princetown from about 1934 to 1939, although it was not included in a 1935 listing and the vehicle doesn't appear in photos of the site taken that year. The coach was stabled at the end of the goods shed siding and could be hired for £4.00 per week with a condition of hire being that railway tickets had to be taken to and from the hirer's destination.
G.W. Magazine

Fig. P12 No. 4407 at Princetown with the usual single coach train and still bearing its GWR livery in 1951.

W.A. Camwell

Fig. P13 No. 4410 runs past its train.

R.C. Riley

Fig. P14 The eastern end of the station building c. 1935. The station is believed to have still been oil lit at this time but gas lighting was provided in later years and supplied from the prison gasworks.

S.R. Loxton

Fig. P15 According to the original plans the station building was constructed of rendered stonework with brick dividing walls between each room and a slate roof. The timber screens at each end of the canopy were not included on the plans but were obviously erected to provide extra shelter from the harsh Dartmoor weather. The door in this end of the building served the gentlemen's lavatories and the remaining accommodation was as follows: the first entrance in the platform elevation, hidden by the screen, boasted double doors and served a waiting room through which access was gained to the ladies' lavatories; the second doorway beneath the canopy led into a booking hall and waiting room with the traditional ticket window. Two further doorways beyond the canopy, hidden in this view but illustrated above, served the office and the station stores respectively whilst the last room, which was originally intended as a lamp room, served as a parcels office and was entered by a door in the end of the building. The entrance to the station stores was bricked up about 1947 and converted to a window (as seen in *Fig. P39*) thereafter access to this room was gained via the office or through a new connecting doorway from the parcels office. The chimney stack from the parcels office was also removed at this time.

The goat on the platform was one of those kept by Frank Price, a guard on the line for many years, who also kept poultry and had an allotment at the site.

Lens of Sutton

Fig. P16 No. 4542 clears the crossover before running back past its train on the 22nd September, 1955. The cattle pen had been reconstructed since 1951 and the timber palings finally replaced with concrete posts and wire. Cattle traffic was very heavy for the Princetown cattle fair which was held each year on the first Wednesday in September, there was also a large pony sale within six weeks of this event.

M.B. Warburton

Fig. P17 Looking towards the buffer stops from the station platform with the yard entrance gate just visible beyond. The small building to the right of the yard approach was built in 1909 to serve as a stable, but in later years this was leased by one of the staff. A corrugated iron carriage shed had originally stood over the headshunt and can just be seen in *Fig. P25*. This structure was removed around 1930 but coaches continued to be stabled at this site.

After the removal of the carrriage shed the coaches provided for branch services were usually due for 'shopping' or semi-condemned stock the reason for this presumably being a combination of the harsh weather conditions and severe curvature of the line. Only one coach was normally used with a standby vehicle being kept at Princetown and brought into use as required.

The engine release turnout was permanently sprung in favour of the loop to protect the running line from vehicles stabled beyond.

J.H. Moss

Fig. P18 The goods shed was again constructed of rendered stone with a slate roof and housed the usual light purpose crane. The entrance on this side of the building was protected with a small canopy evident in earlier years, but this was removed about 1947 and the sliding doors patched up with corrugated iron, possibly at the same time. The canopy over the road vehicle entrance survived until closure.

J.H. Moss

Fig. P19 Just prior to demolition, this photograph clearly shows the small crane and the 'lock-up' inside the goods shed.

There was a small weighing machine inside the 'lock-up' but as there was no weighbridge at Princetown larger loads were sent to Horrabridge for weighing. The doorway in the west facing wall of the office was bricked up just before the Second World War and the flight of steps removed.

E.T. Day

Fig. P20 Looking towards Yelverton from the station platform with No. 4524 easing towards its train. The nearer and larger of the two corrugated iron huts was used for the storage of station coal and had acquired a wooden door, the other was used as a lamp hut. The gangers' hut beyond was probably provided about 1933 when the motor trolley system of maintenance was installed on the branch around 1930 and was subsequently enlarged at the end of the Second World War to accommodate two P.W. trolleys the smaller of which was used for the inspection of the branch and the other to take the P.W. Gang to the nearest stabling point to the location of their work. The Princetown P.W. men often teamed up with the Yelverton gang to work elsewhere on the Tavistock branch.

J.H. Moss

Fig. P21 The signal box was an unusual design substantially constructed of rendered stonework with a slate roof, sliding window casements and a small cast iron framed window in the opposite end of the base. The stovepipe had replaced the original brick chimney by 1926 and the building apparently received some exterior renovation about 1948. A porter/signalman manned the box as required.

R.J. Sellick

Fig. P22 No. 4410 approaches the signal box on its way to the platform.

R.J. Doran

Fig. P23 This view shows the west elevation of the cabin with No. 4542 detaching the wagons from the early afternoon mixed train from Yelverton on the 22nd September, 1955.

M.B. Warburton

Fig. P24 An early view of the terminus taken about 1910. W. Bolt was the local coal merchant at Princetown and used the large timber shed on the right for the storage of coal until they found an alternative site in the village, after which wagons were unloaded straight onto their lorry and the shed subsequently removed. It seems that their business could often bring three or four wagons a week from Messrs. Reid & Son and the Plymouth Coal Company. Another local coal merchant was J. Crocker who was also a carrier for the railway. The prison gasworks also brought considerable coal traffic to the branch. The former wooden loading gauge and the original siting of the fire buckets on the screen at this end of the station building are also visible.

Lens of Sutton

Fig. P25 The carriage shed is featured in the background of this photograph of No. 4403 placing wagons in the yard on the 15th June, 1926.

Lens of Sutton

Fig. P26 An unidentified 44XX class 2-6-2T can be seen in this view which was taken about 1935. The more obvious changes include the new P.W. hut beyond the signal box, the removal of the carriage shed and the replacement yard levers. Notice the standby clerestory coach in the yard.

S.R. Loxton

Fig. P27 An interesting comparison in 1955, again showing the entire width of the site. The sleeper-built platelayers' cabin in the foreground was built during the early 1940's (see *Fig. P34*) and is shown here in its final condition, having been clad with roofing felt. The remains of the previous cabin can still be seen in the right hand foreground of the picture.

R.J. Doran

Figs. P28 & P29 Again the engine shed was constructed of rendered stonework with a slate roof and differed very considerably from the official plans which showed a much shorter design. A smoke hood ran through the entire length of the building and projected through an aperture in the glazing above the entrance, just visible in *Fig. P32*, however little remained of the projection when these views were taken circa 1935. The slate roof was later replaced with boards and roofing felt leaving only the centre smoke hood ventilator in position and the area over the main entrance was also boarded over, this work probably being carried out about 1944. The water tank mounted above the entrance was fed from a well that was situated opposite the coaling stage. Water was raised using steam from the branch loco via a copper pipe coupled in place between the steam fountain and a connection along the inside of the shed wall, but in latter years steam was taken from the train heating pipe by means of a new connection in the shed pit. Besides the nearby water crane, the tank additionally fed the station's 'NOT DRINKING WATER' supply and a hydrant that was positioned half way along the inside of the shed on the right hand side; this was used to top up the boiler level if it was too low for lighting up.

S.R. Loxton

Fig. P30 The wooden building just outside the engine shed was used as a loco dept stores but disappeared soon after this date, loco stores were subsequently kept in the engineman's cabin at the rear of the shed. The two chicken houses alongside the shed were owned by the staff who kept the area alongside fenced off as a chicken run. (Photo 13th April, 1936.)

W.A. Camwell

Fig. P31 The engine shed again in the final condition in 1955. The sleepers in the foreground of this view covered a site drainage manhole.

R.C. Riley

Fig. P32 A view of the station from the south circa 1924, just prior to the construction of the second terrace of four station houses. A siding projected through the gateway in the boundary fence and into the field in the foreground, this was used for loading timber (mainly pit props) from Brimpts' estate but seems to have been a somewhat temporary arrangement as the necessary land was merely leased from the Plymouth Borough in April 1923. The siding is thought to have been in use by the end of that year but as seen below it had been removed by 1926. The original coal stage which stood outside the engine shed can also be seen here.

Lens of Sutton

Fig. P33 Looking east from the occupation bridge, 15th June, 1926. The coaling stage on the right replaced the earlier version that was situated just outside the engine shed and the truncated spur on the shed approach is all that remained at this time of the siding that extended across the field beyond.

H.C. Casserley

Fig. P34 A falling gradient in the turntable siding protected the shed from runaway wagons and was used to advantage in loading the ashes. Each morning the contents of the ashpan were emptied into the shed pit, then when the locomotive was moved outside, the fireman shovelled the ashes into a wheelbarrow and dumped them beside the water crane. When a sufficient volume of ashes had accumulated to fill a wagon, an empty coal wagon was moved up to the shed using a pinch bar and allowed to return by gravity when loaded. Equipped with snowploughs, the small 19XX class tanks used to clear the line during the hard winter months were turned at each end of their journey to face into the snow, using the 23′ 6″ diameter turntables at Yelverton and Princetown. The reserve coal outside the shed was kept here during the second war. (Photo c. 1945.)

Author's Collection

Fig. P35 No. 4410 alongside the coal stage in July 1955; locos were coaled straight from the wagons whenever possible to save the double movement of coal and fires were dropped here before going on shed.

R.C. Riley

Fig. P36 The corrugated iron sheeting replaced the planking seen in *Fig. P33* and the gutter was a later refinement.

E.T. Day

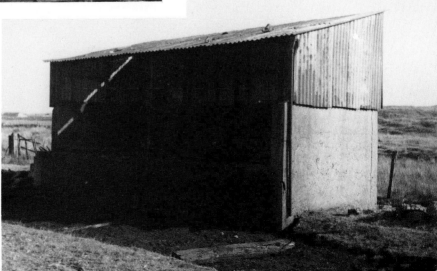

Fig. P37 The occupation bridge at the neck of the site was constructed of local stone with plate girder spans and carried a grassy track which led from the Plymouth road to the open moors. The catch point featured beneath the bridge replaced the headshunt that is just visible in *Fig. P9.* Notice how the telegraph wires are carried under the bridge.

M.B. Warburton

Fig. P38 No. 4410 rolls past the home signal with a mixed train after the stiff climb from Yelverton in July 1955. This picture clearly illustrates the open moorland.

R.C. Riley

Fig. P39 Track removal at Princetown on the 15th October, 1956.

R.J. Sellick

The branch was closed on the 5th March 1956, the buildings at Princetown were demolished and now only the station houses and former stable remain at the site.

Further sources of reference:
   The Plymouth & Dartmoor Railway *by H.G. Kendall,*
      Oakwood Press
   The Tavistock, Launceston & Princetown Railways *by*
      G.H. Anthony, Oakwood Press
   Trains Illustrated *Vol. 9 Page 29 1956*
   Trains Illustrated *Vol. 9 Page 96 1956*

PRINCETOWN CARRIAGE SHED

BUILT IN 1883 BY
FRANCIS MORTON & CO LTD.,
NAYLOR ST., LIVERPOOL.

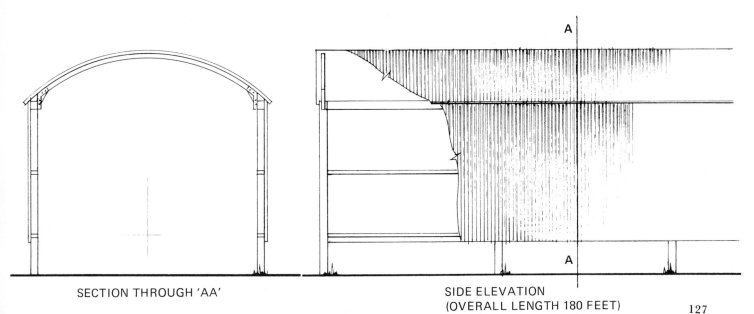

SECTION THROUGH 'AA'

SIDE ELEVATION
(OVERALL LENGTH 180 FEET)

PRINCETOWN SIGNAL BOX

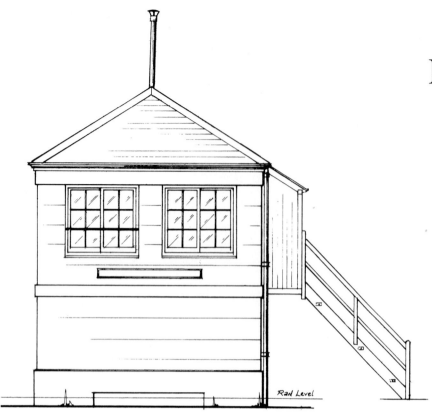

FRONT ELEVATION

ELEVATION TO WEST

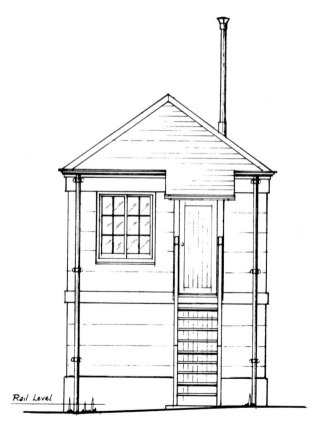

ELEVATION TO EAST

Additional Scale Drawings

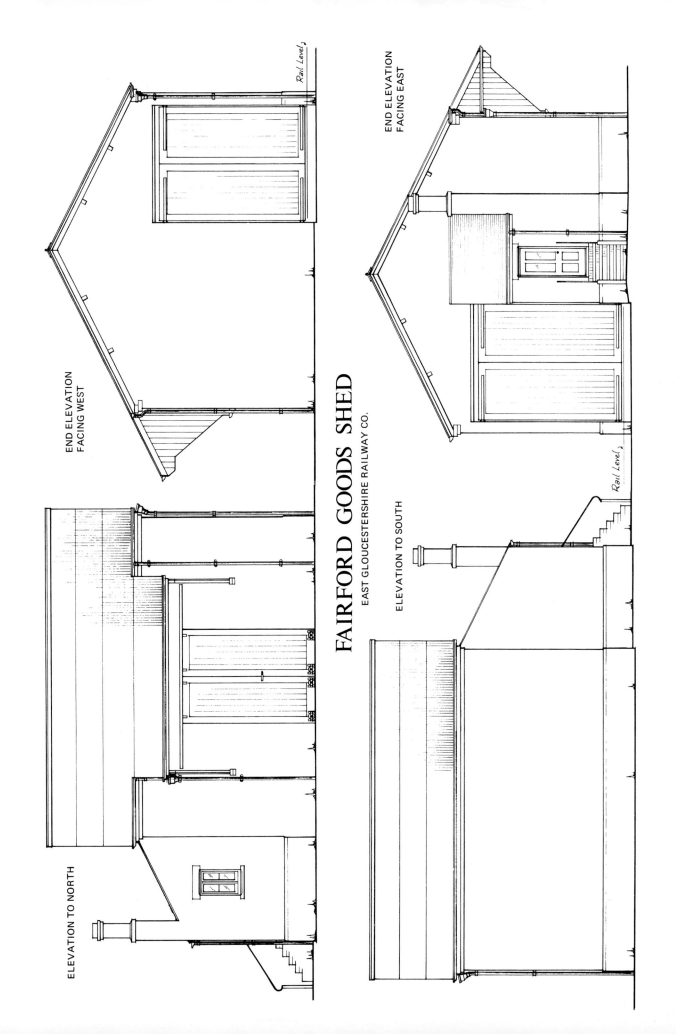

END ELEVATION
FACING WEST

ELEVATION TO NORTH

END ELEVATION
FACING EAST

ELEVATION TO SOUTH

FAIRFORD GOODS SHED

EAST GLOUCESTERSHIRE RAILWAY CO.

Rail Level,

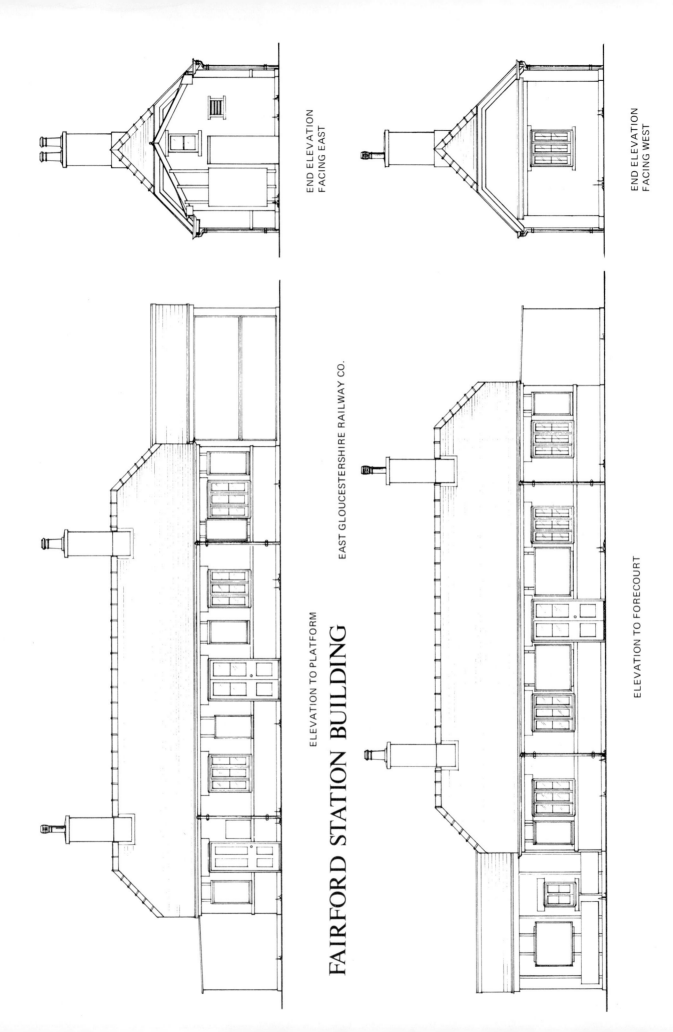

END ELEVATION
FACING EAST

END ELEVATION
FACING WEST

EAST GLOUCESTERSHIRE RAILWAY CO.

ELEVATION TO PLATFORM

FAIRFORD STATION BUILDING

ELEVATION TO FORECOURT

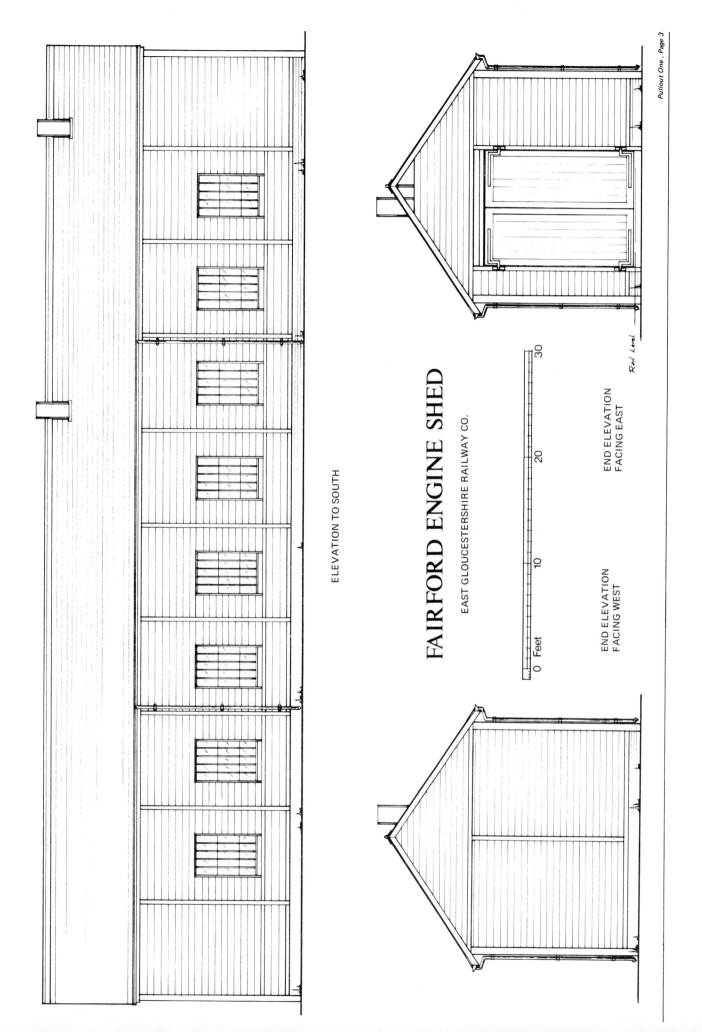

ELEVATION TO SOUTH

FAIRFORD ENGINE SHED

EAST GLOUCESTERSHIRE RAILWAY CO.

0 Feet   10   20   30

END ELEVATION
FACING WEST

END ELEVATION
FACING EAST

Rail Level

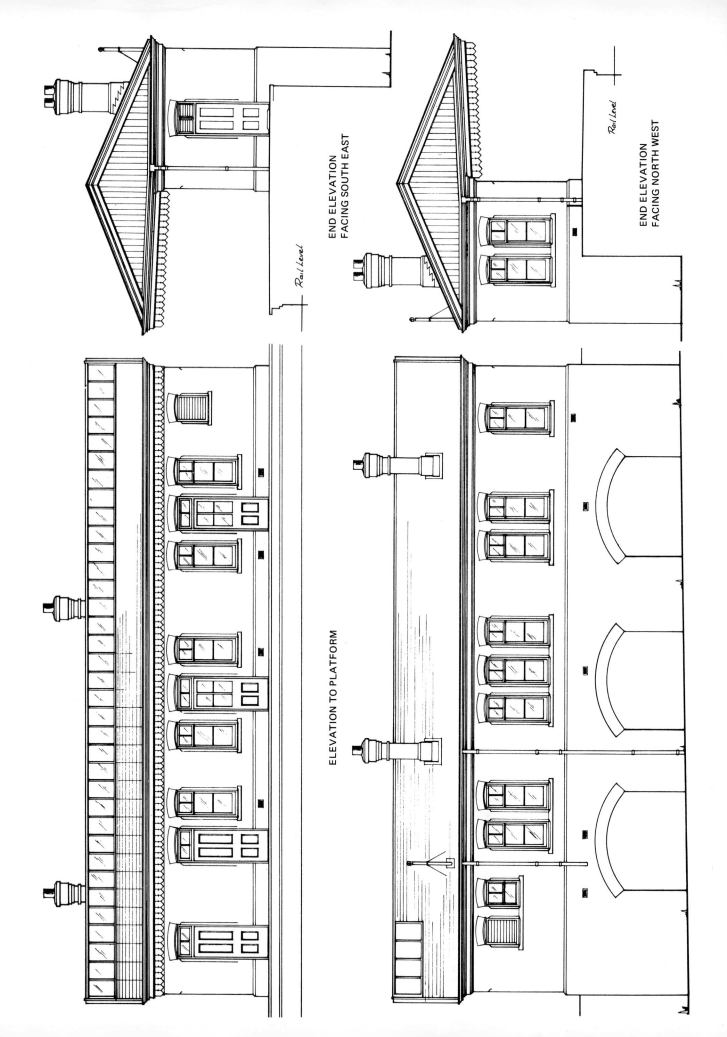

END ELEVATION
FACING SOUTH EAST

Rail Level

END ELEVATION
FACING NORTH WEST

Rail Level

ELEVATION TO PLATFORM

LAMBOURN STATION BUILDING

(REPLACEMENT) G.W.R.

0 Feet 10 20 30

LAMBOURN GOODS SHED

LAMBOURN VALLEY RAILWAY Co.

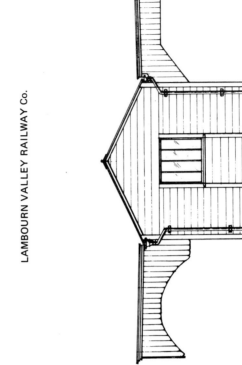

Rail Level

END ELEVATION
FACING SOUTH EAST

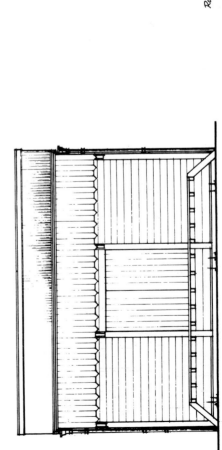

REAR ELEVATION

ELEVATION TO NORTH EAST

ELEVATION TO SOUTH WEST

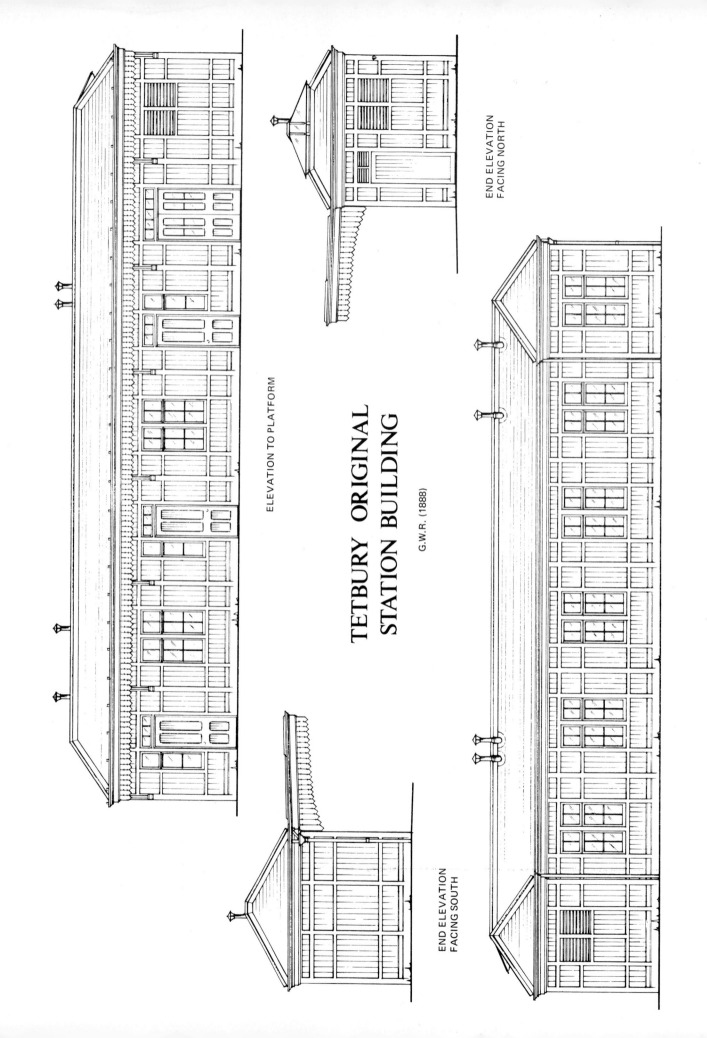

END ELEVATION
FACING NORTH

ELEVATION TO PLATFORM

TETBURY ORIGINAL
STATION BUILDING

G.W.R. (1888)

END ELEVATION
FACING SOUTH

TETBURY GOODS SHED

(ELEVATIONS)

END ELEVATION
FACING NORTH

END ELEVATION
FACING SOUTH

0 10 20 30

Feet

Rail Level

ELEVATION TO PLATFORM

ELEVATION TO FORECOURT

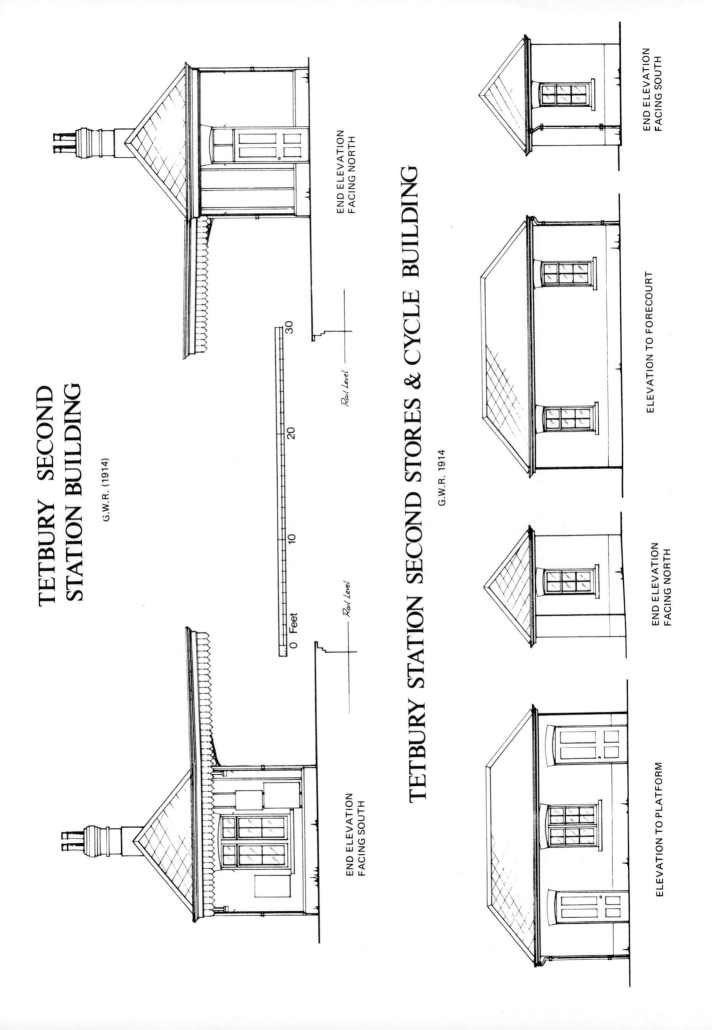

TETBURY SECOND STATION BUILDING

G.W.R. (1914)

END ELEVATION FACING NORTH

END ELEVATION FACING SOUTH

Rail Level

Rail Level

0 Feet 10 20 30

TETBURY STATION SECOND STORES & CYCLE BUILDING

G.W.R. 1914

END ELEVATION FACING SOUTH

ELEVATION TO FORECOURT

END ELEVATION FACING NORTH

ELEVATION TO PLATFORM

TETBURY GOODS SHED

G.W.R. (1888)

30 — 20 — 10 — 0 Feet

ELEVATION TO WEST

ELEVATION TO EAST

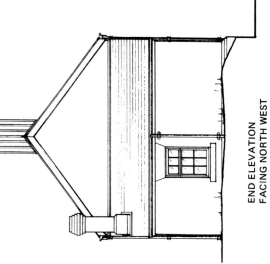

END ELEVATION
FACING SOUTH EAST

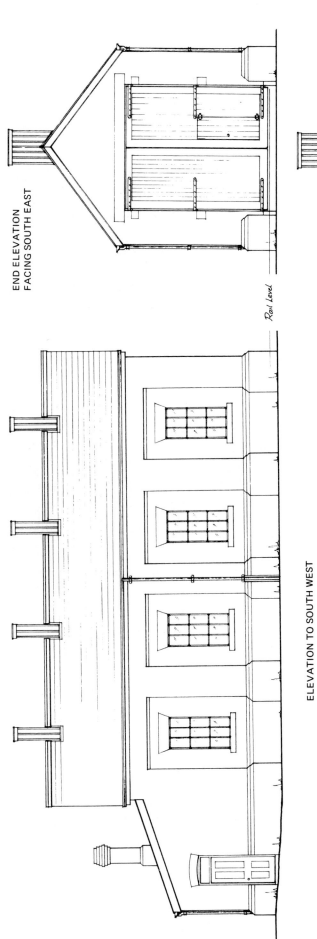

END ELEVATION
FACING NORTH WEST

Rail Level

ELEVATION TO SOUTH WEST

WALLINGFORD ENGINE SHED

(REPLACEMENT) G.W.R.

0 Feet   10   20   30

END ELEVATION
FACING SOUTH WEST

END ELEVATION
FACING NORTH EAST

ELEVATION TO NORTH WEST

ELEVATION TO SOUTH EAST

WATLINGTON GOODS SHED

WATLINGTON & PRINCES RISBOROUGH RAILWAY CO.

WATLINGTON CARRIAGE SHED

PROBABLY CONSTRUCTED BY G.W.R. ON ACQUISITION OF W. & P. R. RLY.

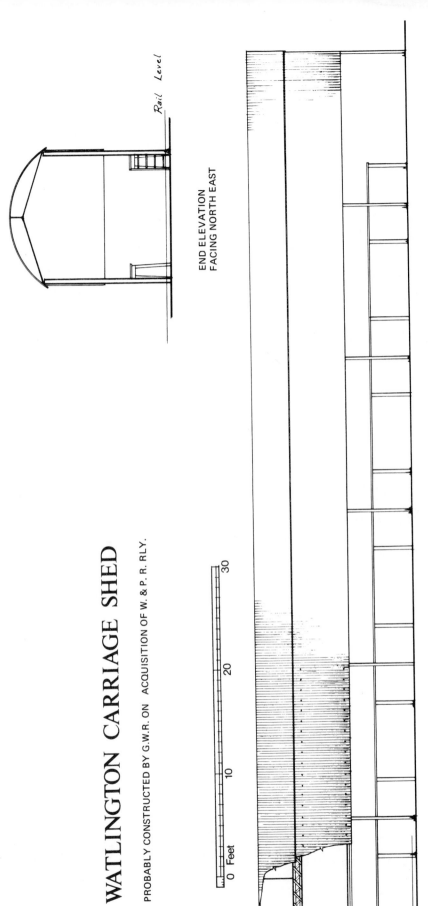

END ELEVATION
FACING NORTH EAST

Rail Level

ELEVATION TO NORTH WEST

0 Feet   10   20   30

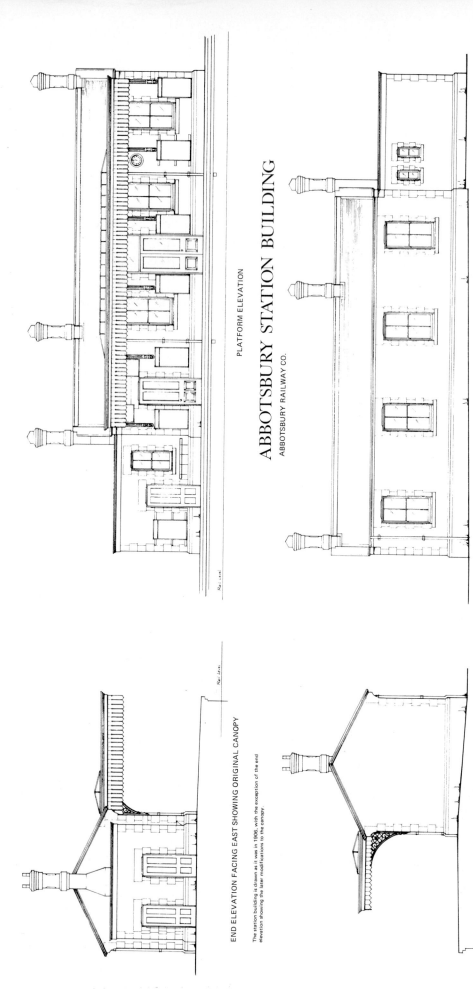

PLATFORM ELEVATION

ABBOTSBURY STATION BUILDING

ABBOTSBURY RAILWAY CO.

REAR ELEVATION FACING SOUTH

END ELEVATION FACING EAST SHOWING ORIGINAL CANOPY

The station building is drawn as it was in 1906, with the exception of the end elevation showing the later modifications to the canopy.

END ELEVATION FACING WEST SHOWING MODIFIED CANOPY

ABBOTSBURY WATER TOWER

ABBOTSBURY RAILWAY CO.

This drawing is based on the condition of the building in 1947 after the removal of the delivery arm.

SCALE

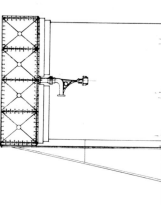

SIDE ELEVATION FACING NORTH

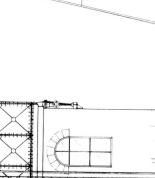

END ELEVATION FACING EAST

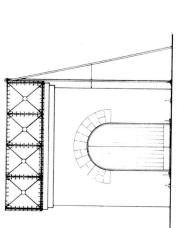

SIDE ELEVATION FACING SOUTH

ABBOTSBURY GOODS SHED

ABBOTSBURY RAILWAY CO.

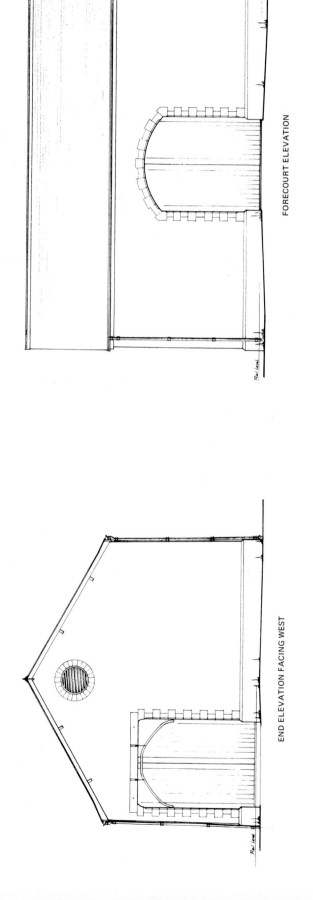

END ELEVATION FACING WEST

FORECOURT ELEVATION

ABBOTSBURY ENGINE SHED

ABBOTSBURY RAILWAY CO.

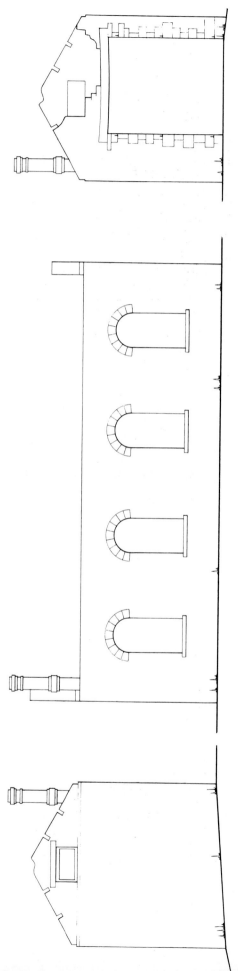

END ELEVATION FACING EAST

SIDE ELEVATION FACING NORTH

END ELEVATION FACING WEST

SCALE

30 feet

This drawing is based on the condition of the remains of the building in 1947.
Details of the roof have not yet been established but the windows were almost
certainly the same as those in the water tower.

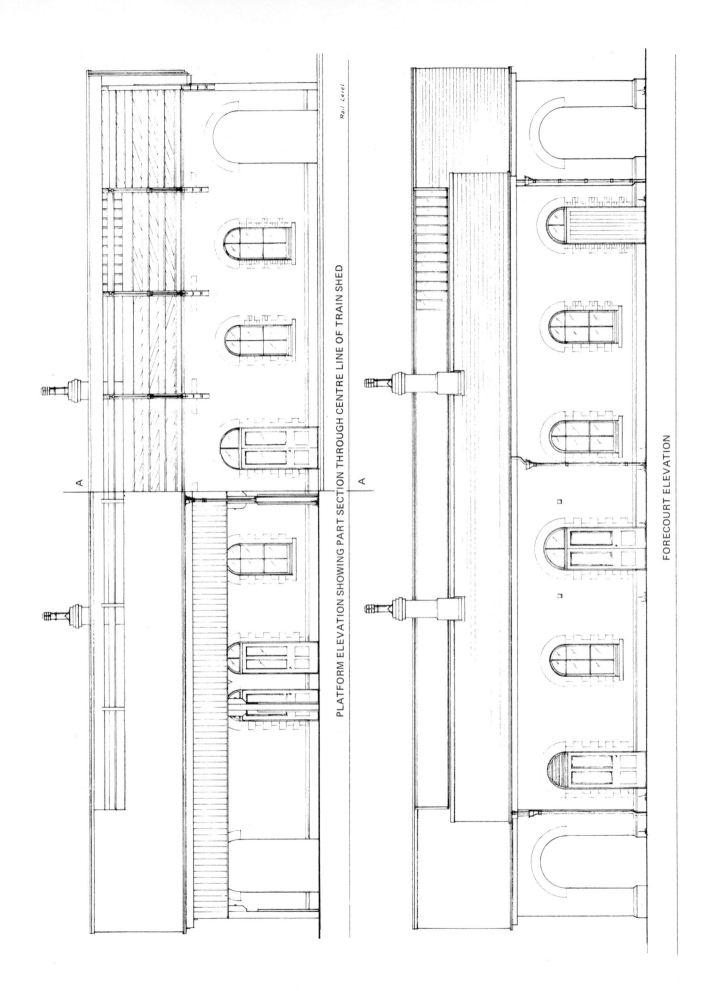

PLATFORM ELEVATION SHOWING PART SECTION THROUGH CENTRE LINE OF TRAIN SHED

Rail Level

FORECOURT ELEVATION

ASHBURTON STATION BUILDING AND TRAIN SHED

BUCKFASTLEIGH, TOTNES AND SOUTH DEVON RAILWAY

The station is drawn in its final condition c1950

Rail Level

END ELEVATION FACING SOUTH

SCALE

0 1   5   10   20   30 feet

Rail Level

END ELEVATION FACING NORTH WITH SECTION THROUGH 'AA' OF TRAIN SHED ONLY

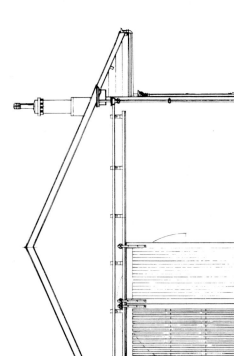

END ELEVATION FACING SOUTH

SCALE

0 1   5   10   20   30 feet

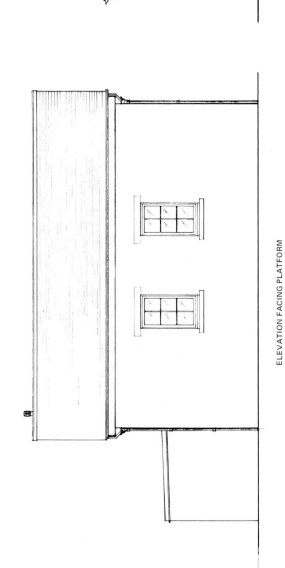

END ELEVATION FACING NORTH

The goods shed is drawn in its final condition with the replacement office shown in *Fig AN 28*

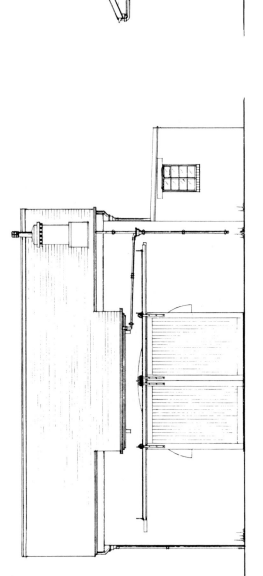

FORECOURT ELEVATION

ASHBURTON GOODS SHED

BUCKFASTLEIGH, TOTNES AND SOUTH DEVON RAILWAY

ELEVATION FACING PLATFORM

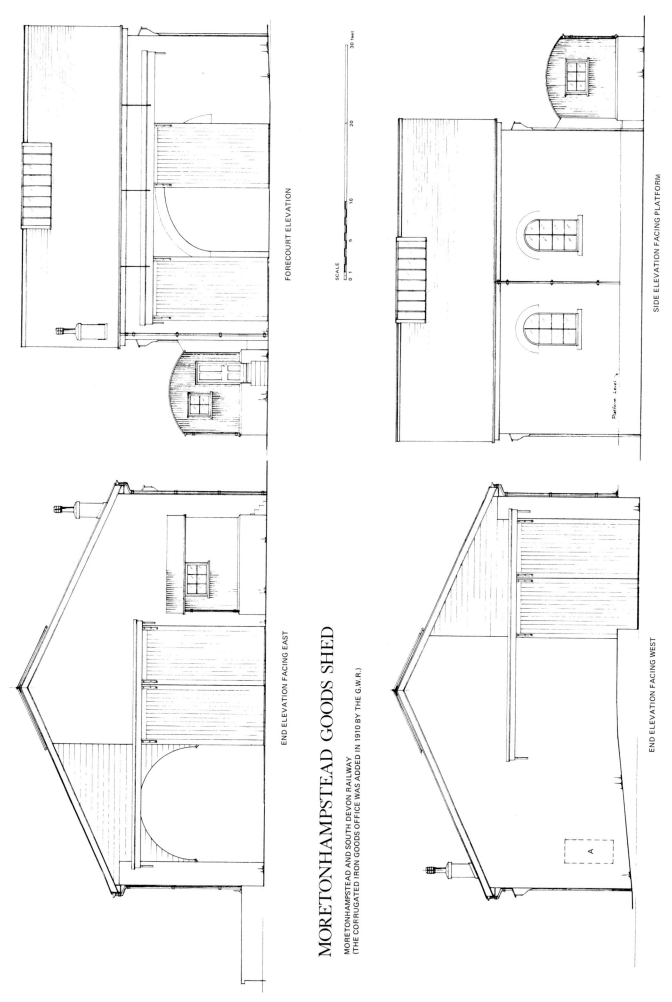

FORECOURT ELEVATION

END ELEVATION FACING EAST

MORETONHAMPSTEAD GOODS SHED

MORETONHAMPSTEAD AND SOUTH DEVON RAILWAY
(THE CORRUGATED IRON GOODS OFFICE WAS ADDED IN 1910 BY THE G.W.R.)

SCALE

0 1   5   10   20   30 feet

SIDE ELEVATION FACING PLATFORM

Platform Level

END ELEVATION FACING WEST

A

The goods shed is shown just prior to the construction of the corrugated iron
warehouse see *Figs. M 25 and 26*. Details are not known of the doorway marked
'A', a similar doorway existed in the opposite end see *Fig. M 23*, but is obscured
by the goods office.

END ELEVATION FACING WEST

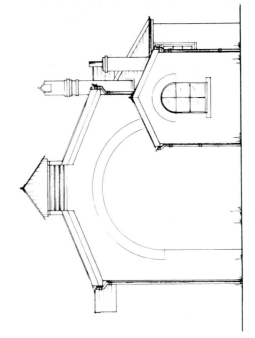

END ELEVATION FACING EAST

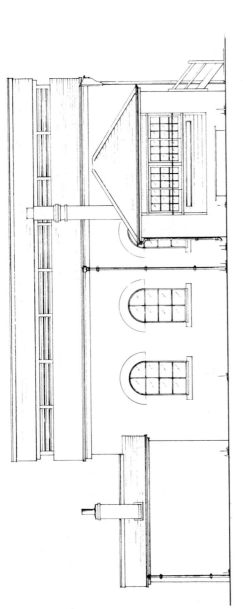

SIDE ELEVATION FACING NORTH

MORETONHAMPSTEAD ENGINE SHED

MORETONHAMPSTEAD AND SOUTH DEVON RAILWAY
(THE SIGNAL BOX WAS PROBABLY A LATER ADDITION BY THE G.W.R.)

The engine shed is shown c1936. The detail of the engineman's cabin shows how the brick wall above the doorway was angled to join the main rear 'entrance'. The door was hung in line with the wall and was protected with its own small roof/piece, although when this arrangement originated is not known.

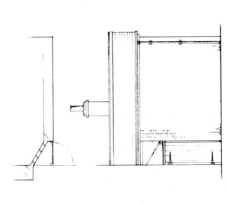

DETAIL VIEW OF SOUTH FACING
WALL OF ENGINEMAN'S CABIN

SCALE

0 1   5   10   20   30 feet

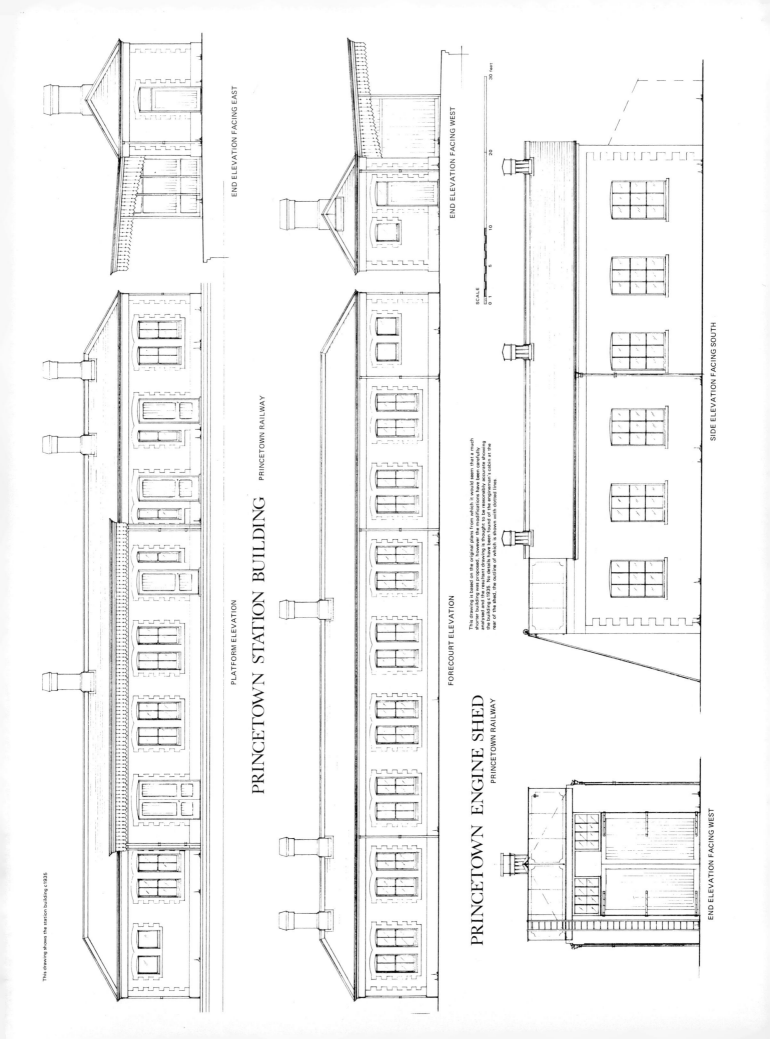

This drawing shows the station building c1935

END ELEVATION FACING EAST

PLATFORM ELEVATION

PRINCETOWN STATION BUILDING PRINCETOWN RAILWAY

END ELEVATION FACING WEST

FORECOURT ELEVATION

PRINCETOWN ENGINE SHED PRINCETOWN RAILWAY

This drawing is based on the original plans from which it would seem that a much shorter building was proposed, however the modifications have been carefully analysed and the resultant drawing is thought to be reasonably accurate showing the building c1935. No details have been found of the engineman's cabin at the rear of the shed, the outline of which is shown with dotted lines.

SCALE
0 1   5   10   20   30 feet

SIDE ELEVATION FACING SOUTH

END ELEVATION FACING WEST

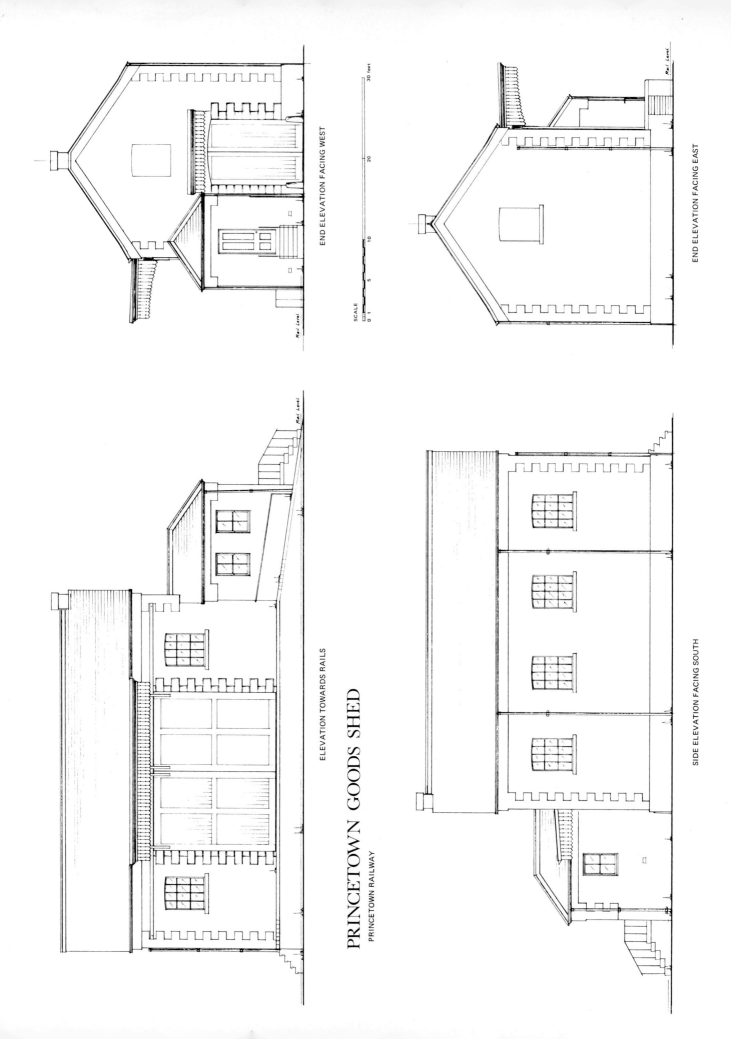

END ELEVATION FACING WEST

SCALE

0 1   5   10   20   30 feet

END ELEVATION FACING EAST

ELEVATION TOWARDS RAILS

PRINCETOWN GOODS SHED

PRINCETOWN RAILWAY

SIDE ELEVATION FACING SOUTH